"*Expert Approaches to Support Gifted Learners* gathers a dream team of practitioners and researchers in an accessible volume full of practical recommendations. Each chapter is well written, engaging, and rewarding. This remarkable collection is comprehensive in the areas covered and in its range of perspectives and should be useful to anyone interested in the education and psychology of gifted students."

—Felice Kaufmann, Ph.D., consultant in gifted education

"Here is our essential resource to nurture our brightest children's spirits and minds with wisdom, respect, and crucial information. These authors deeply know our gifted learners from the inside out."

—Elizabeth Meckstroth, M.Ed., M.S.W.
Senior Fellow, Institute for Educational Advancement
Guiding the Gifted Child, Teaching Young Gifted Children in the Regular Classroom,
and *Acceleration for Gifted Learners, K–5*

EXPERT
APPROACHES
to SUPPORT
GIFTED
LEARNERS

EXPERT
APPROACHES
to SUPPORT
GIFTED
LEARNERS

Professional Perspectives, Best Practices, and Positive Solutions

A Collaboration with the California Association for the Gifted

Edited by Margaret Wayne Gosfield, *Gifted Education Communicator*

free spirit
PUBLiSHiNG®

Meeting kids'
social & emotional
needs since 1983

Library of Congress Cataloging-in-Publication Data
Expert approaches to support gifted learners : professional perspectives, best practices, and positive solutions / edited by Margaret Wayne Gosfield.
    p.   cm.
    "A collaboration with the California Association for the Gifted."
    Includes index.
    ISBN-13: 978-1-57542-280-0
    ISBN-10: 1-57542-280-8
    1. Gifted children—Education—United States. 2. Curriculum planning—United States. I. Gosfield, Margaret Wayne. II. California Association for the Gifted.
        LC3993.9.E97 2008
        371.95'6—dc22

        2007045930

All essays in this book were previously published in the *Gifted Education Communicator* and are reprinted with permission of the California Association for the Gifted.

Cover and interior design by Percolator

10 9 8 7 6 5 4 3 2 1
Printed in the United States of America

Free Spirit Publishing Inc.
217 Fifth Avenue North, Suite 200
Minneapolis, MN 55401-1299
(612) 338-2068
help4kids@freespirit.com
www.freespirit.com

For Sheila Madsen
In memoriam

ACKNOWLEDGMENTS

I wish to thank the authors of these articles who so generously shared their expertise; the *Gifted Education Communicator* Editorial Board for helping to shape the journal and this book: Barbara Clark, advising editor; Jennifer Beaver, Richard Boolootian, Ann MacDonald, Jim Riley, and Elaine Wiener, associate editors; the California Association for the Gifted for sponsoring the journal; and my husband Amor for his encouragement and support.

CONTENTS

PART 3: SEEKING AND SERVING SPECIAL POPULATIONS 159

PART 4: PARENTS AND EDUCATORS TEAMING TOGETHER 243

FOREWORD

Sally M. Reis, Ph.D.

It's a pleasurable task for me to write a foreword to this book. I have been a fan of the *Gifted Education Communicator* since its inception. One reason is that its editor, Margaret Gosfield, has always worked to keep this journal true to its mission: to present practical applications of best practices for educators and parents of K–12 gifted learners—the target audience for this book. I like this book because of its hopeful outcome: to generate interest in and develop expertise related to best practices in giftedness and talent development and the challenges and decisions that accompany this process. I also like this book because the authors raise many important questions and offer both common sense and research-based responses.

With its wide variety of authors and selections, this book represents a co-mingling of old and new in the field of giftedness and talent development. Widely published respected scholars in the field have written some of the thirty-six articles. A number of selections are written by people who may be lesser known to some readers but have many years of experience, high levels of knowledge, and excellent ideas that can benefit talented children. The book also includes some new voices that present fresh perspectives about growing up gifted and LD (learning disabled), parenting a gifted/LD child, visual-spatial learners, and growing up gifted and gay.

The points of view represented are diverse, and yet they reflect recurring themes: giftedness is multidimensional, it can continue to develop across the childhood and later years, and multiple strategies must be employed to enable more students to develop their gifts and talents; moreover, the expression of giftedness is diverse, and the manifestation and development of talents and gifts occur in diverse ways under very different circumstances for different young people.

This book is a high-quality compendium of past reflections, current strategies, and future directions both for the field and for a very diverse group of high potential children. Parents and educators—and in turn the gifted learners they support—will benefit greatly from this wise, straightforward, and thoughtfully conceived book. It is my hope that it will be the first volume in a series of helpful collections of practical articles to help teachers learn new practices and ideas, and help parents better understand their choices and actions in order to support their children.

Sally M. Reis
University of Connecticut, Storrs

INTRODUCTION

Teaching and parenting gifted children can be exceedingly demanding, and even frustrating, given their tendency to devour information, ask questions endlessly, and embody social and emotional traits of greater intensity than is typical. In addition, their often uneven (asynchronous) development can result in a child with the reading skills of a twelfth grader, the social skills of a second grader, and a chronological age somewhere in between. Adults often don't know how to reconcile these differences. Where can actively engaged and sometimes frazzled educators and parents turn for assistance?

Expert Approaches to Support Gifted Learners provides practical information that busy K–12 educators and parents can use now at home and in school. The authors whose work is compiled here are experienced and experts in the field of gifted education.

The articles in this book first appeared in the pages of *Gifted Education Communicator,* a quarterly journal for educators and parents of K–12 gifted children sponsored by the California Association for the Gifted (CAG). The journal was launched as a national publication in the spring of 2001; it has since published hundreds of articles and columns providing perspectives, strategies, and solutions that parents and educators can use in their daily interactions with gifted learners. *Expert Approaches to Support Gifted Learners* brings this practical information to a wider audience.

The primary focus in this work is on the social and emotional needs of gifted learners. Much has been written about challenging and supporting the intellectual needs of gifted learners, but in order to master and develop their cognitive functioning—and to lead lives of satisfaction and productivity—gifted learners need guidance, encouragement, and support in their affective functioning as well.

The book is divided into four parts:

- **Part 1: Understanding and Nurturing Gifted Learners** addresses social and emotional characteristics of gifted individuals that set them apart from other learners and provides expertise and strategies to address these issues.

- **Part 2: Making Gifted Education Work** focuses on the importance of careful planning for and implementation of programs appropriate for gifted learners. It includes discussions of program design, assessment, identification, and grouping as well as detailed guides for specific classroom activity.

- **Part 3: Seeking and Serving Special Populations** concentrates on subpopulations within the larger pool of gifted learners who are marginalized in a variety of ways. These students include those who come from minority and low socioeconomic families, gay and lesbian youth, visual-spatial learners, and English language learners.

- **Part 4: Parents and Educators Teaming Together** emphasizes the need for educators and parents to work together in providing the support gifted learners need in order to reach their high potentials.

Read the whole book to get an overall guide to caring for gifted learners. Or, if you have a specific or pressing concern right now, skip to an article that addresses that issue. Each article is briefly introduced so you can quickly discern whether it covers information you need at the moment. Though some articles may seem geared toward one audience or the other, all of them can be of use to parents and educators both.

It's true that raising and educating gifted children can be challenging, but armed with knowledge—and a healthy dose of respect for the kids—it also can be extremely rewarding.

Margaret Wayne Gosfield

PART 1

UNDERSTANDING AND NURTURING GIFTED LEARNERS

Gifted children tend to experience feelings more intensely than most children. As a result, they may feel deep concern for justice or unfairness and deep empathy for others, have a higher capacity for reflective and global thinking, and feel great frustration when the pace or level of learning is slow or low. All kids deserve an understanding and nurturing educational environment, and for gifted kids that need is no different. But the intensity of gifted kids' feelings requires that parents and educators use different approaches with gifted kids than they do with mainstream kids. This is paramount and necessary for gifted learners in order for them to engage in and demonstrate well their intellectual abilities and talents.

The writers in Part 1 share techniques, strategies, and knowledge that can help educators reach their gifted students. In the following essays you'll learn ways to support and encourage gifted learners to more fully realize their potential and actualize their dreams.

Lessons from Bright Learners About Affect

Carol Ann Tomlinson | SPRING 2002

Carol Ann Tomlinson, Ph.D., teaches at the University of Virginia in the Curry School of Educa-tion. She is program coordinator for the Educational Psychology/Gifted Education department where she teaches both Educational Leadership, Foundations, and Policy and Curriculum and Instruction. She serves as codirector of Curry's Institutes on Academic Diversity. She is the author of twelve books on the topics of differentiated instruction and curriculum, as well as many profes-sional development materials and more than 200 articles. She is a past president of the National Association for Gifted Children.

The social and emotional well-being of gifted learners is often neglected in pre-occupation with their cognitive abilities. Carol Ann Tomlinson reminds us that "bright kids are kids first." And as bright kids, they have special challenges not faced by other young learners. Among these are misperceptions about uneven development; the need for self-efficacy; the use or misuse of "intellectual power"; and negative images. She reminds teachers that we must never take "for granted my role as one who shapes the human psyche as surely as I shape the human mind."

I'm on board with Robert Fulghum *(All I Really Need to Know I Learned in Kindergarten)*. Nearly everything I know that's important in life, I learned in some classroom or other. Mostly, however, the lessons I retained seem to have taken root when I was a teacher—not a student. That's the case when it comes to my perspective on the affective needs of bright kids. Bright kids were the ones who quietly (well, sometimes quietly) and patiently (nearly always patiently) taught me about their feelings and emotions—just as they were my mentors in learning about their bright minds.

Here are a few of the principles they taught me. The lessons have served me well.

Bright kids are kids first. Bright happens to be a trait they have, but it is not who they are. It's important to look for and acknowledge all the things they are. Not only is that honest, but it's freeing. If I get the sense that there's only one trait that really matters to other people—one trait on which I am constantly judged—that trait becomes a heavy burden.

Bright kids have basic needs. Because bright kids are kids first, they have the same basic affective needs all other kids have: safety, security, belonging, achievement, affirmation, and so on. They may learn quickly, but they still need to feel like the teacher invests in them—just like all other kids need that sense of investment. They may talk a good game, but they still suffer self-doubt, as do all humans. They need partners in a long journey to share their joys and fears alike. In other words, bright kids need sensitive teachers—no more than do other kids—but no less either. We often see verbal prowess as a sign that a student is immune to the sorts of affective yearnings we recognize in other kids. Not so. (And be careful with young kids who are both tall and bright. They're doubly likely to be dismissed as past needing us.)

Bright kids vary in their affective needs. Because bright kids are like other kids in most ways, most of them will not have serious emotional problems. Some bright kids will have remarkably few problems. Some will have some problems at some times. Other bright kids will have more of an on-going struggle with affect and emotions. Adults make a mistake when they assume that if a kid is smart, emotional problems will be part of the package. Adults also make a mistake when they assume that smart kids have it made, and will work through everything on their own.

Affective Snares Bright Kids Encounter

Most of the affective snares bright kids encounter are a result of a negative interaction of two variables: brightness and basic human need. In other words, all people need to feel a sense of belonging. If a student's speed or level of thought causes him to feel rejected, there is a negative interaction between high ability and the basic human need to belong. All humans need to feel safety. If a highly able learner consistently feels insecure asking questions important to her in a class, she will not feel safe, and there is a negative interaction between a need generated by her ability and a basic human need. A great teacher continues to ask the question, "What can I do to make certain that each student in this classroom feels safe, valued, accepted, and challenged?" Such a teacher understands that what feels safe to one student may not to another, and what is a celebratory achievement for one student is not for another. Nonetheless, using benchmarks such as Maslow's hierarchy of human needs provides us a lens for examining what is going on in our classrooms and how a student's particular profile can interact with needs of every individual to create a unique perspective on the classroom.

Simultaneous maturity and immaturity. It's okay if a bright kid is both too mature and too immature at the same time. The same third grader who ponders questions related to cosmology may get the giggles as a result of the most inane humor imaginable. The same middle schooler who wows you with his adult-like judgment may also want to curl up next to a parent on the couch. The same high school student whose knowledge of computers astounds everyone in the school may not be able to make sense of the theme of a short story or read social signals from peers. Advancement in one area is no guarantee of advancement in another—or even of "typical" development in other areas. That unevenness in encounters with the world can be frustrating for some bright kids. It's helpful if adults "get it," and aren't frustrated, too. Parents and teachers who give such kids ample opportunity to soar where they can—as well as acceptance, safe haven, and gentle guidance for growth in the trickier areas of development—are the most helpful. In other words, the child needs to know if you can happily participate with him in a very adult-like conversation and get a charge out of his giggles, too!

The need for self-efficacy. One of the greatest affective needs of many bright kids is one we seldom identify or address; that is the need for self-efficacy. Self-efficacy develops when a person encounters challenges that seem beyond grasp, but which the person surmounts after all. For highly able learners, it's possible—indeed likely—to progress through year after year of schooling with no genuine challenges in view. The bright student excels on tasks that are challenging for someone else, and we reward that "achievement" with an A—our hallmark of excellence. Over time, a series of outcomes evolves. The bright student has a sense, whether tacit or explicit, that something dishonest is taking place. Not only do teachers look dishonest, but school also looks fraudulent, and the students themselves know they are accomplices to the fraud. Simultaneously, the students are becoming addicted to "easy success"—an oxymoron in the arena of real life. They come to fear challenge, to resent it, to avoid it, and they fail to develop the coping skills necessary to do battle with the complex challenges that would give them a sense of honorable achievement, and power in the face of life's inevitable hurdles. A great teacher for bright kids insists on challenge, and is also a full partner in the sometimes frightening journey toward accomplishment at a new level of demand.

The issue of intellectual power. Bright kids often need some guidance in "the care and feeding of power." High ability is a kind of power. Finding oneself in possession of that power can be exhilarating, frightening, and confusing—especially for someone who, like all school-age learners, is young. Bright kids may thus need adults who help them determine that power itself is neither inherently good nor inherently bad, and that the outcomes of power depend on the use that is made of it. Bright kids need teachers and parents who help them understand that the mental power they possess is fine. They need teachers and parents who help them place limits on their use of the power, so that it does not seem overwhelming. That is to say, some young people can make articulate arguments in favor of doing things they are not experienced enough to handle. Adults often need to look beyond the verbal acuity and understand the need for "fences" that say, "No trespassing here." These sorts of fences separate young people from terrain that is too perilous for inexperience—albeit verbally impressive inexperience. These fences define safety, even though they may be encountered with protest.

Bright young people often need teachers and parents who help them understand that their mental power will affect both themselves and others. Sometimes the effect will be positive, sometimes negative. Bright young people need teachers and parents who help them "read the signs" of impact and make decisions about the use of mental power in reasoned and sensitive ways. In a way, brightness is a sort of currency and bright young people need help in understanding how to invest it in ways that both honor the holder of the currency and reflect a sort of philanthropic respect of others.

The problem of negative images. We place some bright young people at a disadvantage in school because we do not understand that the negative affective messages they receive are virtually impenetrable barriers standing between them and patterns of achievement. That is the case for many low economic and minority learners for whom school is anything but the gateway to recognition and development of their high ability. In a time when special education classes are often disproportionately overrepresentative of low economic and minority learners, and when gifted education and advanced classes are often disproportionately underrepresentative of low economic and minority learners, the affective message impedes cognitive development. Students of color and poverty hear the message clearly, "Achievement is not really yours. This won't work for you." The message is reinforced when my face and my history are not in books I read. It is reiterated when school does not connect with my language, my neighborhood, my family, and so on. It is likely that understanding the imperative of building affective bridges to cognitive achievement for bright kids from low economic and minority backgrounds is our next step in the very steep learning curve for educators who truly care to make schools and classrooms doorways to self-actualization for all who come our way.

Watch the Kids

They bring notebooks and laughter and backpacks to school. They come with minds—ready or not—for learning. They come also with emotions, spirits, and affect—invisible and essential in becoming what they are becoming each day of their school lives. We're understanding more and more fully the power of ongoing assessment of student understanding and adjustment of instruction based on those insights. We aren't fully teaching until we also understand and practice the power of ongoing assessment of student affect and adjustment of what we do in the classroom based on those insights.

In the end, that's what the kids taught me about affect and bright learners (and others)—caring, watching, reflecting, asking, adjusting—and never taking for granted my role as one who shapes the human psyche as surely as I shape the human mind.

Reclaiming Teaching as a Helping Profession: Seven Rules of Counseling for Classroom Teachers

Meredith Greene | SPRING 2006

Meredith Greene, Ph.D., *was a high school teacher and guidance counselor for twenty years and is currently an educational consultant in Nova Scotia, Canada. She is also adjunct faculty with the University of Connecticut; an instructor at Confratute, a summer program for training educators in gifted education; and a member of the National Association for Gifted Children's (NAGC) Counseling and Guidance division. She specializes in the social, emotional, and career development of gifted youth and counseling training for teachers.*

Most teachers are not trained as counselors, and yet they are called on regularly to assist their students in nonacademic matters. This is especially true of teachers of the gifted, who often are the only educators on their campus trained to recognize the special affective needs of gifted learners. Meredith Greene shares seven guidelines that classroom teachers can use in helping students in need without going beyond their responsibilities as classroom teachers.

Many gifted and talented children and youth spend the majority of their time in mixed-ability classrooms with teachers who have no specific training in gifted education. Other gifted students are in classes designed with their unique academic and intellectual needs in mind, taught by educators with gifted education training and certification. In both of these scenarios, it is unlikely that these classroom teachers have had any comprehensive training in social and emotional development, communication, or counseling theory and practice. Yet, teachers spend a good portion of their time and energy each day helping students with concerns that are not academic in nature and for which they have not been prepared in preservice or in-service training in curriculum and instruction.

Unanswered Questions

After more than ten years as a classroom teacher, I began my graduate studies in counseling. I realized almost immediately that I, and more importantly my students, could have benefited from everything I was now learning. I was distressed to think that I had not known any of this before I started teaching. Were counseling skills supposed to be kept separate from teaching skills? Did counseling only mean psychotherapy and psychological testing? I looked up the definition of the verb *to counsel*: to advise, to recommend, to provide guidance, to give suggestions, to provide direction. I searched for the meaning of the verb *to teach*: to instruct, to train, to develop, to enlighten, to prepare, to nurture, to guide. Counseling and teaching did indeed overlap, at least in the dictionary.

Teachers have a long tradition of helping students with personal issues, with students coming to them for advice, guidance, and support. Teaching is, after all, a helping profession. We teach children, not content. Why then were there no required courses in interpersonal interaction, human relations, counseling, or communications in my education degree? Why did no one teach me what to do when a student stood before me crying about a problem at home? Why did I not learn how to speak to families in crisis? How was I to help students who came to me when I was afraid I would do something wrong, make the situation worse, or overstep my role?

Teachers with gifted education training at least have knowledge of unique developmental challenges facing some gifted and talented students, including internal unevenness in development (asynchrony), advancement and maturity compared with age peers, and the special needs of gifted students with simultaneous membership in one or more other groups (i.e., with learning disabilities, ethnic minorities, females) (Robinson, 2002). But do they know what to do when these challenges are manifested in a classroom? All teachers have the opportunity to establish very close relationships with their students, an essential step in the counseling or helping process. Educators do not have to become professional counselors, but they can learn basic counseling rules of thumb to guide their classroom practice.

Paradigm Shift: From Instructing to Helping Mode

Many of the same skills are essential for effective educators and counselors: the ability to tune in to people, empathy, energy, learning through experience, and making on-the-spot decisions. However, teachers are conditioned to talk more, be directive, multitask, and correct or fix things. Counselors, on the other hand, are trained to do quite the opposite: to listen more than they talk, never give advice, to focus, to be receptive, and to allow "clients" to find their own solutions (Kottler & Kottler, 2000).

The first and most important change for a teacher adopting a helping mode is to foster a mindset that requires a nonjudgmental attitude and an understanding that the goal should be to empower students and guide them through the decision-making process, not to make decisions for them.

Seven Rules of Counseling for Classroom Teachers

1. Listen. Listen more than you talk. Listen actively. To listen, one must first attend. Attending is the act of giving a speaker your total, complete, and undivided interest using your body, face, and eyes. It is important to take a deep breath or practice another effective technique to allow concentration and focus. You need to resist distractions, face the speaker fully, and maintain appropriate eye contact (there are cultural differences in amount and type of respectful eye contact). This is no easy task in a classroom environment. One of the easiest ways to show you are attending is to simply put down your chalk or pen and look at the student who is talking to you. You would be surprised at how seldom this is done. It is rare and powerful to have someone's undivided attention.

Active listening is an essential exploration skill that can be quite difficult for teachers because of time pressures and classroom distractions. Active or deep listening requires intense concentration so that the helper can collect the information needed to interpret the situation being presented. This is done by reframing, rephrasing or paraphrasing, reflecting content and feelings, and summarizing what the student has said. The helper has to concentrate on the words spoken, the message, and the nonverbal and contextual cues that may contradict each other. Helpers don't ask too many questions and keep the ones they do ask as open-ended as possible. For teachers of gifted students, this can be a challenge since they are used to asking many questions and getting quick responses. It is important to allow for silence so that students can think and to let students determine the pace and direction of the conversation. Wait-time is even more important when asking questions about feelings.

You are listening to find out what the concern really is. Some students will be able to present their concerns in a direct and articulate manner, but some will not know what is at the bottom of their presenting symptoms. Many teachers don't have to spend as much time as counselors do building positive, open, and respectful relationships with students before helping them, because teachers have already established those relationships in and out of the classroom. Teachers do, however, have to spend time exploring the issues, rather than jumping to a quick diagnosis and an even quicker fix.

People who demonstrate good listening behaviors are remembered and valued. We make particular mention when we meet someone who is a "great listener." People with good attending behaviors are often described as nicer, more caring, and more sensitive than distracted listeners. But being a truly good listener in a helping role entails more than just looking interested and letting the other person talk. Stay as neutral and accepting as you can. If the student senses criticism or disapproval, you've lost him or her.

2. Don't give advice. Most adolescents don't listen to advice anyway, and the last thing a helping teacher should want to do is to make the student more helpless! Besides, most students who ask for your advice will ignore it, especially if it is not what they wanted to hear. If things go well, you will only reinforce their indecision or helplessness or impose your own value system. They will do what you tell them to do, to please you or because it is easier than figuring out what to do for themselves. If things don't go well, they may not only blame you for the bad advice, but your efficacy as a helper may be called into question. They may not come to you again for help, nor will their friends.

3. Slow down. Practice counseling skills. Completing the stages of the counseling process can take years or hours, but classroom teachers often have only minutes. Counseling or helping students is not easily scheduled according to school or teacher schedules. It takes time for students to unburden themselves to you, and rushing the process is not helpful.

Ask yourself questions as you listen.

- Listen carefully. Do you hear what the person is saying or are you making your own interpretation?

- Assess systematically. Organizing the information you are hearing is like conducting an Internet search. Do you know the context? How do you know what is important? How do you find meaning? How do you wade your way through everything a student tells you to find the real concern?

- Analyze logically. Are you jumping to conclusions? Are you making too much of an innocent comment? Do you hear the real message? Listen to students' explanations for their problems; watch for discrepancies in their behavior.

- Respond empathically and avoid self-disclosure. You must be sincere in your responses and genuine in your care and respect for the students you are helping. You are not helping them by expressing sympathy or pity. Self-disclosure is also not very helpful, unless in quite general terms. (For instance, "I used to get frustrated when I made mistakes, too," or "I remember being very sad once when I wasn't invited to a party.") Some well-intentioned adults believe they are helping by sharing personal anecdotes, but when they talk too much about themselves, they are ignoring the student's need to be heard.

- Problem solve creatively. Once you have critically processed the information, what type of approach or solution would work best? Should you even be intervening, and when, for how long, and which issue do you tackle first? You'll have to help students learn that making personal life changes is not as easy as memorizing vocabulary or solving equations.

4. Focus on the present and the future. Work on actions, goals, consequences. There is no point in dwelling on the "couldas, wouldas, and shouldas" of life. The basic principles of brief counseling interventions can be applied in classroom situations. Emphasis on the present, action orientation, specific objective for small incremental changes, focus on strengths, finding exceptions—this is the language of teachers. This action phase of the helping process is similar to lesson planning, in that specific, attainable and reasonable goals must be established, but in the counseling process, goal-setting has to be student-driven.

It is not necessary to probe deeply into a student's past history to help him or her move forward. We can ask simple questions such as: What is not working for you now? What do you want the situation to look like? When has this not been a problem? What were you doing differently? How will you change your situation? How will you know when the "problem" is gone? We need to help students understand that they are choosing their behaviors and therefore, have control over changing those behaviors.

Students have to expect setbacks, and for academically gifted students, this can be a big risk since they often expect instant success. You should not force or expect action. You can encourage, support, and reassure, but ultimately you have to accept that some students, for a host of reasons, would prefer to remain mired for the moment.

Probably the biggest underlying concept for this kind of helping is the conversational shift that is necessary. Conversation is not problem-dominated but solution-oriented and for good reason. The word *problem* is the problem; it implies that something can be fixed. The "problem" may have taken years to develop, and therefore is likely complex and even unsolvable. You may not be able to change the student's home life, socioeconomic situation, or previous experiences. In fact, many of their troubling personal challenges or issues may continue, but educators can help students learn to adapt to, cope with, ignore, or overcome them. The focus, then, is on the construction of a solution, not the deconstruction of the problem. This is good news for teachers who fear bringing up disturbing events from students' pasts. Most students come to teachers for help with temporary and even predictable issues, not deep psychological problems. You can help students keep things in perspective and encourage them to talk to you about neutral or happy times, not just difficult ones. You can help them figure out things for themselves.

5. Know yourself. Critically examine your helping behaviors, overuse of interrogatory questions, and need to fill silences. Know your own unresolved or touchy issues. It can be very difficult to put aside your own tendencies toward being judgmental or critical of others, but if you cannot do this, you cannot be a true helper. You have to consider your own strengths and personality type.

It is important to pay attention to the influence of our Western value system on what goes on in schools. Helpers, be they teachers, social workers, or others in helping professions, are almost always middle class. The Western, white, educated, middle-class perspective is still dominating school and counseling domains, even though the student population is changing dramatically.

In heart-to-hearts with students, you might be told things you wish you had never heard, and you might have strong personal reactions that will influence the questions you ask, the actions you take, or the goals you wish the students would set. Knowing yourself well is one of the first steps to being able to help students.

6. Respect your own and your students' boundaries. As mentioned previously, it is difficult to predetermine time limits for a helping conversation. Equally difficult is that students may not want your help, even if they came to you in the first place. Being heard might have been their only intention. You have to postpone your own agenda. For instance, your student with great potential who is underachieving may not want your help, no matter how frustrating the situation is to you and to his or her parents. You might want to help but meet resistance on every turn. You must respect the students' desire to disclose and back off when it is necessary and/or appropriate. Your need to know or help is not the deciding factor and you should not take it personally when students are recalcitrant, defiant, or unresponsive.

Teachers have too much else on their plates to take on major counseling responsibilities. You have to preserve your energy, your spirit, your time. You already have multiple roles, and you need to set your own boundaries, not to mention complying with the internal school politics of who does what for whom. Teachers of gifted students can be like mother bears with their students, assuming that they are the only adults who know enough or care enough to deal with "their kids." This attitude can be divisive for a staff in a heterogeneous school (i.e., contains regular and gifted education programs) with unnecessary and detrimental bad feelings between Gifted and Talented program teachers and regular classroom teachers or between teachers and counselors.

7. Refer easily and often, and respect the need for closure. Know the resources available in your area. A caring adult who listens and guides is a wonderful asset to a gifted and talented student who is looking for direction or help with the typical problems of growing up and/or being gifted, but teachers are not equipped to take on serious student problems. It is important to learn when and to whom to refer. Being ready with that information and offering to be the liaison or to accompany the student to the other professional will make you a more effective and efficient helper.

Know your limitations. Students come to teachers whom they trust. They may ask for the conversation to be kept confidential, or you may assure them that they can trust you to keep things to yourself. We need to help students understand that they are choosing their behaviors, and therefore have control over changing those behaviors. Confidentiality is absolutely not a guarantee that you can give them. Confidentiality may have to be breached for reasons of safety, legality, competence, and more. Students have to know you are an ally and advocate, but that you cannot shoulder all the responsibility in certain situations. You have to let students make their own choices once you help them sort through their options. They can choose to do nothing.

Closure issues can arise at the end of a simple conversation or at the end of a term. Take some time with students with whom you are close. You are their confidant and at the end of the school year, summer may seem interminably long for students who have relied on you for emotional support. Closure is even more important if your students are leaving your school. They might not seek you out, but you should find them to say good-bye and help them make plans for support systems in their new settings.

Conclusion

Until enough trained professionals are available in schools, the brunt of the responsibility for meeting students' emotional needs will rest on classroom teachers. Whether we like it or not, teachers fill some of the void for gifted children and adolescents who need help with personal and developmental issues. For dedicated, caring educators, teaching is not a job but a lifestyle. Increasing your role as a helper carries additional hazards. You may learn more about your students' lives than you care to know. Your own feelings of helplessness can increase when you learn of some of the incredible personal challenges your students face. You see people at their worst yet you are expected to always be at your best. It can seem daunting, but there is much hope. Gifted educators do not have to become counselors, but they can do "counseling" activities in their classrooms: class meetings, group discussion, brown bag lunches, guided viewing of selected film or television clips, stress reduction exercises, curriculum modification.

The single most important counseling skill to practice is to listen genuinely, without judgment, with full attention. Gifted students come to you to be heard and to have their experiences normalized instead of pathologized. Teachers must recognize their counseling boundaries, but at the same time they can practice good counseling habits in classroom situations. These practices will help gifted and talented students learn the skills necessary to manage and maintain their own positive social and emotional development.

References and Resources

Greene, M. J. (2004). Teacher as counselor: Enhancing the social, emotional, and career development of gifted and talented students in the classroom. *Gifted Education International* 19: 213–235.

Kottler, J. A., & Kottler, E. (2000). *Counseling skills for teachers.* Thousand Oaks, CA: Corwin Press.

Peterson, J. S. (2003). An argument for proactive attention to affective concerns of gifted adolescents. *The Journal of Secondary Gifted Education* 14: 62–70.

Robinson, A. (2002). Introduction. In Neihart, M., Reis, S. M., Robinson, N. M., & Moon, S. M. (Eds.). *The social and emotional development of gifted children: what do we know?* Waco, TX: Prufrock Press.

Experiencing in a Higher Key: Dabrowski's Theory of and for the Gifted

Michael M. Piechowski | SPRING 2002

Michael M. Piechowski, Ph.D., author of Mellow Out, They Say. If I Only Could: Intensities and Sensitivities of the Young and Bright, *has collaborated with Kazimierz Dabrowski, and has written extensively on development potential and emotional development of gifted youth. Since 2002, he has been involved with the Yunasa summer camp for highly gifted youth organized by the Institute for Educational Advancement, of which he is a senior fellow. He lives in Madison, Wisconsin.*

One of the most noticeable traits of gifted learners is the intensity with [which] they live their lives. Michael Piechowski delineates five dimensions of psycho[log]ical life as originated by Kazimierz Dabrowski, a Polish psychiatrist: psycho[mo]tor, sensual, intellectual, imaginational, and emotional. Piechowski encourages educators to view intense manifestations of these elements as "normal" traits of gifted students, and to use them to further their development and learning rather than viewing them as pathological and in need of "fixing."

Kazimierz Dabrowski (1902–1980), a Polish psychiatrist and psychologist, studied the mental health of intellectually and artistically gifted youths. He took the intensity of their emotions, their sensitivity and tendency toward emotional extremes, as part and parcel of their psychophysical makeup. In their intensi-fied manner of experiencing, feeling, thinking, and imagining, he perceived a potential for further growth (Dabrowski, 1967, 1972). He saw inner forces at work generating overstimulation, conflict, and pain, but also a search for a way out of the pain, strife, and disharmony. Dabrowski's life mission was to save and protect those who are tuned to the pain of the world and who see its dangerous trends, and those who being open to higher realities are poorly adapted to living in this world and thus at risk.

Dabrowski lived through both world wars. During World War II, putting his life in danger, he helped Jews to hide from the Nazis. He suffered Nazi impris-onment. After the war, the Communists put him in prison for two years because he spoke for individual self-determination and against subjugation by the state. His theory grew out of his own encounter with death, suffering, and injustice and his desire to understand the meaning of human existence. As a teenager during World War I, he witnessed acts of self-sacrifice in the midst of incom-prehensible inhumanity and puzzled how both could exist in the same world. From early youth, Dabrowski was repelled by the cruelty, duplicity, superficiality, and absence of reflection he saw in those around him. He went on a quest for enduring, universal values and for individuals who lived them. He found inspi-ration in Socrates, Gandhi, and Kierkegaard, and in the great saints. He found, too, that they went through agonies not unlike his own.

In his clinical practice, he began to see artists, writers, actors, and people whose inner conflicts were spiritual in nature. In the past, and even still today, those whose emotional richness, creative vision, and spiritual striving bring to them experiences of unusual nature, are easily labeled as abnormal, imma-ture, neurotic, or even delusional and psychotic. We are still, for the most part, chained to the narrow view which limits reality to everyday reality and ignores the extraordinary potentials of the human mind and the verifiable intuitions of the heart. There is room for hope, however, as out of humanistic psychology grew transpersonal psychology, and with the advent of emotional intelligence we have made the further step toward spiritual intelligence (Emmons, 1999; Noble, 2000; Piechowski, 2002).

Dabrowski developed his theory over many years. In its initial cast he laid two concepts at its foundation: developmental potential and multilevelness. The first describes the endowment and the properties of the system that enables us to feel and experience things: the nervous system. The second introduces the notion that human emotions, motivations, values, strivings, and behaviors have to be looked at through a prism of levels. Dabrowski described five such levels. The theory as a whole is too complex to be quickly summarized; other sources may be consulted for a fuller description (Dabrowski, Kawczak, & Piechowski, 1970; Hague, 1976, 1986; Nelson, 1989; Marsh and Colangelo, 1983; Piechowski, 1975, 1991, 2002; Silverman, 1993).

Developmental Potential

Dabrowski's concept of developmental potential includes talents, specific abilities, and intelligence, plus five primary components of psychic life: psychomotor, sensual, intellectual, imaginational, and emotional overexcitabilities (see Table 1).

Table 1: Developmental Potential

1. Talents and Abilities
2. Intensity and Sensitivity Overexcitability (OE)
   (Original Equipment)
   P   Psychomotor
   S   Sensual
   T   Intellectual
   M   Imaginational
   E   Emotional
3. Capacity for Inner Transformation

Conceived broadly as five dimensions of psychic life, these components have many possible expressions:

psychomotor (P)—movement, restlessness, drivenness, and augmented capacity for being active and energetic

sensual (S)—enhanced refinement and aliveness of sensual experience

intellectual (T)—avidity for knowledge, discovery, questioning, love of ideas and theoretical analysis, search for truth

imaginational (M)—vividness of imagery, richness of association, facility for dreams, fantasies and inventions, endowing toys and other objects with personality (animism), liking for the unusual

emotional (E)—great depth and intensity of emotional life expressed in a wide range of feelings, compassion, responsibility, self-examination

Without some degree of intensity in these areas, talent is mere technical facility lacking heart and fire. To varying degrees, these five dimensions give talent its power of invention and expression (Piechowski, 1979, 1986, 1999). They may be thought of as modes of experiencing or as channels through which flow the color tones, textures, insights, visions, currents, and energies of experience. These channels can be wide open, narrow, or barely present. They indicate a more alert, more easily, and more strongly excitable nervous system. To emphasize the above normal, higher pitch of felt experiences, Dabrowski called them "overexcitabilities." They ring loud and clear in gifted children. Kurcinka (1991) had the felicity of calling them spirited—"children who are more intense, sensitive, perceptive, persistent, energetic." Although she did not use the terms "gifted" or "overexcitability," her eminently practical book clearly is about both.

It is unfortunate that the stronger these overexcitabilities are, the less peers and teachers welcome them, unless they, too, are gifted. Children who exhibit strong overexcitabilities are often made to feel embarrassed and guilty for being "different." Criticized and teased for what they cannot help, they begin to believe there is something wrong with them. Sometimes they learn to disguise their intensity, sometimes they seek refuge in imaginary worlds of their own creation, sometimes they try to "normalize" it and as a result suffer depression or ill-defined anxiety. These reactions are the consequences of being forced to deny their own potential.

Table 2: Forms and Expressions of Overexcitability

PSYCHOMOTOR

Surplus of energy

rapid speech, marked excitation, intense physical activity (e.g., fast games and sports), pressure for action (e.g., organizing), marked competitiveness

Psychomotor expression of emotional tension

compulsive talking and chattering, impulsive actions, nervous habits (tics, nail biting), workaholism, acting out

SENSUAL

Enhanced sensory and aesthetic pleasure

seeing, smelling, tasting, touching, hearing; delight in beautiful objects, sounds of words, music, form, color, balance

Sensual expression of emotional tension

overeating, self-pampering, buying sprees, wanting to be in the limelight

INTELLECTUAL

Intensified activity of the mind

thirst for knowledge, curiosity, concentration, capacity for sustained intellectual effort, avid reading, keen observation, detailed visual recall, detailed planning

Penchant for probing questions and problem solving

search for truth and understanding, forming new concepts, tenacity in problem-solving

Reflective thought

thinking about thinking, love of theory and analysis, preoccupation with logic, moral thinking, introspection (but without self-judgment), conceptual and intuitive integration, independence of thought (sometimes very critical)

IMAGINATIONAL

Free play of the imagination

frequent use of image and metaphor, facility for invention and fantasy, facility for detailed visualization, poetic and dramatic perception, animistic and magical thinking

Capacity for living in a world of fantasy

predilection for magic and fairy tales, creation of private worlds, imaginary companions, dramatization

Spontaneous imagery as an expression of emotional tension

animistic imagery, mixing truth and fiction, elaborate dreams, illusions

Low tolerance of boredom

need for novelty

EMOTIONAL

Feelings and emotions intensified

positive feelings, negative feelings, extremes of emotion, complex emotions and feelings, identification with others' feelings, awareness of a whole range of feelings

Strong somatic expressions

tense stomach, sinking heart, blushing, flushing, pounding heart, sweaty palms

Strong affective expressions

inhibition (timidity, shyness), enthusiasm, ecstasy, euphoria, pride, strong affective memory, shame, feelings of unreality, fears and anxieties, feelings of guilt, concern with death, depressive and suicidal moods

Capacity for strong attachments, deep relationships

strong emotional ties and attachments to persons, living things, places; attachments to animals

difficulty adjusting to new environments, compassion, responsiveness to others, sensitivity in relationships, loneliness

Well differentiated feelings toward self

inner dialogue and self-judgment

The many expressions of overexcitability listed in Table 2 are easily observed. They fall into two basic categories: the natural expression of a given intensity and sensitivity and the way emotional tension may be funneled through them. When gifted children are asked which expressions apply to them, they readily give examples of corresponding behaviors and feelings. Cindy A. Strickland (2001) at the University of Virginia developed a wonderfully detailed unit for gifted middle and high school students, "Living and Learning with Dabrowski's Overexcitabilities," for the exploration, understanding, and acceptance of these often unsettling traits. She quotes Pearl Buck who said:

> The truly creative mind in any field is no more than this: A human creature born abnormally, inhumanly sensitive. To him . . . a touch is a blow. A sound is a noise. Misfortune is tragedy. A joy is an ecstasy. A friend is a lover. A lover is god. And failure is death.

Because this manner of experiencing is often viewed as overreacting, it is treated as something to be cured for the "good" of the child. It is true that a high level of intensity and sensitivity creates problems for many people who don't know how to respond and how to help the child with it. It must be remembered that the problem is often even more acute for the young person. A student of mine once wrote:

> I am a "deviant." I am often considered "wild," "crazy," "out of control," "masochistic," "abnormal," "radical," "irrational," "a baby" . . . or simply too sensitive, too emotional, or too uptight. "Mellow out," . . . they say, to which I can only respond, "If I only could . . ." At birth I was crucified with this mind that has caused me considerable pain, and frustration with teachers, coaches, peers, my family, but most of all with myself. (Piechowski, 1989, p. 99)

What helps is first to accept and acknowledge that this is the natural way of experiencing for the child. Some allowances and adaptations go a long way as was done in a preschool class that was open to the free expression of the children's overexcitabilities (Tucker & Hafenstein, 1997). A restless child endowed with a high level of energy focuses attention best when free to move around and use his or her hands. An emotionally sensitive child may at times be overwhelmed by great tension and stress, and holding the hand, or even only the finger, of an understanding adult, may be enough to provide relief. A warm bath and rubbing the child's back are also effective methods of soothing to restore balance. In some children emotional and sensory sensitivity are so high that noise, bright lights, unpleasant smells or tastes may be extremely upsetting. One then needs to take the child out of the noxious environment (shopping malls can be unnerving in the extreme) or remove the offensive stimulus. Because this is how the child's nervous system reacts, it is critical to not demand that the child "get over it."

Lind (2000) and Kurcinka (1991) offer strategies to help children and parents to cope with these intensities in an understanding and accepting way. Parents and teachers must show considerable patience to see that this "overreacting" comes from the child's sensitivity and need for his or her own order of things to be preserved. That children need order and predictable routines is well known. To a sensitive and intense child who may be disequilibrated, often by his own emotions and vivid imagery, a departure from routine (for instance, in the way a story is told), may be extremely upsetting because the need for reliable markers of consistency and support is all the greater. Without doubt, the strongest support is the parent's loving patience and acceptance.

New situations are best handled with advance preparation. When the nature of the occasion, the people involved, and the general flow of the event are explained to children, it removes the uncertainty that usually is the source of stress and difficulty for the children. However, one should not expect too much from a sensitive child, and if he or she reaches a point of wanting to leave, it is best to leave within a short time.

In the aftermath of 9/11, children are particularly affected by the general feeling of insecurity and the anxieties that adults cannot hide. But even a mention of the tragedy itself can evoke an overwhelming reaction. A twelve-year-old friend of mine, two months after the event, suffers nausea and has difficulty breathing whenever anyone begins to talk about what happened. In children, the initial reaction is often hidden, only to emerge weeks or months later in nightmares, slipping in schoolwork, or listlessness and withdrawal. Tolan's *Pride of the Peacock* depicts what happens to an emotionally gifted teenager, who, despite her supportive family, feels entirely alone with the crushing realization of the threat to the survival of the human race. Thousands of children are feeling this way today.

What helps is first to accept and acknowledge that this is the natural way of experiencing for the child.

The degree of emotional intensity is a stable individual characteristic and quite independent of what actually evoked the emotion. Emotional intensity, or its lack in unemotional people, is a characteristic of temperament observable early in life (Larsen & Diener, 1987).

Emotionally intense individuals can also be very sensitive to the feelings of others, to others being hurt, to injustice, but also to criticism and pain. If an emotionally sensitive child grows up with too much criticism and ridicule, the child will begin to seek self-protection in emotional withdrawal, and perhaps create an inner shield. The price for such withdrawal and denied feeling is high: loss of emotional vitality, lack of enjoyment of one's successes and achievements, and lack of the sense of who one is—in short, a process of emotional deadening.

A child with vivid imagination will often be upset by images seen on television, scary movies, stories in the news, or sensational gossip. Some children cannot get the disturbing images out of their minds. One then tries to suggest that more positive pictures be put in place in their mind so that the bad images be put in files and locked away. Many gifted children have a hard time stopping their thinking to go to sleep. It is worth discussing with them their methods of slowing down and quieting their mind. It is also very useful to introduce them early to effective methods of relaxation. Some gifted children know some form of meditation that brings them to a peaceful and joyful state (Piechowski, 2000). Young children benefit from five-minute meditations that progressively can be extended to twenty minutes.

It is a common mistake to take something exceptional as being abnormal. What looks abnormal, and creates difficulties for the individual, mental health professionals tend to see as something to be cured. But as Tolan astutely observed, "some of the very greatest gifts bring an inevitable downside which you cannot 'cure' without curing the gift at the same time" (in Strickland, 2001, p. 22). One of the most common misjudgments is to label as hyperactive a child full of energy and vitality.

Developmental potential includes also the capacity for inner transformation. This has to do with the ability to consciously engage in the work of personal growth to become a better person. It also has to do with the realization of all that one can become—in other words, self-actualization. It is this kind of personal growth that Dabrowski called multilevel because of the tension between what one is and the inner ideal of what one can become. The direction is from down low to up high within oneself, or, one could say, from one's current self to one's higher self.

Multilevelness

In human life there is joy and sadness, anger and compassion, aggression and cooperation, love and hate, despair and hope, fear and courage, attachment and loneliness, death and rebirth. If we take manifestations of joy, we could see, for instance, this kind: joy from winning a football game, feeling superior, defeating an opponent, succeeding by cunning, feeling of power when cleverly manipulating others. But to many people such joys would be offensive because of total lack of consideration for others. A different kind of joy is the joy that the name of a loved one brings, the joy of overcoming one's bad habits, the joy of self-discovery, the joy of a creative moment and inspiration, the joy of being able to help another. In the first case, the experiences of joy are egocentric, self-serving, self-protecting, and power-seeking. In the second case, they arise from love and empathy toward others, and from positive changes in oneself, and from expansive feelings of a higher order.

The first case represents joy on a low emotional level, the second case represents joy on a high emotional level. This comparison can be extended to all emotions and behaviors. Emotional level means here inner growth rather than the usual maturation through the life span. It is quite possible for a young person to operate on a higher emotional level than a so-called mature adult.

Dabrowski refined the distinction of levels to five, which space does not permit going into. It is enough to keep in mind that the idea of levels comes from the experience of higher and lower in oneself. Failing a person in time of need is something lower, something we are ashamed of and feel guilty about. Helping a person without any expectation of reward or even token gratitude is something higher in ourselves, and all the purer if no one knows about it. The yardstick here is the nature of our intentions and motives.

Standing by one's beliefs and ideals is a common experience for gifted teens. Here is an example picked from responses to the Overexcitability Questionnaire (Piechowski, 1979).

The responses, two years apart, are from a boy confronted with asking himself, "Who am I?" When he was 15 he wrote: "I feel that I am a person who is on the earth that is destined to use his abilities and talents to his fullest. This is simply what I think I really am." This is a typical, though erroneous, egocentric view of self-actualization as *self*-fulfillment. At 17 he recognized a moral conflict between getting ahead and being considerate of others:

> The answer to this question has changed over the past few years. A few years ago I was a person who wanted things for himself. Now I am trying to change that person to a person who wants to contribute to others and the world, not just himself. Obtaining this type of person in this world is not that easy. The one thing that is a roadblock is competition. Not necessarily losing to other people, but beating them. How can I compete to get into medical school when a doctor is supposed to build people's confidence and restore their sense of security? The process is self-defeating.

This young man's moral conflict is an inner conflict. He discovered a contradiction between competing in order to win, which meant defeating others in the process, reducing them to no more than obstructions on the way to victory, and caring for others which is relating to them as persons no less valuable and worthy of consideration than ourselves. The stance he took Dabrowski called positive maladjustment because as an adjustment to higher values it rejects compromise with lower ones.

Observing the people around them and the way things work in the world, gifted youngsters reflect, evaluate, and question. Selfishness, conceitedness, phoniness, pushing ahead of others offend them. Seeing the easy contentment of the "normal" others, their uncomplicated view of life, and easy camaraderie, they question their own "differentness" and suffer a malaise, the source of which isn't always clear in the beginning. The dissatisfaction with the world and with themselves become a source of inner turmoil. Also seeing what is wrong and how it could be corrected but being powerless to do it, can lead to depression (Jackson, 1998). There are gifted children who feel it is their responsibility to save the world (Roeper, 1995). They might do well to heed the Peaceful Warrior that to be effective one needs the right leverage at the right time (Millman, 1984, 1991).

Dabrowski's theory describes the process of inner growth in which the guiding principle is to be true to oneself. In the search for self-knowledge, the process entails inner struggles, doubts, even despair about one's emotional and spiritual handicaps, and yet always picking up again the task of gaining more understanding of others, ridding oneself of prejudices, and becoming more self-determined in the light of an inner ideal. Self-knowledge, as Eleanor Roosevelt observed, is not easily won:

> You must try to understand truthfully what makes you do things or feel things. Until you have been able to face the truth about yourself you cannot be really understanding in regard to what happens to other people. But it takes courage to face yourself and to acknowledge what motivates you in the things you do.
>
> This *self-knowledge develops slowly.* You cannot attain it all at once simply by stopping to take stock of your personal assets and liabilities. In a way, one is checked by all that protective veiling one hangs over the real motives so that it is difficult to get at the truth. But if you keep trying honestly and courageously, even when the knowledge makes you wince, even when it shocks you and you rebel against it, it is apt to come in flashes of sudden insight. (Roosevelt, 1960, pp. 63–64, emphasis added)

Because this process is not unlike dismantling an inner personality structure and replacing it with a better one with more light in its moral core, Dabrowski called it *positive disintegration.* One can get a better understanding of this type of inner growth from the study of cases than from a dry theoretical description. The lives of Eleanor Roosevelt, Etty Hillesum, self-actualizing people (Brennan

& Piechowski, 1991; Grant, 1996; Piechowski, 1990, 1992), or gifted adolescents (Jackson, 1998; Peterson, 1997; Peterson & Rischar, 2000) illustrate the process in enough detail for thoughtful young persons to see how it may apply to them.

Inner growth of this nature, once it starts, does not stop. The inner forces at work push for new challenges and development of clarity of purpose, and with this of the will to take the necessary steps. Much attention is given to setting goals, but it is knowing what one must do at every step to get there that secures reaching the goal. Just visualizing the achievement of the goal is not sufficient (Taylor, Pham, Rivkin, & Armor, 1998). We can be of great assistance to young people when we help them to know in concrete detail the steps toward their goals. Then the great energy of youthful idealism can become a positive force in the world. Techniques fostering personal growth are simple and accessible to practice (Ferrucci, 1982, Murdock, 1988; Wilson, 1994).

References

Brennan, P. T., & Piechowski, M. M. (1991). A developmental framework for self-actualization: Evidence from case studies. *Journal of Humanistic Psychology* 31: 43–64.

Dabrowski, K. (1967). *Personality-shaping through positive disintegration.* Boston: Little Brown.

———. (1972). *Psychoneurosis is not an illness.* London: Gryf.

Dabrowski, K., Kawczak, A., & Piechowski, M. M. (1970). *Mental growth through positive disintegration.* London: Gryf.

Emmons, R. A. (1999). *The psychology of ultimate concerns.* New York: Guilford.

Ferrucci, P. (1982). *What we may be: Techniques for psychological and spiritual growth through psychosynthesis.* Los Angeles: Jeremy Tarcher.

Fugitt, E. D. (1983). *"He hit me back first!" Creative visualization activities for parenting and teaching.* Rolling Hills Estates, CA: Jalmar Press.

Grant, B. A. (1988). Four voices: Life-history studies of moral development. Ph.D. thesis, Evanston, IL: Northwestern University.

———. (1996). "There are exceptions to everything": Moral relativism and moral commitment in the life of Hope Weiss. *Advanced Development* 7: 119–128.

Hague, W. J. (1976). Positive disintegration and moral education. *Journal of Moral Education* 5: 231–240.

———. (1986). *New perspectives on religious and moral development.* Edmonton, Alberta: Publication Services, Faculty of Education, University of Alberta.

Jackson, S. (1998). Bright star—black sky: A phenomenological study of depression as a window into the psyche of the gifted adolescent. *Roeper Review* 20: 215–221.

Kurcinka, M. S. (1991). *Raising your spirited child: A guide for parents whose child is more intense, sensitive, perceptive, persistent, energetic.* New York: HarperCollins.

Larsen, R. J., & Diener, E. (1987). Affective intensity as an individual difference characteristic: A review. *Journal of Research in Personality* 51: 803–814.

Lind, S. (2000). Overexcitability and the highly gifted. *Gifted Education Communicator* 31(4): 19, 45–48.

Lovecky, D. V. (1993). The quest for meaning: Counseling issues with gifted children and adolescents. In L. K. Silverman (Ed.), *Counseling the gifted and talented.* Denver: Love.

Marsh, C. S., & Colangelo, N. (1983). The application of Dabrowski's concept of multilevelness to Allport's concept of unity. *Counseling and Values* 27: 213–228.

Millman, D. (1984). *Way of the peaceful warrior.* Tiburon, CA: HJ Kramer.

———. (1991). *Sacred journey of the peaceful warrior.* Tiburon, CA: HJ Kramer.

Murdock, M. H. (1978). Meditation with young children. *Journal of Transpersonal Psychology* 10: 29–44.

———. (1988). *Spinning inward: Using guided imagery with children for learning, creativity, and relaxation.* Boston: Shambhala.

Nelson, K. C. (1989). Dabrowski's theory of positive disintegration. *Advanced Development, a Journal on Adult Giftedness* 1: 1–14.

Noble, K. D. (Ed.) (2000). Spirituality and giftedness. *Advanced Development, a Journal on Adult Giftedness* 9.

Peterson, J. S. (1997). Bright, tough, and resilient—and not in a gifted program. *Journal for Secondary Gifted Education* 8: 121–136.

Peterson, J. S., & Rischar, H. (2000). Gifted and gay: A study of the adolescent experience. *Gifted Child Quarterly* 44: 231–246.

Piechowski, M. M. (1975). A theoretical and empirical approach to the study of development. *Genetic Psychology Monographs* 92: 231–297.

———. (1979). Developmental potential. In N. Colangelo & R. T. Zaffrann (Eds.), *New voices in counseling the gifted.* Dubuque, IA: Kendall/Hunt.

———. (1986). The concept of developmental potential. *Roeper Review* 8: 190–197.

———. (1989). Developmental potential and the growth of the self. In J. VanTassel-Baska & P. Olszewski-Kubilius (Eds.), *Patterns of influence on gifted learners: The home, the school, and the self.* New York: Teachers College Press.

———. (1990). Inner growth and transformation in the life of Eleanor Roosevelt. *Advanced Development, a Journal on Adult Giftedness* 2: 35–53.

———. (1991). Emotional development and emotional giftedness. In. N. Colangelo & G. Davis, (Eds.), *Handbook of gifted education* (pp. 285–306). Boston: Allyn & Bacon.

————. (1992). Etty Hillesum: "The thinking heart of the barracks." *Advanced Development, a Journal on Adult Giftedness* 4: 105–118.

————. (1993). Is inner transformation a creative process? *Creativity Research Journal* 6: 89–98.

————. (1999). Overexcitabilities. In M. Runco & S. Pritzker (Eds.). *Encyclopedia of creativity.* New York: Academic Press.

————. (2000). Childhood experiences and spiritual giftedness. *Advanced Development, a Journal on Adult Giftedness* 9: 65–90.

————. (2002). From William James to Maslow and Dabrowski: Excitability of character and self-actualization. In D. Ambrose, L. Cohen, & A. J. Tannenbaum (Eds.), *Creative intelligence: Toward a theoretic integration* (pp. 283–322). Cresskill, NJ: Hampton Press.

Roeper, A. (1995). *Selected writings and speeches.* Minneapolis: Free Spirit Publishing.

Roosevelt, E. (1960). *You learn by living.* New York: Harper.

Silverman, L. K. (Ed.). (1993). *Counseling the gifted and talented.* Denver: Love.

Strickland, C. A. (2001). *Living and learning with Dabrowski's overexcitabilities: A unit for gifted middle or high school students.* University of Virginia.

Taylor, S. E., Pham, L. B., Rivkin, I. D., & Armor, D. A. (1998). Harnessing the imagination: Mental simulation, self-regulation, and coping. *American Psychologist* 53: 429–439.

Tolan, S. S. (1986). *Pride of the peacock.* New York: Fawcett Juniper.

Tucker, B., & Hafenstein, N. L. (1997). Psychological intensities in young gifted children. *Gifted Child Quarterly* 41: 66–75.

Wilson, L. O. (1994). *Every child, whole child: Classroom activities for unleashing natural abilities.* Tucson, AZ: Zephyr Press.

No Wonder They Behave Differently

Barbara Clark | WINTER 2002

Barbara Clark, Ed.D., is a professor emeritus in the Charter College of Education at California State University, Los Angeles. She is the author of the widely used text, Growing Up Gifted, now in its seventh edition (2007). Dr. Clark is a past president of the World Council for Gifted and Talented Children and the National Association for Gifted Children, and is on the Board of Directors and is a past president of the California Association for the Gifted. She is a recognized scholar and has presented major addresses and workshops throughout the United States and the world.

Recent brain research reveals that differences in male and female brains already exist while still in utero, dispelling the notion that differences in male and female behavior is due to the cultural environment in which they are raised. Barbara Clark identifies the learning advantages of males and females and encourages use of this knowledge when designing classroom environments and developing lesson plans that will support both male and female students.

"Sugar and spice and everything nice;
frogs and snails and puppy dog tails"

From the beginning of their children's lives, moms and dads have noticed that little girls and boys seem to behave differently, so they have treated them differently. Of course, researchers have noted that moms and dads have treated boys and girls differently and have assumed that that was why they behave differently. While it may be that both of these observations are true and both assumptions contribute to the observed differences between genders, the growing knowledge introduced from the brain research during the past four decades helps parents, teachers, and educational researchers to better understand what these differences are, how they may originate, and how we might use this knowledge to improve education for all students.

Research on Gender Differences

Much of what scientists knew about the brain prior to the late twentieth century came from animal studies and the study of adult male brains. For example, studies of the results of shrapnel wounds to the head of war veterans established that the most posterior parts of the cerebral hemispheres are the final destination of the nerve fibers involved in vision. Animal studies provided general biological information, however, the behavior of animals was less accurate in its ability to provide principles of behavior for humans. Even with the studies on male brains, researchers often wondered if the results they were getting from men would be duplicated in women or if, perhaps, there might be significant differences in the brain functioning between men and women.

Usually differences that could be seen between boys and girls were explained on a cultural basis—that is, how the child was reared. Boys were expected to be aggressive and rowdy, girls encouraged to be gentle and passive. It was much later that psychobiological research indicated that many of the differences in brain function between the sexes are innate, biologically determined, and relatively resistant to change through the influences of culture. The bulk of the evidence suggests that the effects of sex hormones on brain organization occur so early in life that from the start the environment is acting on differently wired brains in males and females. While the differences are small, they are highly significant.

One must remember when discussing research results, however, that research on sex differences is usually statistical research—that is, it is based on samplings of large numbers of people for the purpose of discovering trends. It does not accurately describe individuals and should not be used to make conclusions about any one person. In this case we are discussing two generalized groups of people, males and females. There is large individual variation within groups. No one person will exhibit all of the characteristics of either specified group, however, an individual will show a high percentage of characteristics of the group to which he or she belongs. Having said that, let us look at what research on large numbers of males and females indicates.

Differences in Behavior and Ways of Thinking

Generally, male and female brains differ in anatomy and biochemistry. It is believed that the hormone testosterone may delay the development of the left hemisphere of the brain in male fetuses, giving female fetuses a head start in their use of their left-brain hemisphere. The left hemisphere is more specialized in verbal functioning and in sequential analysis. Thus, boys rely more on their right-brain hemispheres resulting in greater development of the visual-spatial skills. Females show less lateralization of the hemispheres, that is, less distinction between their right- and left-brain functions, using both to support their characteristically more developed verbal skills. This also results in a more unified double mind that may assemble information more quickly than can males, creating the source for what is often called female intuition.

While a review of the research will show advantages in some areas for females and in other areas for males (see Table 1), these differences should not be equated with either sex being seen as superior or inferior. Just as there are differences in abilities between artists and historians, historians and psychologists, and psychologists and dancers, one professional group is not superior to the other. They are just different.

Female Advantages

Females are found to be more efficient than males in the development of their left hemisphere; therefore, females seem to be at an advantage compared to males in verbal functioning, and in a wide range of abilities that require organizing data in sequence. Females speak sooner, possess larger vocabularies, and rarely demonstrate speech defects. Stuttering occurs almost exclusively among males. Females exceed males in language and linguistic abilities allowing them

Table 1: Skills and Abilities Identified as Having Gender Differentiation

ADVANTAGES FOR FEMALES:

Are less lateralized in brain hemisphere functioning and use functions of both hemispheres to support thinking and learning.

Are more efficient than males in the development of their left hemisphere that is more specialized in verbal functioning and in sequential analysis.

Speak sooner, possess larger vocabularies, and rarely demonstrate speech defects.

Are more sensitive to sounds than males with enhanced hearing performance persisting throughout life. Girls can sing in tune at an earlier age.

Develop the sense of touch more rapidly than do males.

Are more proficient at fine motor performance than are males.

Carry out rapid sequential movements more quickly and more efficiently than do males.

Are more attentive than males to social contexts such as faces, speech patterns, and tones of voice, and perceive more details.

Exceed males in language and linguistic abilities, both spoken and written, allowing females to read sooner and learn foreign languages easier.

Develop interpersonal skills at an earlier age and maintain them throughout their lifetime.

Perform higher than males on psychological measurements of brain functioning in the areas of similarities, vocabulary, and digit-symbol substitution.

ADVANTAGES FOR MALES:

Are highly lateralized in brain hemisphere functioning developing right-brain functions very early.

Specialize in right-hemisphere visual functions and show superiority over females on visual-spatial tasks, spatial analysis, and higher mathematics.

Show early development of visual acuity, a difference that remains throughout life.

Are better at manipulating three-dimensional space. They can mentally rotate or fold an object overwhelmingly outperforming females.

Perform better than females in gross total body movement especially those requiring fast reaction times.

Are more curious than females, especially in regard to exploring their environment; touching and handling anything that they can reach.

Perform higher than females on psychological measurements of brain functioning in the areas of information, arithmetic, and picture and maze completion.

to read sooner and learn foreign languages easier. They develop a greater facility with language, both spoken and written. However, females seem also to use the left hemisphere for both verbal and spatial functioning; this may create an interference so that the result is slowed, incorrect, or even absent in areas of spatial functioning.

From birth, female infants are more sensitive to sounds, particularly their mother's voice. They will find comfort in sounds and voices earlier than will males. Female babies orient more to tones and are more startled by loud noises. Females can sing in tune at an earlier age than males. The enhanced hearing performance of females persists throughout life with the falloff in hearing occurring at a much later age than with males. Females are more proficient at fine motor performance than are males and develop the sense of touch more rapidly than they do. Females develop more sensitivity to odor, and to taste. Rapid sequential movements are carried out more quickly and more efficiently by females than by males and they exhibit manual dexterity and fine muscle coordination that exceeds that of males.

Females are more attentive than males to social contexts such as faces, speech patterns, and tones of voice. By four months, female infants can distinguish photographs of familiar people. Even more important, females understand the meaning of facial expressions, have better face recognition, and identify the affective implications of the tone of voice. They can read affective and motivational states of others better than males and show empathy and interest in people to a higher degree. Females favor a communicative mode in their approach to gain knowledge about the world and tend to conform by relying more than males on social cues. For this reason, interpersonal skills appear at an earlier age and are maintained throughout their lifetime.

On psychological measurements of brain functioning, females perform higher than males on similarities, vocabulary, and digit-symbol substitution.

Male Advantages

Males specialize in right-hemisphere visual functions, show early development of visual acuity, and show higher skill than females on visual-spatial tasks. They deal analytically with spatial relationships and with math, especially geometry and trigonometry. They are more interested in and are better at manipulating three-dimensional objects and space than are females. This difference remains throughout life. They can mentally rotate or fold an object, overwhelmingly outperforming females on such tasks.

Males perform better than females in gross total body movement, especially those requiring fast reaction times. They are found to be more curious than females, especially in regard to exploring their environment. They will begin more quickly to explore their surroundings, touching and handling anything that they can reach. On psychological measurements of brain functioning, males perform higher than females on information, arithmetic, and picture and maze completion.

The Importance of Biology Interacting with an Enriched Environment

In all discussions of how the brain organizes and functions, research consistently finds that the sex-related patterns are significantly affected not only by the anatomy of the brain but also by the sex hormones. The female hormone estrogen may play an important role in reading and in memory, for example. Research studies on women who have experienced menopause or surgical removal of their ovaries and uterus and have, therefore, deactivated the production of the hormone estrogen, find that the brains of those treated with estrogen behave like brains of younger women, while those not treated suffered lapses in memory and deterioration of their reading ability. The behavioral differences found between males and females that are related to the anatomy and chemistry of the brain are impressive and seem to indicate certain cognitive advantages and disadvantages for children of each sex.

However, the brain is not a closed system; it is highly malleable and can be dramatically influenced by experience. Experience includes not only encounters with the outside world, but also such things as mental attitude, determination, beliefs regarding self, and the sense of well being. "All aspects of experience or one's environment can alter brain circuits and induce changes that may diminish or even reverse the cognitive organization originally established by biology" (Restak, 2000, p. 65).

More in keeping with our interest in education, it is of great importance to understand that in addition to the biological contributions of anatomy and hormones, the functions of the brain of males and females also respond differently depending upon the environmental conditions. Enriching environmental stimulation can change brain patterns, thereby mitigating many of the disadvantages established by the response to anatomical and hormonal predispositions. This is especially important when related to the organization of teaching and learning opportunities currently available in our schools. Some researchers claim that parents and teachers play a larger role than nature in differentiating between the sexes. Studies have shown that teachers tend to favor boys by calling on them more often and pushing them harder. Girls seem to do better when teachers are sensitized to gender bias and refrain from sexist language, an example of which is the use of "man" when referring to all humans. Single-sex classes in math and science are proving valuable in boosting female performance by eliminating favoritism and male disapproval of female achievement, and increasing female risk-taking behavior and confidence.

We have seen that the male brain learns by manipulating the environment, yet the typical student must often sit still for long periods of time in the classroom. While it has been found that males have difficulty with fine hand coordination, they must learn to express themselves in writing at an early age. Males excel at gross motor movements and rapid muscular responses, yet there is little opportunity for expression of such ability in classrooms. Combine this need to move around, to touch, and to examine with the male reliance on sight as a major learning tool, one can see that the continued use of lectures given while students sit in rows of chairs becomes a real obstacle to equity in the classroom.

The classroom seems to be organized for skills that come naturally to girls with their enhanced hearing, question asking, and analytic listening, all skills that develop slowly in boys.

The classroom seems to be organized for skills that come naturally to girls with their enhanced hearing, question asking, and analytic listening, all skills that develop slowly in boys.

We know that behavioral differences in learning unevenly affect boys. For example Restak (2000, p. 62) reports comparisons such as, "severe mental retardation—1.3 males for every female; speech and language disorders 2.6 to 1; learning difficulties 2.2 to 1; dyslexia 4.3 to 1, and autism 4 to 1." However, at more advanced levels of instruction, especially in subjects such as physics, engineering, and architecture, where male skills are highly valued, females are at a disadvantage. In these areas, where visual-analytic, spatial, and manipulative skills are needed, the teaching methods could and should be changed to incorporate more verbal and linguistic approaches.

Testing is another area that needs reconsideration. Many of the standardized tests used to check ability and learning have been shown to favor males and their strong spatial sense and facility with math. Males have been found to outperform females in tests that require rotating an object, manipulating objects in space, mathematical reasoning, and navigating through a route. Even in professions where math is rarely used, such as law, tests used as identifiers for eligibility discriminate against those less able in math. Women are better at identifying matching items rapidly, working with details, and calculating arithmetic problems. Perhaps restructuring schools and testing to take better advantage of the skills of both males and females would give both groups a better chance at success over a broader range of subjects and with more equity in producing quality learning outcomes.

Integration as a Solution and a Step to Optimizing Learning

While the hemispheres of the brain do show specialization, the entire brain is capable of performing all the activities exhibited by any of its divisions. It would therefore be more accurate to speak of one hemisphere leading the other during certain tasks rather than viewing a person as right-brain dominant or left-brain dominant. The goal would be to have available the leadership from the hemisphere whose processes would be most appropriate to the effective solution in any situation. The ability to use the strategies from either hemisphere effectively when needed would be ideal. When we are using our left-brain mode we show preference for written directions, structured places, organized tasks, lists that can be crossed off when things are accomplished, successful results, control, and closure. When we are using our right-brain mode we can more easily tolerate a lack of closure and large amounts of ambiguity, desire lots of space, see the whole problem or situation, appreciate an artistic and aesthetic focus, and enjoy spontaneity.

For instructional purposes the functions of the brain can be organized into four areas: cognitive, with both linear and spatial processes; affective, including social and emotional processes; physical, which includes movement to support learning; and intuitive, which includes the creative processes. Planning lessons to include activities and strategies in each of these areas of brain function provides for growth in all areas of human ability and all areas of brain development. With an integrative presentation of lessons it is possible to teach the whole brain to work together.

It seems important to integrate all of these functions if all students are to have the advantage of their full ability and creativity. If we are concerned about the optimal growth of intelligence, we must provide within the environment the opportunities for the use of both right- and left-brain processes. More nerve connections exist between the halves of the brain than from the brain to the rest of the body so we are biologically supported in using this more coherent approach. To actualize the potential we possess, we must develop both types of brain function and integrate our learning experiences. The teacher or parent who has been unaware of the need for such integration and who has believed that the only valid learning comes from rational inquiry, the cognitive analysis, and in-depth, complex thinking will need to reconsider the possibilities. For most activities both mental and physical, humans require both hemispheres to function in close integration, thereby allowing the understanding of both the computation and the conceptualization of mathematics, the structure and the melody of music, and the syntax and the poetry of language.

Students that we label gifted show evidence of having this brain integration process more developed than other students. Because of increased stimulation, there is an increase in the production of neural cell growth, both biochemical and physical, allowing accelerated processing and more complex patterns of thought. More coherence and integration of functions within the brain result in more effective and efficient brain processing. The observation that very bright children seem to be more androgynous may show that this integration of function has developed and is indeed possible and highly preferable. Remember, the brain changes in anatomy and in function as a result of experience. The environment in which a brain operates determines in large part the functioning of that brain. An enriched environment is critical to determine whether gender differences are limitations or contributions to the lives of our children.

The recognition that males not only behave differently, but also think differently from females can lead us to a greater understanding of gender differences and the development of environments that can make all learning and development more effective.

References and Resources

Clark, B. (2002). *Growing up gifted* (6th ed.) Columbus, OH: Merrill/Prentice Hall.

Diamond, M. (1988). *Enriching heredity: The impact of the environment on the anatomy of the brain.* New York: The Free Press.

Diamond, M., & Hopson, J. (1998). *Magic trees of the mind.* New York: Dutton.

Jensen, E. (1998). *Teaching with the brain in mind.* Alexandria, VA: Association for Supervision and Curriculum Development.

Kimura, D. (1992). Sex differences in the brain. *Scientific American* 267(3): 118–125.

Restak, R. (2000). *Mysteries of the mind.* Washington, DC: National Geographic Society.

Siegle, D. J. (1999). *The developing mind.* New York: Guilford Press.

Sylwester, R. (1995). *A celebration of neurons.* Alexandria, VA: Association for Supervision and Curriculum Development.

Comfortably Numb:
A New View of Underachievement

Jim Delisle | WINTER 2004

Jim Delisle, Ph.D., is distinguished professor of Education at Kent State University in Ohio, where he directs both graduate and undergraduate programs in gifted child education. He also teaches middle school students in Twinsburg, Ohio, one day a week. He publishes and speaks widely.

Successful intervention of underachievement patterns is one of the most difficult challenges facing teachers of gifted students. Jim Delisle suggests there are actually two different types of underachievers: (1) conventional underachievers with low self-esteem who doubt their own intelligence and abilities, and (2) those he calls "selective consumers," who do well on tests but *choose* not to complete unchallenging or busywork type homework assignments. He identifies distinctive differences and shares supportive strategies appropriate for each type.

"It's really not fair that Joel is allowed to go on your field trip today. He hasn't done any of his assignments all week in his regular classes."

Any conversation that contains the words "it's not fair" is bound to work to the detriment of the child who is its focus. When that child is a gifted child, and the work not completed is standard-issue curriculum that, truth be told, offers little intellectual sustenance, the result is universal disappointment. Classroom teachers are offended that a child so bright refuses to complete required work. The gifted child is confused: why is he or she being asked to do assignments that are void of purpose; and the gifted advocate is chagrined that more than half a century after the first book on underachievement was published, little progress has been made in effectively addressing this condition.

As a teacher of gifted adolescents for much of my career, I have met many smart teenagers who opt out of performing highly in school. Usually, these kids are seen as smart, but not working "up to their potential." Frequently disengaged from curriculum that they believe focuses on others' needs, not their own, kids who are labeled as underachievers continue to learn. However, their learning often takes place in areas apart from the curriculum (video games, animals, sports, theater), in venues that don't look very much like school (at debates, with a mentor, while employed at the local bookstore or surf shop), or in that rare classroom where the teacher pronounces: "Joel, since the regular work is stuff you already know how to do, let's find something more engaging for you to study."

What can we learn about the dynamics of situations that cause underachievement to occur in the first place? How can we address the underlying issues involved in gifted students performing at low levels so that a win/lose situation is avoided? And what can we glean from five decades of research and practice on the topic of underachievement that can help Joel and countless others like him who may have to miss a field trip as a punishment for not playing well the game called school?

Cloud Cover

The biggest problem in addressing the issue of underachievement is that no two people can seem to agree where achievement ends and underachievement begins! Do we use a mathematical formula and gauge the child's IQ and compare it to everyday school achievement, calling it underachievement when a discrepancy is noted? If so, how big a discrepancy? Or, do we look at school grades and determine that when a B is earned by someone capable of A work, that shows underachievement?

Further, not only can we not come to a common definition of underachievement, we do not even understand why it occurs. Perhaps underachievement is seen as the rebellious behavior of students who don't comprehend the importance of repetition in education, or as an illogical reaction to something so challenging that it might actually cause a student to think hard or earn a less than perfect grade. Interestingly, in one of the earliest reviews on underachievement (Raph & Tannenbaum, 1961) where more than ninety empirical studies of underachievement that had been conducted as early as 1931 were analyzed, the only conclusion the authors could make . . . was no conclusion. The results of the studies were contradictory, making generalizations about ways to prevent or reverse patterns of underachievement impossible. Sad to say, but almost fifty years later, the same situation exists: underachievement is a phenomenon as complex and confounding as are the children and adults to whom this label has been attached.

On the Nailing of Jell-O to the Wall

> I was in school and I wanted to learn so much, but both students and teachers seemed not to care, and that bothered me. At 10 years old, I was frustrated because I was ready and willing to learn, but I observed teachers who knocked themselves out trying to teach kids who didn't want to learn, while ignoring me who wanted to learn so badly. (Turk & Campbell, 2002)

Even though no one wakes up in the morning and states "Gee . . . I can't wait to be bored today!" there is no question that boredom occurs—in school, at work, throughout life in general. When boredom occurs in our jobs, we have the ability to pack up and leave, finding employment that is more stimulating. When everyday life grows tedious, we take up a new hobby, seek a new relationship, or add spark to an existing one.

In school, however, when a student is bored, the opportunity to pick up stakes and go home just isn't there. The bright, bored student tolerates hour after hour, month after month, feeling intellectually isolated. Eventually, unless some type of acceleration or enrichment is provided, the student succumbs to behaving in ways that cause others to apply the label of underachiever: "a smart kid who just won't apply himself." As in Pink Floyd's classic lyric, the student becomes comfortably numb. Learning in school occurs sporadically, if at all.

Perhaps the problem is that the term itself—underachievement—is too broad to apply to every case where high ability is not matched by equally strong performance. Consider these two example of children who have both been labeled as underachievers:

Cassie is a seventh grader who fears that she is not as smart as everyone claims she is. A quiet girl with a pleasant demeanor, Cassie wants to please her teachers. She pursues her work with caution, and when her teachers distribute assignments or projects, Cassie thinks to herself, "This is too hard. I can't do this." A perfectionist by nature, Cassie would rather "forget" a homework assignment than turn one in that is not flawless. Often, Cassie is her own worst enemy, for when she receives praise or a high grade she attributes it to "being lucky," yet when perfection is not attained, she internalizes this failure and calls herself dumb. Due to her erratic performance, teachers reluctantly award low grades to Cassie, telling her all the time, "We know you can do this, Cassie; you've just got to believe in yourself."

Doug is an eighth grader about whom teachers cannot agree. The math teacher complains that "Doug only does work when he feels like it. He may be smart, but he needs to play ball by my rules." The social studies teacher praises Doug's astute observations: "If ever I want a great discussion on a controversial topic, I turn to Doug. If you approach him just so, he's the ideal student." Doug dislikes "busywork" and teachers who assign it, and the threat of getting a low grade for lackluster performance doesn't bother Doug at all. He enjoys learning what he likes to learn, and Doug sees grades as artificial lures to try to hook him in to do something he wouldn't otherwise complete.

So, when teachers say to him, "Doug, you have an A average on tests and quizzes, but you have twelve missing homework assignments. That'll lower your grade to a D," Doug shrugs his shoulders and says "Whatever." Most everyone is frustrated with Doug's sporadic performance except one person: Doug. He knows he's smart, and he realizes that if he played the game by the teachers' rules, he'd be a straight-A student. Somehow, though, no one has yet convinced Doug that getting straight A's when you are learning next to nothing is a worthwhile goal. Doug loves learning, but it doesn't necessarily follow that all of his eighth-grade classrooms are places where lots of learning occurs.

Cassie and Doug both are labeled by their schools as underachievers, yet, despite similar report card grades, they are as different as chalk from cheese. . . .

Enter the Selective Consumer

In previous writings (Delisle, 1992; Delisle & Galbraith, 2002), I have distinguished between the Cassies and Dougs of the world by calling one (Cassie) an underachiever and the other (Doug) a "selective consumer." The importance of this distinction can best be illustrated by comparing both the personal qualities and the motivational intentions of the two. Table 1 shows these differences at a glance.

Table 1: Characteristics of Underachievers and Selective Consumers

UNDERACHIEVERS	SELECTIVE CONSUMERS
do not fully understand the causes or possible solutions to low grades	can explain both the problems and cures of their low grades
are dependent and reactive	are independent and proactive
tend to withdraw when faced with challenges	tend to rebel when faced with "busywork"
respect or fear authority figures	see most teachers as adversaries
need both structure and imposed limits	require less structure and more "breathing room"
exhibit uniformly weak school performance across subjects	exhibit performance that varies relative to the teacher and/or curriculum area
often require family intervention	can usually be dealt with by flexible classroom teachers
experience positive change usually over the long term	experience positive change sometimes "overnight"
are often perfectionistic despite no pressure from others to be so	
have a poor academic self-image	

It should be obvious that categorizing these students together and attempting to change their school performance or attitude by using the same strategies and techniques will often result in either outright failure or only short term improvement. For example, using a contract that specifies the expected outcomes of an assignment and provides firm deadlines will be perceived by the underachiever as an aid to academic success while a similar contract with a selective consumer will be looked at as yet another attempt at coercive education! Further, telling an underachieving student that she can do a project on any topic might cause anxiety and aimless topic searching while providing this option to a selective consumer often results in a successful exploration of an area of the student's interest.

In her classic text on underachievement (1980), Joanne Rand Whitmore proposes a variety of strategies for working with underachieving students that she categorizes as supportive, intrinsic, and remedial, defined thusly:

> **Supportive strategies:** "those which affirm the worth of the child in the classroom and convey the promise of greater potential and success yet to be discovered and enjoyed." (p. 256)
>
> **Intrinsic strategies:** "strategies . . . designed to develop intrinsic achievement motivation through the child's discovery of rewards available to him as a result of efforts to learn, achieve and contribute to the group." (p. 265)
>
> **Remedial strategies:** "those employed to improve the student's academic performance in an area of learning in which he has evidenced difficulty learning, has experienced a sense of failure, and has become unmotivated to engage in learning tasks." (p. 271)

In considering the cases of Cassie and Doug, strategies that may be effective could include ideas found on Table 2 (Delisle & Galbraith, 2002). A note of caution, however: the possibilities for working effectively with both students who underachieve and those who fit the cluster of attributes more common to the selective consumer are rife with possibilities . . . which means that they are also the feeding ground for failure. For example, a student like Cassie will need the tender loving care of a teacher who understands and respects the fears about the abilities everyone (except Cassie) believes she has. Curriculum will matter, but only after a relationship of trust is established and maintained.

Table 2: Supportive Strategies for Underachievers and Selective Consumers

SUPPORTIVE STRATEGIES	
For Selective Consumers	**For Underachievers**
Eliminate (or reduce significantly) work already mastered.	Hold class meetings and one-on-one meetings to discuss student concerns/progress.
Allow independent study on topics of interest and teach through problem-solving methods.	Use predictable and concrete instructional method.
Establish a nonauthoritarian classroom atmosphere where student/teacher roles sometimes blur.	Establish a directive classroom atmosphere with clearly delineated teacher and student roles.
Permit students to prove academic competence via multiple methods.	Establish daily, weekly, and monthly written contracts of completed and assessed work.
INTRINSIC STRATEGIES	
For Selective Consumers	**For Underachievers**
Allow students to help determine class rules and procedures.	Teacher determines both rules and rewards structure.
Encourage students to design assessment methods that go beyond grading by letters/percents.	Allow students to evaluate and grade their own work before discussing it with teachers.
Encourage open dialogue about the merits and worth of particular assignments.	Engage in frequent and positive contact with student and family regarding academic progress.
Schedule regular meetings to review "how things are going" from the student's perspective.	Include praise for self-initiating behaviors and teacher-led discussion about progress.
REMEDIAL STRATEGIES	
For Selective Consumers	**For Underachievers**
Establish self-selected weekly goals for basic skill acquisition, set jointly by student and teacher.	Allow students to grade their own assignments immediately upon completion.
Provide private instruction/tutoring in areas of academic need.	Encourage peer tutoring of younger students in areas of strength or interest.
Use humor and personal example to approach academic weaknesses.	Provide small-group instruction in areas of basic skill deficiency.
Teach students about learning styles/preferences and incorporate these into learning tasks.	Encourage students to work on projects/tasks that have no grades or assessment at all.

From Delisle & Galbraith, 2002

For students like Doug, a successful teacher will be one who is willing to erase the artificial barrier often existing between teacher and student, alternating these roles as time passes and school options are attempted. Cassie will be more forgiving than Doug when a teacher "messes up," but Doug will be more forthcoming in letting you know that you are no longer reaching him. Still, the ultimate benefit of adjusting both our demeanor and our demands to those that will allow us to reach previously unreachable kids is rich with rewards. Consider the case of a real Doug—Doug Campbell.

Spinning Gold from Straw

Doug Campbell, now a 24-year-old college graduate, went through much of school comfortably numb. Breezing through classes that had no meaning took its toll early on Doug, a student identified as twice exceptional (gifted and ADHD) in preschool. In two of the most stunning articles of giftedness I have read in quite some time (Turk & Campbell, 2002, 2003), Doug Campbell and his teacher of seven years, Thomas Turk, reveal the attitudes and approaches to schooling it took to reach Doug, a highly gifted individual with a precocious ability to detect when the educational emperor was wearing no clothes. It started with small incidents of trying to share his intellectual excitement . . . that went unanswered:

"In grade school my hand was always up with the answer to a question and teachers always avoided me; they always wanted someone besides Doug to answer" (2002, p. 49).

As middle school approached, Doug's disenchantment with school escalated into confrontational exchanges between himself and his teachers:

Since the teachers would not let me talk, I ended up correcting their mistakes. When I realized they weren't going to let me talk, I would sit in the back and I raised my hand only when they made a mistake . . . not all teachers were adversaries; several encouraged, supported, and challenged my intelligence. Many tried to help yet most gave up. (2002, p. 50)

By the time high school began for Doug, he had virtually written off the education system as personally purposeless:

I found high school academics to be a joke, so I used all my extra time to cultivate my social life. I went to a lot of parties because I didn't have to learn. This was a dangerous thing for a person my age to have so much free time on his hands. (2002, p. 53)

Still . . . Doug learned: "I started reading Machiavelli, Dante, Shakespeare—they had nothing to do with class, but I read anyway. It got to the point where I couldn't bring myself to do anything the teachers wanted me to do" (2002, p. 53).

Not unexpectedly, this academic despondency led to the temporary refuge of substance abuse: "Weed started out as an escape from my anger. I would come home from school upset, feeling that I had wasted an entire day. But, when I went to class stoned, I didn't notice; I didn't care" (2002, p. 53).

This downward spiral was arrested by Thomas Turk, a teacher who first met Doug in ninth grade and taught him for seven years (including college) in English, history, and four years of Latin. Under Turk's caring guidance, and using many of the interventions that parallel the supportive, intrinsic, and remedial strategies highlighted earlier, this student-teacher partnership created in Doug a new sense of purpose to move forward and succeed. Outside interventions, including group counseling, time management skills acquisition, physical exercise, and the effective use of medication to address his ADHD combined with Turk's belief in Doug to transform a life. On the last day of Doug's sophomore year in college, Turk received a call:

At ten minutes after 5:00 on deadline day when University offices had closed, I got a call from (Doug) telling me that everything was done . . . it was the best news I had heard from him in a long time. But, there was more: He told me that he had achieved a 4.0 grade-point average. I knew right then that this was a major benchmark in his life. I felt **we** had come out of Plato's Cave into the sunlight. (2003, p. 45)

In the above paragraph, I took the liberty of doing something the first author of this article did not do: I put the word "we" in boldface; for, indeed, Doug did not succeed alone. The guidance and care of a teacher who believed in Doug enough—and for long enough—to see the gold beneath the straw resulted in a story of success that could have ended otherwise, as another sad chapter in the life history of the "kid who got away," slipping through the cracks of an educational system that would rather ignore Doug than address his multiple needs.

On Righting Wrongs

One of my favorite quotes is from novelist John Cheever: "How far one little candle throws its beam. So shines a good deed in a naughty world."

Whenever a teacher takes the time to put aside the traditional teacher roles to address personal and meaningful student concerns, a candle is lit. Whenever a teacher swallows hard and keeps inside the admonition to an underachieving child to "work up to your potential . . ." and, instead, reaches out to listen, rather than preach, the beam shines brighter. Whenever a teacher takes the time to see education from an angry, rebellious, unmotivated, or insecure student's point of view, the naughty world becomes a slightly nicer place.

With all students, these are the keys to mutual success. With children whom I call underachievers or selective consumers, the road is tougher, the path to success less clear, the obstacles more prominent, and the struggles more exhausting. But then, with glorious hope underpinning all the hard work, Doug will emerge as a 4.0 student with a smile on his face, and Cassie will begin tomorrow more confident in her success than she ever thought possible. No longer comfortably numb . . . simply comfortable.

References

Delisle, J. R. (1992). *Guiding the social and emotional development of gifted youth.* New York: Longman.

Delisle, J., & Galbraith, J. (2002). *When gifted kids don't have all the answers.* Minneapolis: Free Spirit Publishing.

Raph, J. B., & Tannenbaum, A. J. (1961). *Underachievement: Review of literature.* Mimeo. Talented Youth Project, Horace-Mann-Lincoln Institute of School Experimentation. New York: Teachers College, Columbia University.

Turk, T. N., & Campbell, D. A. (2002). What's wrong with Doug: The academic struggles of a gifted student with ADHD from preschool to college. *Gifted Child Today* 25(4): 48–65.

———. (2003). What's right with Doug: The academic triumph of a gifted student with ADHD. *Gifted Child Today* 26(2): 40–45.

Whitmore, J. R. (1980). *Giftedness, conflict and underachievement.* Boston: Allyn and Bacon.

Squelching Enthusiasm

Elaine S. Wiener | WINTER 2004

Elaine S. Wiener is associate editor for book reviews for the Gifted Education Communicator, *for which she also writes a regular column, "Carpe Diem." She is retired from the Garden Grove Unified School District Gifted and Talented Education (GATE) program in Southern California.*

Elaine Wiener laments the reality that gifted children must often hide their abilities to prevent mistreatment at the hands of other children and by the attitudes of society at large. She suggests ways to minimize the impact of this mistreatment and counsels moderation, but considers it a "sad commentary" that intellectual passion is not appreciated or encouraged in our society.

Chris Van Allsburg's *The Polar Express* is a favorite book in many classrooms, and now it is an exquisite film with the most modern animation process. Everything about this film is beautiful—except a stereotype of one of the characters. Perhaps I am being overly sensitive; see what you think. There is a youngster on the train who is selfish and greedy and rather overbearing and obnoxious. If that were all, he would blend into a stereotype of a spoiled child. However, in addition, he wears glasses and spouts off memorized information like a smarty. He bores the other children with his incessant factual outpourings. And I believe this places him into that stereotyped nerdy kid that our society makes fun of and does not value.

I wish the film had allowed him to simply be insufferable without adding the propensity to share factual information and without also wearing glasses.

I know we all have had students in our classrooms or our own children who rattle off information. I am not speaking of spoiled children or rude children or tediously incessant children, but children who are so full of passion for knowledge that it overflows. I have seen these children try to share their information on the yard at recess while children from other classrooms make fun of them. I have also seen children on the yard make derogatory comments simply because a child was in a gifted classroom.

Jeanne Delp, a cofounder of the California Association for the Gifted, used to tell her teachers to refrain from speaking too much about their students in the faculty rooms to prevent other teachers from resenting their students' accomplishments. Her phrase, "When what you are makes others reflect upon what they are not, you get hostility," used to sadden me because it seemed so small and so petty for any human being to want others to be less instead of taking pride when they are *more*.

Even today's politics denigrate outward scholarliness. There is a desire for our president to be homespun. On one hand, some people want our president to be cultured and well read and articulate. They want our president to be a West Wing president a la the TV program. But others want a president who is "of the people." They would rather see him down on the ranch than at a Beethoven concert. They think the average man can't relate to an intellectual; others believe our president should not be an average man. The disagreement occurs in the definition of what "smart" means. Some people want a smart president who doesn't look or behave as though he were smart. They want a "closet" gifted person.

And that is what our precious gifted children have to become to get along: be smart but don't sound smart, don't volunteer in class so there is no teasing later, and hide your passion for learning so you can be one of the guys or gals. This has always been, but it seems to be getting worse because the outside world values *erudition* less and less. Those students fortunate enough to be in peer groups of gifted students are free within those walls to share knowledge, but when they step outside they have to be cautious. Most of them don't know how to switch gears so they pay the price of being put down; sometimes they pay the price of being knocked down.

The attempts to remedy this problem seem to be the same everywhere:

- teach our gifted children to be humble with their gifts and to respect the gifts of others

- provide them opportunities to be with all kinds of students in addition to being in gifted classrooms

- encourage children to be friendly, and teach those matching language patterns

- show them how to persevere regardless of events

- and when possible, involve them in sports of any kind because this is an easy crossover with all kinds of other students

These are ideas which have limited results, however, and the reality is that our children will "suffer the slings and arrows of outrageous fortune" nevertheless. Wise teachers will continue to have discussions with their students and suggest ways to blend into society. That sounds like a good idea. But is it? Is that not a sad commentary when intellectual passion is so rare? To squelch it seems sinful. And to allow it too much freedom brings such pain to our students. As always, the answer is in moderation, and if you've ever had to watch your weight, you know what a fine line moderation is.

PART 2

MAKING GIFTED EDUCATION WORK

Successful gifted education requires careful planning and implementation of all elements of the program. The authors in Part 2 address the following issues with insight and practicality:

- Deliberate program design yields far greater satisfaction and effectiveness than haphazard program development.

- Assuring intellectual peer interactions with appropriate groupings leads not only to happier students but greater cognitive accomplishment.

- Educators and parents of gifted learners can only be optimally successful when they receive quality training.

- Identification procedures that include a range of different types of giftedness with inclusive search and assessment procedures assure fairness and integrity.

- Challenging, purposeful curriculum results in engaged and enterprising students.

- Assessment using measures that match the goals and components of curriculum designed to meet the needs of gifted learners allows for furthering student progress and refining and improving of the program as a whole.

Authors in Part 2 share specific and often detailed examples of classroom activities that have been classroom-tested and successful.

Stacking the Blocks:
The Importance of Program Design

Barbara Clark | SPRING 2005

Barbara Clark, Ed.D., is a professor emeritus in the Charter College of Education at California State University, Los Angeles. She is the author of the widely used text, Growing Up Gifted, now in its seventh edition (2007). Dr. Clark is a past president of the World Council for Gifted and Talented Children and the National Association for Gifted Children, and is on the Board of Directors and is a past president of the California Association for the Gifted. She is a recognized scholar and has presented major addresses and workshops throughout the United States and the world.

Many programs for gifted learners have developed haphazardly and are less effective than they might be. Barbara Clark provides an important rationale for constructing a carefully thought-out program design as a necessary foundation for serving gifted students well. Key components of design include: (1) philosophy and goals, (2) administrative groupings, (3) continuous assessment, and (4) articulation of the program for gifted learners with general education.

One of the most important tasks involved in planning a program that meets the needs of gifted and talented students is the development of a comprehensive design for a school district's program. As early as 1968, beginning with Renzulli's report of the most important components of gifted programs, research has shown that such an overall design is necessary if a program is to be successful.

An analogy could be made to the blocks children use to make a variety of structures. Consider each separate block analogous to elements within a gifted program such as identification practices, appropriate curricular experiences, instructional strategies, and assessment instruments. Program design is the result of stacking the blocks to form a strong, diverse, and exemplary gifted program. Past and future articles found in the *Gifted Education Communicator* give the readers much information on the topics each block represents. This issue will explore ways in which the blocks can be brought together to form the structure of a district's program design.

Philosophy and Goals

One of the most important elements of the program design is the written statement of the philosophy, goals, and standards the district supports and around which the gifted program will be built. The success of the program depends on the efforts and cooperation of all who are involved with the participating gifted students. Therefore, it will be important to discuss these issues with all of the participants and find a shared consensus. The result will allow a focused effort that can strengthen and support the district program.

The design for a gifted program will define the identification process and the types of gifted students that the program will serve. This will depend on the resources, both personnel and materials, which the district can make available. The program design must clearly communicate the continuum of services and program options that the district will provide to respond to the needs, abilities, and interests of the students who are to be served.

Identifying students whose needs cannot be met by the district's resources would be a disservice to the students and to the professionals who must work with them. It is inappropriate to identify students with advanced ability in fine arts, or creativity, or any other area if higher levels of educational opportunities in those areas cannot be provided. Placement in classes that focus on areas of learning that a student has not yet developed is not challenging, but highly frustrating to the unprepared student and to any advanced colleagues with whom the student may be grouped. The program design will reflect the district's commitment to the areas of the curriculum into which gifted students can be placed.

Administrative Groupings

Decisions regarding administrative groupings and structures to be used to deliver educational services must also be a part of a program design. Among those appropriate for gifted education are clusters of gifted students within a regular classroom, homogenous classrooms, or special schools. Such groupings and structures should be part of the regular school day, be flexible enough to promote continuous progress for the students who take part, and make it easier for teachers to provide for educational experiences at the level of student growth. Continuity and balance between cognitive and affective learning must be built into the program design.

Stating an agreed-upon assessment process in the program design can make the ongoing evaluation of the students and the gifted program more dependable, more available, and more consistent with the program's philosophy, goals, and standards. Including decisions regarding when and how data are to be collected and reported, how the results are to be used, and what instruments and methods are to be part of the procedure will contribute to both improvement of the gifted program and higher levels of student performance. Such practices are necessary to the success and the longevity of the gifted program.

Continuity between the gifted program and the general education program is another benefit of a well-planned program design. The gifted program can be planned and organized to provide articulated learning experiences across subjects and grade levels. Teachers at all levels of learning can be offered opportunities for professional development in the education of gifted learners and resources made available in a way that has been designed from teacher input and professional need. Involvement among the home, the community, and the gifted program can be better ensured when the methods and opportunities for such involvement have been thought out and articulated in a previously established plan.

How these blocks are stacked is clearly up to the teachers and administrators in the district and depends on the unique needs they and their students have. What is important is that time and effort are spent in developing a program design, and that it is then made available to all of those who are working with or interested in the gifted program and the students it serves. When all of the blocks represent a knowledgeable consensus of the program constituents, there is a greater opportunity for everyone to support and help further the program's goals, resulting in a far greater possibility for those goals to be realized. A well thought-out program design ensures a successful gifted program and higher levels of success for the gifted students it serves. You can find two examples of the components of exemplary program design in the standards developed by the National Association for Gifted Children and by the California Association for the Gifted.

Considerations in Evaluating Gifted Programs

Joyce VanTassel-Baska | SUMMER 2002

Joyce VanTassel-Baska, Ed.D., is the Jody and Layton Smith professor of education and executive director of the Center for Gifted Education at The College of William and Mary in Virginia. She has published widely, including twenty books and more than 345 refereed journal articles, book chapters, and scholarly reports. Her most recent book is the third edition of Comprehensive Curriculum for Gifted Education (2006) with Tamra Stambaugh. She is currently president of the National Association for Gifted Children (NAGC).

Many of us have negative mindsets when we consider evaluation of programs. It may be required and so we do it—but we don't like it. As a result, many school districts do it poorly. Joyce VanTassel-Baska presents a positive view of program assessment. She puts the emphasis on improvement of programs rather than viewing assessment as a district "grade" or required approval for continued funding. She provides a logical, step-by-step process that is valuable for all program assessment.

"In human affairs the logical future, determined by past and present conditions, is less important than the willed future, which is largely brought about by deliberate choices."
—Rene Dubos

The epistemological orientation for gifted evaluation study draws upon Stake's (1976) idea of "responsive evaluation" and is framed by three key beliefs:

1. The fundamental role of evaluation is to provide information that can be used to improve and advance the state of the art of gifted programs.

2. Evaluation research is a collaborative process among stakeholders including the state department, local school districts, and the contractor.

3. The use of multiple data sources helps to illuminate the complexity and salience of issues needing to be considered.

Evaluation teams also need to recognize that rational decision-making is mediated by values and that the structural, social, political, and symbolic dimensions of a given context (Bolman & Deal, 1991) influence the nature and degree of change that can be made. Thus, conducting district and state level evaluations of gifted programs requires placing strong emphasis on what is working well in a program and what areas need improvement.

Evaluation also needs to be seen as part of the overall program development cycle that flows naturally out of planning and implementing programs. Moreover, it is a prelude to action planning that becomes the basis for a new cycle of program implementation. Annually, gifted programs need to experience the process of evaluation and be able to learn from its results. Programs for gifted learners will not improve until evaluation is incorporated as a logical part of this program development process.

For the past five years, I have served as a principal investigator for five local, two state, and one international evaluation of gifted programs. These experiences have led me to reflect on important understandings that educators must have about the process and the common core of findings that emerge from evaluation work. The purpose of this article is to share insights on both the processes to be applied in conducting an evaluation and the common outcomes to be considered.

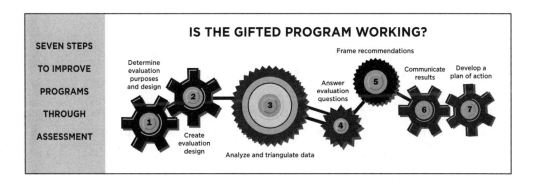

Step 1: Determining Evaluation Purposes and Questions

A first important stage for any evaluation of gifted programs is determining why it is being done and what answers an educational agency wants about a program. Usually a representative group from the district or the state is a good body to determine the right focus for an evaluation. Most evaluations are done with an eye to program improvement as part of a larger district or state initiative to upgrade all programs and services. Some may be done when key individuals running these programs are leaving the system through retirement or for other reasons. Sometimes problems are so visible in the program that an evaluation appears called for. Some sample stated purposes or objectives of evaluations are:

- To identify the effectiveness of gifted services within and across levels of the system

- To identify strengths and weaknesses, and to make recommendations regarding the most appropriate (best) delivery model for the program

- To make recommendations for gifted program improvement and for further development of each program model and service within existing resources

  Additional common questions that may be answered by evaluations include:

- To what extent are the stated mission and goals of the gifted program fulfilled in their actual operation?

- To what extent is the gifted program meeting the needs of identified students as perceived by relevant groups?

- What evidence exists to document positive student performance trends for students participating in the gifted program?

- What are the program strengths and weaknesses in relation to the state of the art or best practices in gifted education?

  A "goal-based" evaluation is almost always a major consideration and approach, driven by the question of the discrepancy between stated program goals and evidence of implementation of those goals through various data sources.

Step 2: Creating an Evaluation Design

Once evaluation questions and objectives have been articulated, it becomes important to decide on approaches to evaluating each objective or question. These strategies can range from research designs that are experimental or quasi-experimental in nature—where one compares the performance of teachers in the gifted program to those not in the program on a common observation scale, for example—to assessment of important differences in instructional delivery, to interviews with key stakeholders. The approaches to evaluation are solidified by using multiple strategies and matching the strategy to the question in an appropriate way.

Another phase of creating the evaluation design is to decide how to operationalize the evaluation approach in respect to instrumentation. In a typical evaluation, some instruments are created, others are "tailored" to the requirements of a particular context, and others are reused for multiple evaluations, based on relevance and technical adequacy considerations. When designing or selecting measuring instruments, stakeholder groups who will complete or experience the instruments of choice must be considered. Common instruments that I have employed in the conduct of evaluations include the following types of instruments:

SURVEY QUESTIONNAIRES

This type of instrument typically contains multiple-choice and Likert items, with one or two open-ended questions. It should be limited to approximately thirty items and designed for electronic scanning. It should parallel best practices emphases in identification and assessment, curriculum and instruction, organizational arrangements (i.e., grouping), evaluation, and administration. In addition, it should probe staff development and personnel qualifications and parent communication. Tailored versions of such a survey should be developed for teachers, administrators, parents, and a modified version with more targeted questions for students.

CLASSROOM OBSERVATION SCALE FORM (COS)

This instrument has been developed by the Center for Gifted Education and used in a variety of program evaluation and research projects. It involves using trained observers to script an observation and then confirm the presence or absence of forty behavioral indicators grouped into nine categories. These indicators focus on general teaching practice, elements of educational reform, and differentiation for gifted learners. The content validity of the instrument was established by expert review and calculated at 0.97 and the medium kappan for inter-rater reliability at 0.82 (Feng, 2001), although the use of a team strengthens this psychometric property even more.

ADMINISTRATOR INTERVIEW FORM

This structured interview form is used to gather specific data about the features of a local gifted program and the context for on-site data collection. It supplements and verifies the information received on the local district survey. It also probes more deeply the interviewee's sense of program development and resource impact. Typically, it is employed with program coordinators, principals, and superintendents.

FOCUS GROUP PROTOCOL

The focus group protocol typically involves five to seven open-ended questions, tailored to participants' perceptions of their endemic situation. A small group of individuals, usually eight to twelve, would be invited to participate in each focus group (Morgan, 1998). The facilitator hands out note cards and asks participants to respond to the first question. After everyone has had an opportunity to respond, the facilitator records group responses on a flip chart. The process is repeated for each question. Participants are asked to build on the conversation that unfolds, rather than sequentially share their own written responses. Students are grouped separately from adults in order to promote more open communication. Guidelines are provided to the district about representative selection for focus group participation among teachers and parents.

DOCUMENT REVIEW FORM

This form is used to ascertain the extent and quality of program documentation. Separate forms are used for policy or administrative documents and curriculum documents. These forms provide narrative and (in the case of the curriculum unit reviews) quantitative data on the nature of the written material. Document review is primarily used to confirm or support perceptual data provided by stakeholders and classroom observation data.

Step 3: Analyzing and Triangulating the Data

Once the design of the evaluation is carried out through a series of on-site visits to schools and off-site assessment of program documents, it must be followed by analysis of the data collected using techniques appropriate to the instruments employed. A quantitative analysis is conducted of all test score data, questionnaires, and observations. A qualitative analysis is conducted for all interviews, focus groups, and open-ended questions or written surveys. Content analysis of program documents is also conducted. Individualized sets of data obtained are then examined individually in respect to findings that can be discerned.

At the next stage of analysis, the evaluator engages in a cross-checking process to see how the separate findings begin to coalesce across data sources. This process, called triangulation, allows one to begin to discuss "patterns of understanding" that are revealed through multiple data sources (Yin, 1989). It is preferable to treat findings that emerge from two or more data sets as more important or relevant for program improvement than those findings that emerge only from one source. However, the issue of varied stakeholders who share a common perspective coupled with strong reactions to particular program dynamics may occasionally lead evaluators to violate that rule in favor of a strong unitary finding that may emerge. Table 1 is an example of three themes that emerged from an evaluation and the triangulation of data sources that documented their importance.

Table 1: Results of a Sample Program Evaluation

FINDINGS	EVIDENCE
There is a lack of equity and consistency in programs and services across buildings within one district as well as across districts within the state.	Supportive Data Sources Surveys, focus groups, document review
Gifted students are under-identified in the majority of school districts, given the national incidence rates (5–15 percent).	Interviews, document review
Curriculum emphases are derived from individual teacher preferences, with the majority of emphasis areas being project work and critical or creative thinking.	Classroom observation, document review, surveys

Step 4: Answering the Evaluation Questions

Once all data have been triangulated and themes identified, it is now imperative to return to the core evaluation questions and construct a response that
incorporates the derived themes and "layers" them appropriately in light of the
questions asked. Frequently, evaluation questions require disaggregating the
data sources in order to respond appropriately. For example, a question on how
key stakeholders perceive the program would require focusing on the results of
questionnaire, interview, and focus group data by stakeholder groups and across
stakeholder groups to answer it appropriately. A question on student learning
impacts might focus on data collected on student performance, modulated with
stakeholder perceptions of learning benefits derived.

Step 5: Framing Recommendations

A critical stage of any evaluation is the end-game. What are the recommendations to be left with program personnel and how should they use them? It is my
practice to limit the number of recommendations to a manageable number so that
action planning can move forward expeditiously. Across all evaluations, there are
some common weaknesses we have found in gifted programs, regardless of state
or district involved. These general weaknesses include the following areas:

- Lack of attention to the curriculum structure of the program, such that
  curriculum frameworks and scope and sequence elements are nonexistent.

- The lack of a strong curriculum base being used in the program. Teacher-
  developed units are limited. Many times the curriculum employed is
  neither sufficiently differentiated nor accelerated for gifted learners.

- A lack of attention to assessment of student learning as a direct outcome
  of the gifted program. There appears to be little systematic collection of
  student product data or program-specific student assessment data that can
  demonstrate program effects.

- A lack of a systematic counseling and guidance program that supports
  and nurtures the development of gifted learners over the K–12 years
  of schooling.

These weaknesses are also revealed when program coordinators complete a self-assessment, using the NAGC program standards as a guideline for best practice.

Step 6: Communicating Results

The results of the evaluation should be made available in written and oral form to all audiences that participated in data collection efforts. In many contexts, a series of meetings are scheduled to provide different audiences access to the results, and the evaluator presents the study and answers questions from the audience. Typically, there is also a final presentation to local and state boards. This oral and written communication process is a central part of ensuring that clients understand the findings and recommendations in light of their own experiences and hopefully can become part of a representative task force to move the recommendations forward.

Step 7: Developing a Plan of Action

The more successful the evaluation, the more likely the client will immediately utilize the recommendations for effective program improvement. Too frequently, evaluation data are under-utilized in respect to program involvement avenues (Avery & VanTassel-Baska, 2001). The best way to ensure strong utilization is for the evaluator to sit down with a planning group and help them develop a plan of action for the next few years, based on the recommendations received. A sample set of recommendations that have been worked into such a plan at the local level follows.

Anticipated Action Steps

ELEMENTARY LEVEL

- Provide staff development for classroom teachers on teaching gifted students in the regular classroom.

- Continue to revise/modify curricula to include more hands-on activities.

- Continue to modify curricula to offer more alternatives in assignments, etc.

MIDDLE SCHOOL LEVEL

- Continue process of bringing curricula into alignment with state content area standards.

- Study the content areas used in the middle school model to determine if changes need to be made.

- Encourage all middle school teachers to take a gifted course.

- Provide staff development for middle school teachers on the learning needs of high-ability students.

BOTH LEVELS

- Train all teachers in a critical thinking model.

- Continue summer curriculum development for gifted teachers.

- Conduct staff development for gifted teachers on using state standards at higher, more complex levels of thinking.

- Establish a longitudinal database that can easily access all data on gifted students, including all test scores, grades, high school courses, etc.

- Use off-level performance-based and portfolio-based approaches for classes.

- Collect data annually.

Recommendations

1. Continue differentiation of curriculum and instructional processes in both gifted classrooms and regular classrooms for gifted learners.

2. Continue refinement and development of existing gifted curriculum units of study.

3. Evaluate student impact data annually to assess the nature and extent of learning in gifted at each stage of development.

Conclusion

Gifted program evaluations are central to the continued development and evolution of the field. Without access to good data for making program decisions, we can fall further behind in our efforts to expand and deepen program opportunities for gifted students. Because gifted programs are seriously underfunded and underresourced everywhere, there is a real need to leverage evaluation findings to gain a stronger position within educational contexts for continued and even stronger support. In an era of educational accountability, we must be proactive in our efforts to enhance program services on behalf of gifted learners.

References

Avery, L. W., & VanTassel-Baska, J. (2001). Investigating the impact of gifted education evaluation at state and local levels: Problems with traction. *Journal for the Education of the Gifted* 25(2): 153–176.

Bolman, L. G., & Deal, T. E. (1991). *Reframing organizations: Artistry, choice, and leadership*. San Francisco: Jossey-Bass.

Feng, X. A. (2001). *Technical report on inter-rater reliability of the classroom observation scale*. Williamsburg, VA: Center for Gifted Education.

Morgan, D. L. (1998). *The focus group guidebook*. Thousand Oaks, CA: SAGE Publications.

Stake, R. E. (1976). A theoretical statement of responsive evaluation. *Studies in Educational Evaluation* 2(1): 19–22.

Yin, R. (1989). *Case study research: Design and methods*. Newberry Park, CA: SAGE Publications.

Grouping the Gifted: Myths and Realities

Karen B. Rogers | SPRING 2001

Karen B. Rogers, Ph.D., is professor of Education in the Faculty of Arts and Social Sciences and the director of research for the Gifted Education Research Resource and Information Centre (GERRIC) at the University of New South Wales in Sydney, Australia. She specializes in "best practices" in gifted education and has written two books and numerous book chapters and articles on the subject. She sits on the editorial boards of many journals in the field of gifted education, including the national advisory board for the Gifted Education Communicator.

The debate over whether to group gifted students with their academic peers has raged for years. A host of myths claiming negative results from grouping gifted students has evolved and been used in attempts to eliminate such groupings. Karen Rogers reviewed a massive amount of research on the topic and presents information to dispel nine of those myths. Her article is a powerful tool for advocates of gifted education.

Few topics in education have aroused as much passion, both positive and negative, as ability grouping. Jeanie Oakes' book, *Keeping Track* (1985), spurred a national movement to eliminate grouping practices for students of all abilities. With her powerful appeals to emotion, she argued that tracking students had led to a system for maintaining inequity for the poor, the culturally diverse, and the less able in America's schools. One principal, reacting to her message, wrote in *Educational Leadership*:

The answer to the debate on ability grouping is not to be found in new research. There exists a body of philosophic absolutes that should include this statement: The ability grouping of students for educational opportunities in a democratic society is ethically unacceptable. . . . It should become a moral imperative along with the beliefs that slavery is immoral and that all people are created equal under the law. (Haistings, 1992, p.14)

Then, too, educational writers such as Paul George and Robert Slavin have tried to argue similarly for the elimination of tracking using a somewhat more reasoned approach. At one point, Slavin stated:

Because of the antiegalitarian nature of ability grouping, the burden of proof must be on those who would claim its effectiveness and indispensability. . . . There is much research still to be done to understand the effects of ability grouping . . . on student achievement, and more important, to study the effects of alternatives to between-class ability grouping. However, we know enough after seventy years of research on the topic to justify moving away from tracking and beginning a search for instructional methods capable of enhancing the achievement of all learners. (Slavin, 1993, p. 549)

Why, then, when you read how reason and emotion appear to agree on the "bad effects" of grouping, am I continuing to write this article? Perhaps it is because this issue is of such great importance to gifted children. Moreover, what the general education writers are arguing accounts only for the perspectives of the poor and the culturally diverse who are not gifted. Or perhaps it is because these writers have misled this country's current crop of teachers and administrators, leading them to believe the inequity, moral reprehensibility, and anti-achievement arguments about grouping, with little actual research or even scholarly study to back up the arguments.

It all comes down to the myths about ability grouping, often arising out of emotional, political, and economic foundations, and the realities—what the actual studies about grouping have found out about academic, social, and psychological effects. For the remainder of this article, I would like to take you on a tour of the research, both past and present, to see where the realities lie. I will use my comprehensive meta-evaluation of the fourteen research syntheses conducted on various forms of grouping published by the National Research Center on the Gifted and Talented in 1991. Added to this will be an update of all the research on grouping conducted since that time (an additional fifty-six studies).

Myth 1: Homogeneous grouping is not a "picture" of the real world. In our adult lives, particularly in our work and home lives, we must work together in heterogeneous groups almost continuously.

Reality: A National Public Radio broadcast (1995) studied the work patterns of adults in the Los Angeles area, finding that approximately 35 percent of these adults were working from home, with infrequent trips to a centralized location for meetings with others. The reporter viewed this as a picture of the decades to come, whether because of messy transportation issues, the efficacy of technological/electronic transmissions, or the economic efficiency of fewer business centers and buildings to maintain. In fact, it is likely that the twenty-first century will witness much more individual work done without workers coming to a central place to do business. Each will be accountable for his or her own work, which may be added to other workers' tasks. The "group" project by which all sink or swim may be a dying concept.

Furthermore, at no time in this democracy have adults been forced into having their friends chosen for them. We tend to make friends with others who think and act like we do, people with similar occupations and interests (Schunk, 1996). Yes, we must be able to communicate clearly with all echelons of society in order to buy our groceries, shop, have repairs made on our homes, gas up our cars, and make bank transactions, but this skill is not so pervasive nor so difficult to learn to warrant thirteen years of cooperative/heterogeneous group work in preparation.

Myth 2: Grouping is elitist, undemocratic, and racist. Disproportionate numbers of Asians and whites are found in high-ability groups, and other cultures, such as African American and Hispanic, are underrepresented. "Politically powerful" parents of gifted children insist on maintaining these power inequities for their children's "protection."

Reality: Since 1990 and the inception of the Jacob Javits Act, all federal government funds in gifted education have been focused on finding and educating underserved and underrepresented populations of gifted learners. As a part of the evaluation process, projects funded must enumerate underrepresented students identified and served through the innovative methods undertaken in the grants. In fact, none of these grants has been awarded to any project for which the primary goal was to identify and serve the more "traditional" gifted child.

Furthermore, the majority of projects undertaken involve programs in which gifted children are grouped for instruction. Hence, we can call neither gifted education in general, nor grouping in particular, racist. In fact, the survey studies of numbers of ethnic minorities engaged in grouped programs make the assumption that high-ability groups are formed to separate out the "riff raff" and to maintain the status of the "in group" (Oakes, 1985). Emil Haller (1985), among others, however, has found that group placement is a result of a student's specific and current performance, rather than skin color or economic class. His experiments using student case studies have shown this time and time again, since the mid-1980s. Other factors may be leading educators to under-identify deserving children for gifted grouping opportunities, such as lack of awareness of cultural values that contradict the general notions of giftedness, such as task commitment, desire to achieve, and persistence. This would suggest that major professional development is in order, not that grouping be eliminated.

Myth 3: In schools that use ability grouping, the "good" teachers get the "good" students. The worst teachers are those responsible for low-ability classes.

Reality: The research on effective teachers of the gifted often concludes with a list of personality, experiential, and cognitive characteristics that best match the needs and abilities of gifted students. Often when people outside the field look at this list, they will remark that all students should have teachers like this. But is it true? Look at this list compiled across the work of Clark (1997), Gallagher and Gallagher (1994), and Davis and Rimm (1998) and decide whether these characteristics would be critical to the education of an average child or a child with special needs. Some characteristics, such as training in gifted education, high intellectual ability, expertise in a specific intellectual or talent area, and genuine interest and liking for gifted learners may not be so directly relevant to all learners, but the remainder are.

- extensive training in gifted education

- high degree of intelligence and intellectual honesty

- expertise in a specific intellectual or talent area

- genuine interest in and liking of gifted learners

- recognition of the importance of intellectual development

- strong belief in individual differences and individualization

- highly developed teaching skill and knowledge of how to teach

- self-directed in their own learning, with a love for new, advanced knowledge

- level-headed and emotionally stable

Heath in 1997 canvassed gifted students to find out what they thought made a good teacher. Their list looks like a shopping list for all students, except for "moving through class materials quickly" and "consistent provision of accurate feedback."

- patience

- sense of humor

- moves quickly through learning material

- treats each person as an individual

- doesn't have to be a "sage on the stage" all the time

- consistently gives "accurate" feedback

What is being said here is that there probably is not a single paradigm for the "good" teacher. What makes the teacher of the gifted "good" or "effective" might be highly damaging to a low-level learner and vice versa.

Myth 4: When gifted students are grouped for instruction, this removes the role models at-risk students need to succeed and behave.

Reality: What decades of research on role models has told us, especially the work of Albert Bandura (1964) and Dale Schunk (1996), is that individuals are most likely to choose a "role model" among those whom they perceive to be at about their own level but experiencing some sort of success (attention, financial rewards, praise, or friendship). A low-level student will not choose a gifted student as a role model because (a) he or she doesn't want to be like the gifted student or (b) he or she doesn't think it's possible to be like that—too much change would be involved.

> Observing peers performing a task increases students' self-efficacy for learning. . . . Peers who readily master skills may help teach skills to observing students, but may not have much impact on the self-efficacy of those students who experience learning difficulties. . . . For the latter, students with learning difficulties who have mastered the skills may be excellent models. (Schunk, 1996, p. 113)

What happens when students are grouped with others of similar abilities and interests is most often a function of who becomes the role model in each classroom. It is just as likely that a charismatic severe underachiever might become the role model for anti-establishment behavior in a gifted class as a discipline problem might become the role model for anti-establishment behavior in a low-ability group. Again, there are factors other than the act of grouping that affect the learning climate in grouped as well as whole grouped or ungrouped classes.

Myth 5: Ability grouping is rigid: once you're in one group level, you can't get out.

Reality: There is a reality to this myth for one kind of grouping—tracking, also known as full-time ability grouping. If children are placed in a low or middle track, what chance would they have to acquire all they are supposed to learn in that track and on the side be picking up all they need to learn in order to be successful in the next highest track? It would be close to impossible for children to move up a track. However, lack of focus, underachievement, disciplinary issues, or a developmental plateau could all lead to children moving down a track. Hence, the permanence or rigidity of tracking seems to be a reality.

But as previous research has pointed out, there are many forms of ability grouping that do not seem to be so inflexible. Performance grouping for specific subject instruction, flexible within-class grouping, cluster grouping, cross-grade grouping, and pull-out groups all rely on students' current levels of performance and what they already know about what is being taught as the criteria for group placement (Rogers, 1993). Each of these is defensible as a practice, because up-to-date assessment data are used to place children in the groups they "need" to be in for the best focused and appropriately paced and differentiated instruction. For all of these forms of grouping, the gifted have shown substantial academic effects, ranging from approximately one-third of a year's additional achievement to nearly three-fifths of a year's additional growth. For average and lower achieving groups, the academic effects have been smaller but positive. The key with any form of performance grouping, however, is to focus on what is being taught, not on who is being grouped. The studies since 1990 have pointed consistently to the following conclusions about performance grouping (Rogers, 1998):

1. Advanced students benefit academically more than low-ability students (e.g., Berge, 1990; Gamoran, Nystrand, Berends, & LePore, 1995; Goldring, 1990; Hooper, 1992; Richardson & Fergus, 1993).

2. Homogeneous groups are more beneficial academically for all abilities than heterogeneous grouping (Cohen & Lotan, 1995; Hacker & Rowe, 1993; Lou, Abrami, Spence, & Poulsen, 1996; Slate, Jones & Dawson, 1993).

3. Continuous progress alone (i.e., cross grading, mastery learning) makes no academic difference unless it is combined with a variety of instructional approaches (Hall & Cunningham, 1992; Veenman, 1995).

4. Small-group learning is academically more advantageous than whole-group learning (Hallinan, 1994; Jones & Carter, 1994). One study found this not to be true in teaching basic math facts: whole group drill and practice was found superior for retention (Mason & Good, 1993).

5. What is done when students are grouped (i.e., instructional quality, curriculum coverage, instructional time, class size) is more directly related to achievement than just being placed in a group (Kulik, 1992; Pallas, Entwisle, Alexander, & Stluka, 1994).

6. Low-ability students benefit academically when paired with a high-ability student but the converse is not true (Carter & Jones, 1994; Hooper, 1992).

7. Both high- and low-ability students benefit from more social interactions when grouped within a class with like-ability peers (Berge, 1990; Chauvet & Blatchford, 1993; Hacker & Rowe, 1993).

Myth 6: Low-ability students' self-esteem is irreparably damaged when they are placed with other low-ability students.

Reality: This myth was roundly rejected in Kulik and Kulik's multiple meta-analyses of the 1980s and early 1990s. In each synthesis they found that performance on paper and pencil measures of self-esteem was somewhat more positive for low-ability students in grouped classrooms, with a similar pattern also found for average-ability students. The explanations, although not documented at the time, were that these students were less likely to be intimidated by those who answered the teacher's questions more rapidly and were more likely to experience success when the instruction had been tailored to their needed pace and level of complexity.

Self-confidence, an aspect of self-esteem, has been studied in the decade since the Kuliks' work. Both the research teams of Carter and Jones (1994) and Fuligni, Eccles, and Barber (1995) have found that low-ability students tend to acquire more self-confidence in their abilities when in mixed-ability groups. This leaves us with a dilemma: their self-esteem is not damaged when grouped but their self-confidence improves when they are not grouped. Unfortunately, self-esteem is less high (but perhaps more realistic) for high-ability students when they are grouped but their self-confidence only improves when they are given challenges slightly beyond what they think they can do and then they succeed (Hoekman, 1998). This is not likely to happen when gifted students are placed in a mixed-ability group without the challenge and appropriate pacing they require.

The goal of schools must be to develop the potential of all students as far as possible.

Myth 7: Low-ability and average-ability students' achievement is limited by the groups into which they are placed.

Reality: As pointed out earlier, Slavin's (1993) best evidence synthesis of the research on regrouping by performance level for specific instruction found slight positive gains for low- and average-ability groups when the curriculum itself was appropriately differentiated for these groups. The effects were zero when differentiation could not be documented. Thus, this myth could be true if instruction is not monitored, but it would be wrong to believe that the grouping itself limits achievement. As the more recent research has shown, smaller groups are superior to bigger groups for overall achievement (Cohen & Lotan, 1995; Lou et al., 1996), and homogeneous groups are superior to heterogeneous groups for overall achievement, class participation, and pro-academic behavior (Hacker & Rowe, 1993; Hooper, 1992).

The goal of schools must be to develop the potential of all students as far as possible. We must never choose an instructional management or delivery strategy that limits any child's potential. It is clear, however, that the act of grouping itself is not limiting. Care must be taken when like-ability grouping is used that the curriculum and the instructional delivery practices are appropriate to the group and aimed slightly beyond what students at that performance level think they are capable of—in Vygotsky's "Zone of Proximal Development"—if we are to make the most of the potential in any group.

Myth 8: Too much time is spent on discipline and behavior modification in low-ability groups.

Reality: The argument here is that low-ability groups become behavioral landmines and that teachers must be disciplinarians first and teachers last. Most interestingly, Jeanie Oakes' study did not find significant differences in the amount of instructional time expended when low and high tracks in junior and senior high schools were compared (1985), but the expectations for homework time expenditures were significantly different (forty-two minutes on average for high tracks vs. fourteen minutes for low tracks). Is the myth, then, more an issue of teacher expectations than a grouping issue? Do teachers generally assume that low-achieving students are more likely to misbehave and act out and likewise assume that higher achieving students will not? Perhaps the type of disciplinary or behavioral issue differs in differing grouping levels, but the time spent on discipline and behavior modification is not discrepant. More recently, Chauvet and Blatchford (1993) have found that subjects placed in random mixed-ability groups performed significantly less well than those in either friendship groups or like-ability groups.

Myth 9: Without brighter students in a class, the quality of discussion and pro-academic norms go way down.

Reality: The "quality" of a discussion is a perception of the teacher, who may enjoy having a higher level of thinking going on for personal pleasure. Such discussion, however, may be very intimidating and alienating to lower level students in the class whose pace of learning is considerably slower (Start, 1995) and whose capacity for using higher order thinking may be more limited and infrequent (Nasca, 1983). This brings us to the issue of what purpose gifted students serve in the school system. Are they there to raise the average of the school on measures of school performance and mastery? Are they there to teach those who are struggling with the regular curriculum and its mastery? Are they there to make the teacher's job easier or more pleasurable?

When we think clearly about this, gifted students are there to learn, not to be exploited for the benefit of others. This means that these students' curriculum needs to be compacted in recognition of what they have already mastered, and they need exposure to advanced knowledge and skills at a considerably faster pace and with less review and practice than provided for students of other ability levels. With this new knowledge and skill, they need to apply and produce at higher levels of complexity and abstraction than other students. Compacting could certainly take place in a heterogeneous setting, but the difficulties of appropriate pacing and variable frequency of complex, abstract applications make the heterogeneous setting an impractical placement for most gifted students if their potential is to be fully developed.

The New Realities

Most of the research that has taken place since my foundational paper in 1991 has come to the same conclusions we have seen in this discussion of myths and realities, but three new patterns of research on grouping are emerging and it will be interesting to see what they add to our understanding of the merits of grouping for all ability levels.

Pattern 1: Mixed-ability groups have "mixed" results.

Dyads of low- and high-ability students are now being studied rather than small groups. Thus far, the researchers who have looked at this in the six studies

I have found, conclude that the low-ability students speak out more, behave more appropriately, and stay on task more but with no differences in overall individual achievement. The high-ability dyad members gain little from the interaction (e.g., Cohen & Lotan, 1995; Jones & Carter, 1994). Hence, if our goal is to socialize low-ability students, dyads work. If our goal is to improve their academic achievement, dyads are not the answer. For neither goal are dyads appropriate for high-ability students.

Pattern 2: Like-ability groups produce higher academic effects for gifted learners than mixed-ability groups.

A variety of studies since 1991 have come to this conclusion, from comprehensive syntheses of research (e.g., Goldring, 1990; Lou et al., 1996; Rogers, 1998). There just doesn't seem to be any way around the fact that gifted learners do better in every respect when they are placed together with others who are performing at their levels and share their interests and abilities. At the same time, the achievement effects for other ability levels are not so dramatic or definitive (Richardson & Fergus, 1993). Alternatives to like-ability groups have not produced earthshaking results and more research and experimentation needs to take place to find the best alternatives for these students (students of ability levels other than gifted). At some point, however, educators will have to weigh effort against outcome. Grouping lessens a teacher's efforts to help students master what they have not accomplished by homogenizing pacing and complexity needs. Hence, it is a fairly easy means for developing the potential of gifted learners. The academic gains are substantial and documented. What we want, however, are substantial effects for all students. This means time-intensive individualization/tutoring/mentoring efforts will be required for these other levels of ability. What should not happen, however, is to eliminate performance grouping for gifted students when it does get us where we need to be with academic outcomes.

Pattern 3: Smaller groupings for instruction produce higher academic effects for all students than whole-class instruction.

Only one study in recent years has suggested benefits for whole-class instruction: when it is used for drill and repetition of low-level convergent skills, such as math computation. The direct instruction research of the late 1970s reached similar conclusions. The question, then, is how much of what we aim to teach students in schools today is low level and convergent? If one looks at standards from state to state, the aim has consistently been to move toward higher order learning, patterns, and concepts rather than details and facts.

Many educators have used time as the explanatory factor among differing performance levels for students: some students need more time to learn than others. If this is so, then students will need to be placed in smaller groupings according to the amount of time they need to master the standards. And with standards becoming more and more high end, the need for adequate time to master them becomes more and more critical. We can't expect the majority of students to sit around while the slowest ones begin to master what all can learn. This would fly in the face of full potential development for all. More experimentation must take place with what the composition of these small groupings should look like. Will these be friendship groups rather than like-ability groups? Are friendship groups the same thing as like-ability groups (do we choose others to be our friends based on the similarity of their abilities and interests to ours)? Do dyads prove to be more academically effective than groups of three or four? Do single-gender groups change the complexion of achievement in some subjects, such as math and science?

Our work on the grouping issue and how it impacts gifted children is far from done. We have a strong research base for our current practices, but we also have some responsibility for contributing to an understanding of grouping practices' effects on the achievement of all students, regardless of ethnic origin, socioeconomic class, ability, motivation, and performance levels. Perhaps there are even more effective ways to manage the instruction of gifted learners. Let's be on the cutting edge in finding those ways.

References

Bandura, A., & Kupers, C. J. (1964). Transmission of patterns of self-reinforcement through modeling. *Journal of Abnormal and Social Psychology* 69: 1–9.

Berge, Z. L. (1990, November). Effects of group size, gender, and ability grouping on learning science process skills using microcomputers. *Journal of Research in Science Teaching* 27: 923–954.

Carter, G., & Jones, M. G. (1994, October). Relationship between ability-paired interactions and the development of fifth graders' concepts of balance. *Journal of Research in Science Teaching* 31: 847–856.

Chauvet, M. J., & Blatchford, P. (1993, Summer). Group composition and national curriculum assessment at seven years. *Psychology & Special Educational Needs* 35: 189–196.

Clark, B. (1997). *Growing up gifted: Developing the potential of children at home and at school.* (4th ed.). Upper Saddle River, NJ: Prentice-Hall.

Cohen, E. G., & Lotan, R. A. (1995). Producing equal-status interaction in the heterogeneous classroom. *American Educational Research Journal* 32: 99–120.

Davis, G., & Rimm, S. (1998). *Education of the gifted and talented.* (4th ed.). Boston: Allyn & Bacon.

Fuligni, A. J., Eccles, J. S., & Barber, B. L. (1995). The long-term effects of seventh grade ability grouping in mathematics. *Journal of Early Adolescence* 15: 58–89.

Gallagher, J. J., & Gallagher, S. (1994). *Teaching the gifted child.* Boston: Allyn & Bacon.

Gamoran, A., Nystrand, M., Berends, M., & LePore, P. C. (1995). An organizational analysis of the effects of ability grouping. *American Educational Research Journal* 32: 687–715.

Goldring, E. B. (1990). Assessing the status of information on classroom organizational frameworks for gifted students. *Journal of Educational Research* 83: 313–326.

Hacker, R. G., & Rowe, M. J. (1993, March). A study of the effects of an organization change from streamed to mixed-ability classes upon science classroom instruction. *Journal of Research in Science Teaching* 30: 223–231.

Haistings, C. (1992, October). Ending ability grouping is a moral imperative. *Educational Leadership* 50(2): 14.

Hall, D. P., & Cunningham, P. A. (1992). Reading without ability grouping: Issues in first grade instruction. *National Reading Conference Yearbook* 41: 366–390.

Haller, E. J. (1985, Winter). Pupil, race, and elementary school ability grouping: Are teachers biased against black children? *American Educational Research Journal* Vol. 22, No. 4: 465–483.

Hallinan, M. T. (1994). School differences in tracking effects on achievement. *Social Forces* 72: 799–820.

Heath, W. J. (1997). What are the most effective characteristics of teachers of the gifted? Texas State Report (ERIC Document Reproduction Services, #ED411665).

Hoekman, K., McCormick, J., & Gross M. U. M. (1998). The optimal context for gifted students: A preliminary exploration of motivational and affective considerations. *Gifted Child Quarterly* 43: 170–193.

Hooper, S. (1992). Effects of peer interaction during computer-based mathematics instruction. *Journal of Educational Research* 86: 180–189.

Jones, M. G., & Carter, G. (1994, September). Verbal and nonverbal behavior on ability-grouped dyads. *Journal of Research in Science Teaching* 31: 603–620.

Kulik, J. A. (1992). *An analysis of the research on ability grouping: Historical and contemporary perspectives.* Storrs, CT: The National Research Center on the Gifted and Talented Research-Based Decision Making Series.

Kulik, J. A., & Kulik, C. L. C. (1992). Meta-analytic findings on grouping programs. *Gifted Child Quarterly* 36: 73–77.

Lou, Y., Abrami, P. C., Spence, J. C., & Poulsen, C. (1996). Within-class grouping: A meta-analysis. *Review of Educational Research* 66: 423–458.

Mason, D. A., & Good, T. L. (1993). Effects of two-group and whole-class teaching on regrouped elementary students' mathematics achievement. *American Educational Research Journal* 30: 328–360.

Nasca, D. (1983). Questioning directions for the intellectually gifted. *Gifted Child Quarterly* 27: 185–188.

Oakes, J. (1985). *Keeping track: How schools structure inequality.* New Haven, CT: Yale University Press.

Pallas, A. M., Entwisle, D. R., Alexander, K. L., & Stluka, M. F. (1994). Ability group effects: Instructional, social, or institutional? *Sociology of Education* 67: 27–46.

Richardson, A. G., & Fergus, E. E. (1993). Learning style and ability grouping in the high school system: Some Caribbean findings. *Educational Research* 35: 69–76.

Rogers, K. B. (1991). *The relationship of grouping practices to the education of the gifted and talented learner.* Storrs, CT: The National Research Center on the Gifted and Talented Research-Based Decision Making Series.

———. (1993). Grouping the gifted: Questions and answers. *Roeper Review* 16: 8–13.

———. (1998). Using current research to make "good" decisions about grouping. *National Association for Secondary School Principals Bulletin* 82(595): 38–46.

Schunk, D. (1996). *Learning theories: An educational perspective.* (3rd ed.). Upper Saddle River, NJ: Merrill.

Schunk, D. H., & Zimmerman, B. J. (1996). Modeling and self-efficacy influences children's development of self-regulation. In J. Juvonen & K. R. Wentzel (Eds.), *Social motivation: Understanding children's school adjustment* (pp. 154–180). Cambridge, England: Cambridge University Press.

Slate, J. R., Jones, C. H., & Dawson, P. (1993). Academic skills of high school students as a function of grade, gender, and academic track. *High School Journal* 76: 245–251.

Slavin, R. E. (1993). Ability grouping in the middle grades: Achievement effects and alternatives. *Elementary School Journal* 93: 535–552.

Start, B. (1995, August). *The relationship of instructional pace and ability differences in concept attainment.* Paper presented at the national conference of Supporting the Emotional Needs of the Gifted. San Diego, CA.

Veenman, S. (1995). Cognitive and noncognitive effects of multigrade and multi-age classes: A best-evidence synthesis. *Review of Educational Research* 65: 319–382.

Equity in Gifted Programs: How Do We Measure Up?

Elinor Ruth Smith | WINTER 2001

Elinor Ruth Smith is a freelance consultant specializing in the education of gifted students. In addition to consulting for schools and school districts, she has also been an instructor for the Gifted and Talented Education (GATE) Certificate Programs of the University of California at both the San Diego and Riverside campuses, and, most recently, at San Diego State University.

Many attitudes and practices in our society and schools stand as stumbling blocks to better identifying and serving underrepresented populations in our gifted programs—especially African American, Hispanic, and Native American gifted youth. After a discussion of such attitudes and practices, Elinor Ruth Smith presents a list of do's and don'ts designed to encourage effective change in our schools, including strategies to identify and then retain underrepresented students once they are in the program.

Concerns about equity in gifted programs have been raised periodically since the inception of the programs. Like so many issues in education that arise repeatedly over the years, continued discussions of how to achieve both equity and excellence in gifted education serve as a reminder of our scant progress. Our advances, often hesitant, move us unsteadily toward rather ill-defined goals. Some key factors in our society, our schools, and perhaps in ourselves seem to stand in the way of understanding and dealing with the underlying causes of inequity as we strive to shape programs of the highest quality. What are these factors and what challenges do they pose? What changes can we make to minimize their impact? These are some of the questions I ask as I work and speak with educators, parents, and students in various school districts—questions not too different from those that were asked twenty or thirty years ago.

Addressing inequities in our gifted programs by focusing solely on numbers and on finding the "right" tests sometimes yields improvement in the numbers of students from underrepresented groups. Yet, unless we attend to questions of retention of the students in the programs and how to develop appropriate program services for them, we are likely to have only temporary results.

Roots of Inequity

Desire for immediate results can also lead to the use of indefensible strategies that, in the end, do more harm than good. Inequity in gifted programs has deep roots in the culture of our society and our school systems, as well as in the ways these affect all of us. Willingness to examine these might allow us to come to some longer-lasting, more defensible solutions if, indeed, we truly want solutions.

SOCIETAL FACTORS

It is impossible to deny the stigma attached over centuries to certain ethnic groups in American society. Prejudices against these groups—Native American, Hispanic, and African American—still exist and it is no surprise that they are the groups most overlooked for gifted and other school programs associated with excellence. Though many efforts over time have successfully eradicated some overt forms of discrimination, it is difficult to get rid of all traces of stigma that have for so long seeped under the skin into our very bone. Like True Son in Conrad Richter's *The Light in the Forest* who, perplexed by having to leave his Indian family, wondered if his father had left some tiny trace of white blood in his veins, some of us wonder about the little traces of stigma left under our skin; others are unaware that's even possible. This affects us all.

Culture and society change in many ways. Families today represent an increasingly greater variety of cultures and lifestyles and have widely differing beliefs about and expectations of school and, similarly, of gifted programs. This presents additional challenges for schools and teachers. In areas in which children come from many different language, cultural, and socioeconomic groups, schools and school staffs are called upon to develop greater cultural competence in order to recognize the varied expressions of gifted behaviors and to understand how to serve these children well. We must be willing to give careful consideration to the need to continually revamp our identification and program strategies to accommodate these changes.

School children themselves present varied and ever-changing challenges for school staffs. Changes in the students as a result of societal influences seem to be occurring in much more rapid cycles. At the same time that children are exposed through media and technology to a whole world of ideas and images, both positive and negative, and spend hours alone within the confines of home, many children's opportunities for self-directed experiences outside the home are limited. This is a paradox. Teachers can no longer assume a commonality of prior experiences among students. Effective curriculum planning and instruction require more frequent assessment, both formal and informal, with greater attention to outcomes for individual students.

SCHOOL FACTORS

School systems, whether K–12 or postsecondary, though seemingly dynamic institutions, are hierarchical and accomplish change with great difficulty. They are full of contradictions. Decision making about educational issues is not always in the hands of the educators. In the hierarchy of concerns, those who ought to be the top priority are often not. The amount of money a program draws, rather than the importance of the needs it serves, often determines how much serious attention it receives. In some areas, the gifted program becomes an added responsibility for an already overburdened administrator who may understand little about gifted education. Added to that, frequent changes of personnel with no requirements for prior knowledge, particularly at the administrative level, are common occurrences causing us to lose ground each time rather than make continuous, steady progress. Long-range planning and grooming of future leaders can alleviate some of this.

Public pressure and heightened expectations about what students should know and be able to do at each grade level are placing increasing demands on schools to better educate students, especially in our low performing schools.

Many of these schools serve children of poverty and children from cultural and language groups underrepresented in gifted programs. Accountability is the word of the day. A number of schools and school systems react to this pressure by instituting rigid, top-down, one-size-fits-all programs aimed at rescuing failing students. Some of these instructional approaches are highly scripted, allowing for no variance to meet individual needs for differentiation or for the kinds of student activity through which gifted behaviors become evident. Children who need to learn in a different way are overlooked. Sometimes these approaches tend to penalize the very children we are trying to help.

The current teacher shortage is another factor which impacts most heavily those schools in low socioeconomic areas and diverse communities. These schools, the most difficult in which to teach, have the greatest turnover and, therefore, high percentages of inexperienced teachers. Once trained and more confident, a number of these new teachers opt to transfer to schools in which teaching is less demanding. Instability of staff coupled with greater challenges to meet can make it unlikely that there will be a strong focus on gifted education. Instituting and maintaining gifted programs in these schools is problematic unless they have dynamic leadership committed to serving the needs of all children, including the gifted. Too often the programs are devalued or watered down in the name of equity and fairness and the underrepresented become the most underserved.

Few teacher-training institutions are preparing new teachers for diverse and differentiated classrooms. The range of instructional needs in many classrooms taxes the abilities of even the most experienced teachers. Nor are most schools willing to face the difficulty by adjusting the range from class to class in order to better serve all students and use teachers' talents in more effective ways.

As far as understanding cultural diversity is concerned, we seem to know most about the superficial aspects of the varied cultures we encounter, such as, food, dress, important people in the culture, and important holidays; most of us understand little about what is deeply meaningful to people of those cultures and what they believe defines them. Many educators are unaware of how and when their own values are clouding their perceptions of the children they must educate.

Lack of awareness can cause the best of intentions to miss the mark. The prevailing view among those who have had little experience with gifted children and little or no training in gifted education is that high achievement in school is synonymous with giftedness. This misconception can lead to poor practices with respect to identification procedures, program options, and classroom approaches. In such cases underachieving gifted students in need of differentiated curriculum and instruction will not receive these services, thus compounding their risk for disengagement from school and for continued failure.

Do's and Don'ts

The above are a few of the factors which play a role in our inability to make greater strides and more lasting changes in properly identifying and educating gifted children from diverse, underrepresented populations. How might we change what we do and how we do it to accommodate or minimize any negative impacts of these factors? Based on what I have seen a few schools doing successfully, here are some suggested do's and don'ts for those working with gifted programs.

THE DON'TS

- Don't ask people to perform tasks or services for which they are ill prepared. If classroom teachers are not routinely provided with training in how to recognize gifted abilities in diverse populations, they should not be the main source of referrals for screening and assessment. Similarly, don't place gifted children from underrepresented cultural groups with teachers who have neither the instinct nor the training nor the cultural competence for working with them.

- Don't expect one kind of program or one program option to meet the needs of all gifted students. Even without considering cultural diversity, gifted students are a diverse group with respect to ability levels, areas of strength, interests, learning styles, social and emotional needs, and personality characteristics. For gifted students from diverse backgrounds, successful outcomes, including retention in the program, are more likely if a variety of program options can be combined to meet their needs.

- Don't expect gifted students from diverse backgrounds and their families to share your values about school and the role of education in their lives. Survival needs, loyalty to family, and cultural tradition may take priority over education for some families. Acknowledging the family's values may be the first step to building a relationship of mutual respect. Respect can be the basis for allowing students to make their own decisions at the appropriate time concerning whether to live in one or the other culture, straddle the two, or become bicultural.

- Don't place gifted students from underrepresented cultures in a visual and performing arts option just as a way of quickly increasing their numbers in the program. Legitimate placement of students in visual and performing arts programs is appropriate, but not as a means of avoiding the effort of devising a defensible screening and identification process for all aspects of the program, including the intellectual area.

- Don't focus on identification numbers to the exclusion of program issues. Quality of program, how well the program suits students' needs, retention in the program of those identified, and student outcomes are important. Without these, identification serves no valid purpose.

- Don't wait until upper elementary grades to identify and serve gifted students. Students from diverse cultural and linguistic groups may disengage from school early without the appropriate curriculum and instruction.

- Don't be smug about your or your school's level of cultural competence. Becoming culturally competent requires ongoing self-examination. Refusing to self-examine leaves hidden vestiges of prejudice and stigma deep in one's bones. Subtle forms of prejudice, such as expecting less of children from certain groups in the name of giving them experiences of success that will make them feel good, can be more harmful than overt ones, for they leave children powerless to fight back. Unless we make this effort, all our other accomplishments will be undermined. We are all works in progress.

THE DO'S

- Do make sure that students have equal opportunity to be screened. Opportunity to be screened should not be dependent on age of the student, school attended, classroom placement, socioeconomic level, or cultural or linguistic group. Monitor for equal access on an ongoing basis.

- Do begin identification and program services at the earliest levels. Because children form their view of themselves in relation to school and learning at an early age, gifted students who are at risk are in danger of forming a negative view, which they may carry with them throughout their school experiences.

- Do use multiple measures for identification, including both test and non-test data. At no time in the identification process should one test or measure be the determining factor. In addition to test scores, data collected should include information from parents, the students themselves, and teachers. Other evidence of exceptionality might be anecdotal information and student work samples, as well as information on environmental or personal conditions that might inhibit school performance or depress test scores. All information should be considered together, rather than any one piece of evidence alone determining the outcome of the assessment.

- Do have the data gathered reviewed by a committee or study team composed of trained staff. A team of people working toward cultural competence, who understand giftedness, and who are able to interpret the data should make the recommendations about identification, placement, and appropriate options for program services.

- Do develop a variety of options for program services to meet varying student needs. Traditional program options may not be appropriate for some students. There are those who need a combination of services such as multiage grouping, cluster class placement, mentoring, or interdisciplinary seminars, to name a few. Decisions about these should be made based on student assessment data. Be creative.

- Do seek out parents and community members of diverse backgrounds to participate in some aspects of the program, such as members of advisory groups or in parent education or other activities. Students from underrepresented groups may be hesitant about participating in the gifted program, especially if they see few students like themselves participating. They may have difficulty explaining the program to the peer group from whom they have been separated. Seeing members of their own community involved may increase the chances that they will stay. Invitations by mail may not be enough to get the participation you want. Personal contact may be necessary.

- Do provide ongoing staff development followed by on-site support as programs are implemented. Staff development, whether on instructional practices or recognizing giftedness, requires supportive follow-up in the implementation stages to be effective and have lasting results. Thorough in-depth training over time of small numbers of committed staff from varied sites so that they can become trainers and mentors to others seems to work well. Remember, though, that the trainers themselves need periodic opportunities to come together for support and to further their own learning.

- Do long-range planning that addresses all aspects of the program, paying attention to and prioritizing the trouble spots and how all the pieces of the puzzle fit together. Fragmentation of the program detracts from the success of the whole, particularly for underrepresented students. If those with responsibility for identification, for example, are unfamiliar with curricular and instructional practices in varied program options, retention of students in the program can be seriously damaged, particularly if inappropriate placement decisions have been made. Similarly, those responsible for the instruction need to know the kinds and results of assessment that were done so that instruction can be more targeted and effective for individual students.

Becoming culturally competent requires ongoing self-examination.

- Do consider piloting new program options, identification procedures, and staff development approaches on a small scale before implementing them universally. If piloting is done with volunteer schools and staffs, the cooperative process can help determine what works, what doesn't, and what needs to be altered. It can also help determine whether the approaches are cost effective. Feedback from the users can be extremely valuable to successful use on a wider basis at a later date. When pilot projects are successful, they have the potential to generate positive interest for the next phase of implementation.

- Do build evaluation into all aspects of identification and programming. A particular approach may look good on paper and feel right to those involved. Only by carefully planned evaluation strategies will you be able to identify the intended outcomes and know whether and when they are achieved. As mentioned previously, some school districts focus so much on the numbers of students from diverse backgrounds being identified that they forget to look at whether the students are remaining in the program and whether the program is helping them achieve the expected results.

These are a few ideas gleaned from working with gifted programs in a variety of schools and school districts. The list is not finite. You can probably add to it. These do's and don'ts can be separated into those which are simply good program practices, those which are just common sense, those which require changes in the ways we and our schools succumb to societal influences, and those which require fundamental changes in our own attitudes and behaviors. The latter are the difficult ones. They require determination, resolve, and persistence. Do we have the will power or will we be writing articles addressing this issue again in another ten or fifteen years?

Interdisciplinarity ...
Support and Concerns

Sandra N. Kaplan | FALL 2002

Sandra N. Kaplan, Ed.D., *is an associate clinical professor at the University of Southern California. She is a past president of both the California Association for the Gifted and the National Association for Gifted Children. She coauthored* The Parallel Curriculum Model, *a service publication of the National Association for Gifted Children, as well as other works particularly in curriculum development.*

Curriculum designs that encourage students to make connections between various disciplines are frequently found in programs for gifted learners. Content specialists often oppose such interdisciplinarity, believing that it "diminishes" effective teaching of subject matter. Sandra Kaplan examines some of the reasons for these differences of opinion and suggests ways to reconcile them. She maintains that teachers must find the "intellectual courage" to teach individual disciplines well while also stressing the importance of their connections to other disciplines.

Discussions about interdisciplinary curriculum evoke a combination of concern and support. The concern is often a consequence of content specialists who view interdisciplinary curriculum as diminishing rather than enhancing the accurate and appropriate learning of subject matter in the disciplines. Support comes from educators who understand that interdisciplinary curriculum allows students to weave sophisticated understandings that generalize, facilitate, and sustain the comprehension of subject matter between and across the disciplines. Attempts to reconcile the differences between these individuals may be of less importance than the need to understand that both groups are accurate in their perceptions, and that attending to their concerns and support should underscore decisions to develop and implement an interdisciplinary curriculum.

Facing the Concerns

The first step toward addressing the concerns expressed by content specialists is to understand the major differences between interdisciplinary and integrated curriculum designs. Whereas integrated curriculum uses an organizing element or theme to align subject matter from the various disciplines to achieve continuity, interdisciplinary curriculum presents students with the opportunity to forge understandings between or across disciplines by asking them to seek the areas where the curricular areas are related, connected, and/or associated. For example, the integrated curriculum designed around the study of Native Americans aligns the legends (language arts) with the teaching of the environment (science) and its use to accommodate the life of the people with the anthropological study (social studies) of the tools and customs of the cultures. In this integrated example of curriculum, the curriculum developer has selected the areas of study within the core curriculum that are related to each other.

An interdisciplinary curriculum requests learners to identify how the areas taught in one discipline relate to the areas being taught in other disciplines. The learner is required to analyze the nature of the subject matter that has been taught in order to define, verify, clarify and substantiate how and why these areas are related. In an interdisciplinary curriculum, thorough knowledge of the subject matter is needed in order to be able to make the relationships between and across subject matter from the various disciplines. Providing students with universal concepts such as change, systems, conflict, and power serve to stimulate thinking about how and why connections among disciplines can be made. However, utilizing these universal concepts to make interdisciplinary connections does not eliminate the need to recognize that there are many and varied methods to engineer bridges between and among areas of study in the different disciplines.

Demanding that the interdisciplinary connections be legitimate is another way to counter the critical comments leveled at interdisciplinary curriculum by content specialists. In many situations, teachers accept any relationship stated by students as an authentic association between disciplines. Sometimes this is the result of a teacher's inability to challenge the students by asking them to define what they mean by the stated relationship and to exemplify it for further understanding by the class. Sometimes it is the result of a teacher's inability to recognize the difference between a contrived and viable relationship that exits between and among areas of study in the disciplines. Teachers are often embarrassed that they did not recognize the relationship made by students and perceive the students as smarter and more creative than they are in developing interdisciplinary connections. Teacher acceptance of relationships between and among the disciplines without rigorous inquiry to verify and legitimatize them is one of the reasons why content specialists do not want to support interdisciplinary curriculum.

The premature request to make interdisciplinary connections is still another issue posed by content specialists in their criticism of interdisciplinary curriculum. Too often students are expected to identify the relationship between or among the disciplines without sufficient knowledge of the discipline or sufficient time to have studied the intricacies of the topic under study. Knowing the subject matter and having time to assimilate and understand it prior to making relationships between and among the disciplines are both mandatory and not luxuries to quality interdisciplinary teaching and learning.

Providing the Support

While the literature defining differentiated curriculum for gifted students is replete with support for interdisciplinary curriculum, the realities of contemporary curricular demands mitigate against the nature of interdisciplinary curriculum. The standards-based curriculum movement is interpreted by many to mean the isolated and disjointed teaching of standards in a discrete subject-by-subject manner. Furthermore, the requirement for curriculum pacing that places expectations on the attainment of specific goals within a given time frame is thought to deter attempts at interdisciplinary curriculum designs.

In reality, the selection of standards from different disciplines that complement and or reinforce each other is a more productive way to stimulate student achievement and promote retention. A teacher's first venture into the design of an interdisciplinary curriculum could be to take the standards from the disciplines within their grade level along with a pair of scissors and some glue to cut and paste the standards onto an interdisciplinary chart that indicates how the standards from different disciplines can reinforce one another.

The professional developmental opportunities that are offered to teachers should allow teachers to practice the art of constructing interdisciplinary connections rather than merely telling them about the value of such a curriculum design. Until teachers can experience directly the feelings of frustration, inquisitiveness, and satisfaction found in making interdisciplinary connections, they cannot effectively support the practice of this curricular strategy for their students. Thinking interdisciplinarily is a way of being a scholar. It requires more than knowing about the practice; it requires becoming intellectually familiar with the practice.

Engaging in interdisciplinary curriculum is fostered by clearly understanding that the textbook is a single, but not the only reference for accessing information about the discipline. Constructing interdisciplinary connections requires gleaning information from many and varied sources. Quality as well as abundance of information are necessary in order to detect relationships between and among the disciplines. A single perspective on a subject area and a paltry amount of information concerning the subject area limit the possibilities of making qualitative and authentic relationships between and among the disciplines.

Creating the Design

The classroom environment has to provide the impetus for the development of interdisciplinary connections. The implementation of an interdisciplinary curriculum is dependent on environmental prompts that consistently remind students of the higher order of knowing that is expected as a consequence of the teaching and learning process. Figure 1 illustrates examples of prompts that can be placed in the classroom environment to direct students' attention to the goal of making interdisciplinary connections.

Figure 1: Classroom Prompts to Assist Students in Making Interdisciplinary Connections

CONNECT knowledge across the disciplines.

What ✄ 🍶 📎 **will you use to connect the disciplines?**

Interdisciplinary curriculum is a consequence of design not happenstance and should become a regular feature of the teaching and learning processes. Figure 2 includes examples of how teachers can plan in order to affect interdisciplinary curriculum.

Figure 2: Teacher Planning Sheets for Interdisciplinary Curriculum

LESSON PLANS			GOAL
Discipline	**Discipline**	**Discipline**	
Social Studies	Language Arts	Science	How does the concept of **CHANGE** relate to our studies across the disciplines?
Standard(s)	**Standard(s)**	**Standard(s)**	

Figure 2 (continued)

Interdisciplinary Studies	Universal Concept CHANGE		Generalization	Change has a ripple effect
Core Curriculum Studies	Social Studies	Language Arts	Science	Math

A Point of Recognition

A curriculum that expects students to construct interdisciplinary connections cannot be perceived as a curriculum only for gifted students or one that is a gimmick or a fad. Discussions about interdisciplinary curriculum must begin with discussions about quality curriculum. The separate subject approach prevalent in schools is often more a reflection of teacher requirements for teaching than student needs for learning. It is a natural consequence of human nature to want to make sense out of parts and pieces of learning that are presented to us. The true dilemma affecting the implementation of interdisciplinary curriculum is how teachers find the intellectual courage to teach each discipline to a sophisticated level of comprehension while stressing that the highest level of knowing the discipline is to understand it as a discipline in its own right as well as a discipline that complements and connects to other disciplines.

A Differentiated Rubric to Guide Teaching, Learning, and Assessment

Sandra N. Kaplan | FALL 2002

Sandra N. Kaplan, Ed.D., is an associate clinical professor at the University of Southern California. She is a past president of both the California Association for the Gifted and the National Association for Gifted Children. She coauthored The Parallel Curriculum Model, *a service publication of the National Association for Gifted Children, as well as other works particularly in curriculum development.*

Conventional assessment instruments fall far short when used to measure student mastery of a differentiated curriculum. Sandra Kaplan has devised a rubric that assesses the desired outcomes of differentiated curriculum at various levels. She includes measures of thinking skill mastery, content acquisition, research skills, product development, and scholarly behaviors. A large table illustrates the system for readers.

Assessment is dependent on the relationship between teaching and learning. Answers to the questions: 1) What should be taught? and 2) How well did students learn it? are critical components of this relationship. The Differentiated Curriculum Rubric has been designed to provide teachers with the means to define the curricular experiences appropriately responsive to gifted students while simultaneously providing a guide to assess their progress and achievement in the various areas of a differentiated curriculum. Importantly, this type of rubric sequentially defines and articulates the increasing levels of teacher and student performance expected in implementing a differentiated curriculum.

The rubric reflects the curricular areas commonly identified to differentiate the core curriculum for gifted students.

Table 1: Curricular Areas Used to Differentiate Core Curriculum for Gifted Students

Mastery of higher level thinking skills and inclusive of critical, creative, problem solving, and logic skills.	Thinking Skill Mastery
Acquisition of advanced or accelerated content aligned to standards of the core curriculum.	Content Acquisition
Opportunities to practice skills and use resources related to independent investigations of problems, questions, and topics.	Research Skills
Development of products that are outgrowths of the work of disciplinarians.	Product Development
Understanding of the attributes of scholarly individuals.	Scholarly Behavior

The segments within each area of the rubric (see Table 1) specify the levels of sophistication and expectation for teaching and learning. Segments are arranged from simple to abstract. The specifications of this developmental sequence are crucial for several reasons:

1. It provides teachers with curriculum directionality or a means to set expectations for teaching and learning experiences over time that reinforce each area of differentiation. The developmental sequence underscores the need to develop a comprehensive range of interrelated learning experiences leading to expert-like performance. Too often the quick assimilation of a single lesson is perceived by teachers and students as sufficient success for gifted students resulting in premature cessation of the particular investigation or

study, as well as acceptance of indicators of success that are too cursory or simplistic.

2. The developmental sequence described for each area of a differentiated curriculum defines a means to report to students and parents the pathway of academic achievement expected of a gifted student matriculating through a differentiated curriculum. Each developmental sequence underscores academic success that represents continuous growth rather than a single achievement identified by a discrete score or performance at a definitive point in time.

Unlike the areas of Thinking Skills and Content Acquisition, the areas of Research Skills and Product Development define skills that require more elaboration for teaching and learning. For example, the skill "paraphrase" should be further defined into developmental levels of skill mastery. The ability to express in an oral mode includes giving speeches, participating in a debate, and teaching a lesson. These two areas of a differentiated curriculum require further definition within each segment.

The last column on the Differentiated Curriculum Rubric labeled Evidence identifies means for gathering the assessment data necessary to determine the degree of achievement attained by groups and individual students. These types of evidence are not directly related to the area in the same row. Teachers can mix and match these forms of evidence to the area of differentiation they want to assess. The concept represented by this column is the need to select appropriate alternative measures for assessment and to become less reliant on standardized testing as the sole indicator of determining academic success for gifted students.

Perhaps the most significant application of the Differentiated Curriculum Rubric is the possibility of its use as an outline for developing a scope and sequence for the gifted program. A scope and sequence provides directionality and efficacy to the teaching and learning of gifted students. It avoids the curricular redundancy gifted students too often encounter. It is not unusual for teachers to teach elements of the differentiated curriculum without concern for students' prior knowledge and the need to discriminate between expectations for the outcomes of a differentiated curriculum within, between, and across grade levels. "In what ways does the study of this element of a differentiated curriculum differ at this grade level?" should be a continuing question addressed by teachers of the gifted. "What evidence do we have to measure the outcomes of a differentiated curriculum?" is the other question teachers need to answer. The Differentiated Curriculum Rubric is one way to arrive at responses to these two questions.

Table 2: Differentiated Curriculum Rubric

DIFFERENTIATED CURRICULUM RUBRIC

Thinking Skill Mastery

Define the skill	Describe the purpose for using the skill	Apply the skill in context	Substantiate the use of the skill	Relate the skill to other skills	**EVIDENCE**

Content Acquisition

Know it in relationship to the standard	Know it in relationship to the complex concepts of the discipline	Relate it to big ideas—theories, generalizations, or principles—and make disciplinary connections	Integrate it with Depth/Complexity	Specify Depth/Complexity with Content Imperatives	**CONFERENCE**

Research Skills

Use multiple and varied print/nonprint resources	Paraphrase	Cite correctly	Take notes	Draw conclusions and generalize	**PORTFOLIO**

Product Development

Oral	Written	Graphic	Computer generated	Multimedia/Modality	**TEACHER-MADE TEST**

Scholarly Behaviors

Name the behaviors	Relate behaviors to expertise	Relate traits to heroes and heroines in fiction and nonfiction	Relate to self	Define the self	**WORK SAMPLES**

Drawing on the Inventive Mind: Making Verbal Thinking Visual and Visual Thinking Verbal

Jon Pearson | FALL/WINTER 2003

Jon Pearson is an author, performer, and international creative learning consultant who lives in Los Angeles. He is a regular contributor to Gifted Education Communicator *and at every CAG conference.*

In a lively combination of words and drawings, Jon Pearson makes the case for including drawing in every class and discipline, "even if you can't draw—even if you hate to draw." He delighted in drawing as a child and it defined him as a thinking person. Pearson illustrates the many ways drawing can be used to increase imagination, understanding, and mastery of learning. He even includes tricks for non-drawing teachers to utilize in implementing the practice.

In that magic terrain between words and images, the mind makes sense of the world— outside and in.

When I was 7 years old, I had a love affair with blank paper. It practically called to me from the other room. I didn't draw on it—I dove into it. I split it open with the first crayon mark, and light practically poured out. I didn't draw to "make" something so much as to go somewhere—to a place that defied the laws of logic, gravity, and authority (parents and teachers)—a place where, at four feet tall and sixty pounds, I could be king. In drawing I discovered the first law of learning: *The only way to find yourself is to lose yourself utterly.*

Sitting at the big maroon table in the upstairs bedroom, I drew ships and sailors. My sailors walked all along the sides and tops of the ships as if they wore magnetic shoes. I'd color in a sailor and imagine he was from the Midwest, played cards, loved chess. From my little seat at the big table I commanded a universe of trees and clouds and pioneers and Revolutionary War soldiers and spacemen and insects and lawn furniture and wooded hills. But these weren't pictures as much as "stories," half-stories, backs and fronts, and middles of stories. The gray wolf poised on the crown of the hill was a "topic sentence" and the worn-out barn at the foot of the hill was a "paragraph" of hidden farm animals and implements.

Everything had story—everything was story. The flat rectangular space in front of me rolled forth in living time like a movie. Through drawing, nouns became adjectives. A dog wasn't just a "dog." He was wet, shaggy, proud, ratty, lonely—depending on how I drew him. Nouns came to life as verbs. Space was a form of time. Anything could happen, from anywhere; dogs could snarl or mail checks.

Drawing was always a place I could go where time met space, visual met verbal, spatial met sequential, fact met fiction, inductive met deductive. For example, in my pictures, a cat would require a rug, which called for a sofa, which implied a mom, and a list of chores, that could imply arguments between siblings, which might infer parallel universes and the fact that your sister might, actually, have come from another planet.

I would discuss as I drew. Not out loud, but in a dance of self-talk or pre-talk that bounced between the urge to make a hill, and the thought of who might live on the other side of that hill, and did they like country-western music? Ideas appeared magically from someplace suspended between head, hand, and paper—a place I went to meet myself by getting out of my own way.

Drawing as Thinking

By far the greatest thing was the blank paper: the infinite potential, the igniting and multiplying of worlds and ways of thinking outside the ordinary. Art for me was a grand mixing bowl of philosophy, psychology, and poetry right before my eyes. Drawing was the place I went to stir my thoughts, where I began the lifelong habit of thinking for myself and trusting myself.

Drawing helped me realize I had not just five but ten senses. I had the five "outward" senses of sight, smell, touch, taste, and hearing; but I also had those tangent "imagined" five senses. I could imagine the smell of puppy breath, the racket of birds in a tree—even the "taste" of molten lava in my picture as I drew. I drew with all of myself. Which is the same way I now read.

I could also break the rules. In my pictures birds not only "chirped," churds also burped. Instead of forming my thoughts in words, I forged words in images. Through drawing I could do my best "off-road" thinking. I could go places words couldn't, while at the same time where I went begged for words. Drawing thus made me not only an artist but also a writer and speaker.

The Role of Drawing

Drawing was the world's earliest writing. The letter "A," aleph, began as the image of an ox head. Drawing has become the world's future language in the form of international icons. It is the first language of the most inventive people on earth—children. Children use the drawing process to mix the domains of sensory, emotional, and conceptual knowledge. Drawing takes them beyond surface understanding to enter realms of exploration and appreciation that words and numbers alone cannot convey.

Drawing is language development, brain development, and paradox. Although a drawing of a tree is not itself a tree, it looks far more tree-like than the word does. The magic of drawing can make the emotional sensory and the conceptual perceptual, putting our thinking in front of us and at hand as tangible. Drawing adds nuance and non sequitur—from the accidental and unconscious to the presumed and predictable. Think more routinely in pictures, and you add fluency, flexibility, originality, and elaboration to all your thinking—not to mention depth, complexity, and speed.

Teaching the Art

For the past eighteen years I have had the honor of presenting school assemblies and teacher workshops to over a million students, teachers, parents, and administrators around the world. I have discovered through teaching how to use drawing as a reading, writing, memory, and higher-level thinking tool. There is not a single California State standard that cannot be readily taught through drawing. I have seen drawing used to teach math, social studies, science, language arts, even physical education. Anything that involves seeing or thinking can be facilitated through drawing. Even if you can't draw—even if you hate to draw.

First, forget everything you "know" about drawing. Forget that in third grade someone said your camel looked like a pelican. That "artists draw better than nonartists." That the curriculum is too full. Drawing speeds learning. Drawing makes learning lasting and meaningful by making it creative and personal.

Nearly all young children love to draw. Then, around fourth grade, they separate into "class artist" and "can't draw." Drawing switches from a process of exploration to one of execution—from getting it out to getting it right. Remember when you loved to draw? Gifted children have huge interior worlds. Drawing is an ideal place for more of the brain to speak to more of the brain in order to connect ideas and concepts.

So, you still "can't draw" and are not about to get up in front of students and look foolish. Consider this: if you "can't draw" but do it anyway you are actually giving students personal permission to stretch themselves. Your confident "failure" establishes their collective sense of safety.

Here is a surefire way not to fail. Simply name what you draw after you draw it. Name the outcome, not the intention. This will also build suspense. Does your buffalo resemble a giant garden slug? Turn error into poetry by adding the caption " . . . and they roamed the plains like massive garden slugs." A good drawing may be good not because it looks like something but because it suggests a hundred other things. Error breeds metaphor.

The gifted mind often lurches and gathers through an alternating process of accident and analysis, association and distinction, visual and verbal. Your drawing of a deer might look more like a map of the Great Lakes. A discussion can then ensue on the possible connections between deer and lakes, "great" and animals, two-dimensional figures within three-dimensional worlds.

No time for "accidental" discussions in a busy curriculum? Most thinking is accidental. Can you really predict your next thought? This sort of back-burner thinking is going on constantly with gifted students. Drawing invites it and multiplies learning.

Drawing not only feeds the mind, it seeds the mind. Studying Sir Francis Drake? First, have your students draw his ship, the Golden Hind, purely from imagination. They note any questions they may have as they construct an x-ray drawing of the entire ship—which may finally resemble a space ship. The drawing is less important than the questions generated: How many cannons did it have? Where was the kitchen? Did they have towel racks? Provide a historically accurate picture of the interior of the Golden Hind from the text book or other source. As students finish their drawings and have eight million questions, they can then study the picture—they will view it like hawks. (See Figure 1.) Looking with questions is fifty times more powerful than simply looking. We tend to see what we have already seen; and think we know more than we know. Drawing helps us see what we don't know and don't expect.

Figure 1

The mind craves the unpredictable and particular, variety and detail, the diverting along with the important, the sensory as well as the conceptual. The mind must daydream after such facts: Abraham Lincoln had perfect white teeth. Magellan brought two hundred barrels of anchovies with him on his attempted trip around the world. The Incas used to greet each other with the words: "Don't lie. Don't steal. And don't be lazy." These are all stray details. But details wake up and enlarge the mind as the epicenter of daydreams, the mind's natural drawing process. The trick is to get students to daydream into the subject, not out of it.

The *act* of drawing differs from the *art* of drawing. If you draw at all on the board, you will observe three wonderful things happen: you get better attention, you can massage (repeat) information in, and the message (image) broadcasts long after you have moved on. If you actually sketch a whale while explaining that it has the largest brain of any animal on earth, your students will be able to see what they are hearing. The fact of your drawing anchors the whale facts and puts students' listening in a kind of real time where seeing, saying, and doing (drawing) align themselves. Drawing gets, keeps, and directs attention. It also customizes, personalizes, and adds idiosyncrasy to the lesson.

Much of school is about "getting it right." Have your students draw a picture "all wrong." Try drawing an elk all wrong. I don't just mean with balloon legs, a horse face, and reindeer antlers but with passenger seats, a radar station, and breath that smells like the floor of the New York Stock Exchange. I have no idea what the NYSE floor smells like; the point is that original thinking is full of dead ends, false starts, and unlikely breakthroughs. Want good ideas? Don't simply tolerate error—seek it out. Then use only what you like. Clarity and understanding demand mystery and surprise.

The Uses of Seeing

The creative mind perpetually poses two related questions: What if? and What else? It alternates between the present and the possible, the observed and the imagined, constantly drawing distinctions and connections. Drawing accentuates the process by fostering observation and feeding imagination. Real thinking begins with real seeing, by which the familiar becomes odd and the imagined becomes vivid.

Look at your right hand. Now, really look at it. What did you do differently? For me, I stopped the traffic of words going on in my head and just saw my right hand. Without describing, explaining, interpreting, or judging my hand, I see more of it, until it almost seems to grow before my eyes. What is growing, of course, is my new awareness of it. Paradoxically, afterwards I have much more to say about what I saw. It is also a much-needed vacation from the thoughts in our heads. Sustained looking at something without words is a form of "drawing" it.

Observation and imagination are the brother and sister of reading and writing. Want to be a good writer? Observe more. John Steinbeck wrote *The Grapes of Wrath* in one hundred days. However, he spent five years before beginning to write in observing every possible aspect of migrant life. Mrs. Joad, the central character, isn't one woman; she is a thousand women crushed down diamond-hard into one living, breathing portrait. Observation breeds imagination. Reading, of course, is ninety-nine percent imagination. Good readers read beyond the words to the meanings—to the movies created in their own heads by the writer.

Try this simple activity: Within a large rectangle, students draw whatever they want—perhaps something they are studying. After a few minutes the students stop and write the word "see" to the left of their rectangle, listing everything they can name in the picture. The image of a tree, for example, breaks up into a thousand words: bark, leaves, roots, photosynthesis, diameter—the process is endless. Seeing fosters articulation, articulation fosters seeing. The more you name the more you have to keep looking.

Then have students switch papers with a partner. The partners write the word "imagine" to the right of the rectangle, this time listing everything they don't see in the picture. A scene of a California mission might lack an ox cart—but it also might lack the Taj Mahal or a gazelle or a sleepy Tuesday. It need not make sense; sense can come later. The idea is to see more of what is there—and more of what is not. The drawings are then returned to the originators, who then must weave the list into the scene. Can't draw a gazelle? Draw it hidden in a packing crate. Be either artist or attorney. Make the picture, or make the case for its being in the picture. (See Figure 2.)

Figure 2

Drawing deepens reading comprehension by intensifying the links between inner and outer worlds, bridging the gap between words and their "live" meanings. Both images and words connect deeply into what is not shown or stated.

Encourage your students to experience the rich nature of implication and inference—that most meaning resides below the literal and factual, and must be sought after with deeper tools.

In school we usually talk about a subject, write about it, and if it is Friday or raining, draw something. I often have students reverse this process: draw, then talk, then write. I discovered a simple truth: the better I could see something, the better I could say it; and the better I could say it, the better I could write it; and the better I could write it, the better I could read it. SEE IT—SAY IT—WRITE IT—READ IT, and then see it all over again. Pictures always helped me go "on location" in my imagination. Instead of writing a story and drawing a picture I found I could start with a picture, invent a hundred stories, pick one and write it—a story that was layered and forceful and—most important—mine.

Owning Concepts

In summer 2000, the Catholic Relief Services invited me to teach creative learning techniques to teachers and administrators in Albania. I went to towns whose names were pronounced "Fear" and "Duress" and talked about creativity. Except we didn't just talk. We drew and wrote and talked. At one site, I had the people take just eight seconds to draw an image representing the concept of creativity. Eight seconds—not enough time to think analytically to "get it right." Next, I gave them five minutes to write about their images, and finally, we shared around the room for half an hour.

I'll never forget the images. One man drew an observation balloon and said, "Creativity is like being high in the air objectively looking down." Another man drew a volleyball being spiked over a net and said, "It is like the moment of decisiveness." One woman drew a rowboat in the middle of a lagoon and said, "It is like being afloat on peaceful water; and I wish we could be more on the water." Another man drew a horizontal spiral and said, "Creativity keeps progressing in recurring cycles." One woman drew a garden half on fire. Another drew a dove with its wing chopped off and blood spurting out and said, "Creativity is like freedom and we have been cheated of our freedom." Another woman drew a three-story apartment building and said, "If you live on the top floor you will be shot. If you live on the bottom floor you will be crushed. I tell my children, always, live in the middle, live in the middle." I realized that drawing isn't something we just do on paper. Images in the back of our awareness shape and guide our lives. Drawing moves these images to the front of our minds, where we can own rather than be owned by them.

The drawing became like a little prism that fanned the one word creativity into a spectrum: objectivity, decisiveness, recurrence, freedom, safety. Words passing through pictures fracture into a range of words, generating more pictures. The conversation could then penetrate below the surface, beyond tidy preconceptions.

Have your students draw an eight-second picture of "democracy" without using images of flags or the capitol dome but merely shapes, lines, and colors. An eight-second drawing comes straight from the core of self. Drawing merges senses, feelings, and thoughts: the conceptual becomes perceptual, which becomes sensory, which becomes emotional. What we know, we know with more than just our heads. Have each of your students invent eight completely different icons of democracy. In the end "democracy" will turn into a hundred sub-terms to spark an endless discussion.

Drawings are not only spatial. They can be sequential. Read this story:

Figure 3

It looks like a squiggle. I call it a "shoestring outline." Reading left to right, this is a visual outline of the story *Goldilocks and the Three Bears*. (See Figure 3.) I'll describe the first stanza and you can figure out the rest:

Once upon a time there lived three bears. . . . They were tasting bowls of porridge but the porridge was too hot . . . so they took a walk in the woods.

Now read backwards from the bottom right to left, and the doodle becomes John Steinbeck's *The Grapes of Wrath*: The Joad family left the dust bowl in Oklahoma and bundled their belongings on the back of a truck and made the long, arduous journey to California.

I have students draw shoestring outlines of everything: the lives of great people, science reports, the news—anything with sequence. You can actually draw an entire book on one piece of paper in the form of doodles, then commit the doodles to mind. I have students deliver oral book reports from these visual notes. It forces them to put the story in their own words by first putting it into their own pictures. Students end up making a sort of charm bracelet timeline of icons that represent the story. The squiggles that represent the three bears could be a sentence, a paragraph, or a whole chapter. Between reading the book and writing the report, students should do some drawing and talking; have them make a shoestring outline to narrate to a partner. Since drawing can reveal an entire story in one glance, students can read simultaneously for big picture, sequence, and detail.

I was taught to read by breaking words into sounds and rebuilding the sounds back into words. Now I read for pictures—for the meanings beyond the written word in my own imagination. Pictures provide an overview, inner view, even a side view of the story—even positive and negative space—what was versus what might have been said. I can shuttle between poignant detail and overarching structure.

Moodjees

Usually, people draw the outlines of things and fill in. Here is a fearless way to draw, one that I have shown to probably half a million students. Instead of drawing the outline of something and running the risk of making a mistake at every point, draw from the middle out. Instead of making lines, scribble small circular motions, little "moodjees" as I call them. Working from the inside out there is no way to make a mistake. You just add more moodjees. You end up with a sort of sculpted silhouette of the object. Figure 4 is a typical student drawing that contrasts regular and moodjee.

Figure 4

Mind Exploration

Drawing isn't about getting it right. It's about getting it out—going to places in your imagination that words alone cannot reach, to return with brand new ideas you can put into words more sharply and fluently. It's about merging picture, design, and diagram to make the visual verbal and the verbal visual. Drawing and then talking transforms the visual to auditory and the spatial to sequential. It's about making thinking more lifelike, because although we may think in general concepts, we live in specifics.

Drawing is a loom. The sensory, emotional, perceptual, and conceptual not only "weave" together but "speak" to each other—more of the brain talking to more of the brain—as I did at seven, drawing my magnetic sailors and falling into a picture, as I now fall into the pages of books. Drawing has given me the power to break the surface, drawing more out of reading, more out of experience, helping me to think for myself with more of myself.

PICTURES CONJURE UP WORDS
Ask students to write captions for the cartoons

Responding to Failure

Ann MacDonald and Jim Riley | SUMMER 2002

Ann MacDonald has published curriculum for the LA Times, the Teacher's Edition of a Scott Foresman science series, created curriculum for the Project Success language arts program, and has presented at local, state, and national conferences. She received her bachelor of arts degree from UCLA and master's from the University of LaVerne. A teacher in San Diego for thirty-nine years, she taught Cluster and Seminar gifted classes. She was a local and state recipient of teacher-of-the-year recognition.

Jim Riley taught in San Diego's Gifted and Talented Education (GATE) Cluster and Seminar program for highly gifted students. Postgraduate work includes a master's degree and a three-year Science Leadership Program at UCSD. He wrote for the Teacher's Edition of a Scott Foresman science text, was editor for San Diego's gifted education newsletter, and presented at local, state, and national conferences. He received teacher-of-the-year recognition from the Association of San Diego Educators for the Gifted and the California Association for the Gifted.

Jim Riley and Ann MacDonald, regular contributors to a "Hands-on Curriculum" column, base this set of lessons on the premise that small failures early in life will prepare students to face and successfully meet larger challenges later. Students first identify and define different types of failure; then small groups research and analyze particular failures in topics such as medicine, science, art, business, history, and sports. Finally, students engage in individual research examining reactions to failure.

Failure can be a success in the classroom—a vital topic for students who tend to push the envelope and also for those who should but do not. The teacher must set up lessons sufficiently challenging to include the possibility of failing, realizing that some initial failure in the classroom is protection against the likely head-on collisions of a gifted person's growth. Fear of failure is a hot button that can start lively discussions on assessing the directions life can take. Development of characters in literature, advancements in science or the arts, personal growth—any human endeavor worth considering involves some element of failure.

In this three-part series of lessons, students examine situations where some failure is both inevitable and positive. Begin with the whole class looking at different forms of failure, continue with group work using resources to refine and extend examples of failure, and conclude with individual reactions to risk-taking. Adapt the approach for different ages by using examples applicable to the specific group.

Mistakes Were Made

Defining failure can be therapeutic. The following is offered as a framework to tame fears and note the appearance and habits of the bestiary. It is easy to find cartoons that will supplement class discussion with humorous examples contrasting aspirations with results, as in "What she said, what he heard." It is also easy to find quips and quotes on failure in quotation books or the Internet. The students should be recording concepts and examples as they are brought out in discussion. An alternative form of recording could be on chart paper or a whiteboard.

In this first section of the series, students will examine three types of failure:

- downhill—literally bad news but still a source of guidance

- on the level—a disconnect with society

- uphill—essential to progress

Downhill. Fatal failures are irrevocable, especially for the failure-ee. This category of failure results from lack of information (using a match to check the gas supply), poor moral judgment (if it feels good, do it), or accident (the perversity of inanimate objects).

The class should record examples brought out in discussion and decide what reaction or analysis society utilizes to avoid repetition. The autopsy, FAA investigation, and safety legislation, for example, contribute to hindsight solutions.

On the Level. A person can fail to keep up with society, and, conversely, society can fail to keep up with a person. Both situations appear as not getting anywhere.

Failure of an individual to aspire can occur in education, business, sports, or anywhere the lack of individual growth is contrasted with the growth of others. Formerly successful people can be left far behind if they simply rest on their laurels. It is easy to think of situations where society can pull ahead of an individual; computer technology, clothing styles, menu offerings, and school classes are all good examples. It is difficult, however, to work out practical solutions for the complexity of causes.

Perceived failure occurs when innovation is far ahead of its time. If an individual has really pushed the envelope, the new way of looking at things is bound to meet some—or perhaps total—disapproval. Stravinsky's "The Rite of Spring" and the Tucker automobile did not draw immediate rave reviews. Society might eventually reassess the new changes, but for some time there is failure.

Uphill. Instructive failures happen more often than success and are essential for growth. This is where an effective teacher, coach, parent, diplomat, or trainer helps the learner with analysis to "get back on the horse."

The struggle uphill can be a long one, requiring patience and persistence. Consider the number of failures preceding the present Catholic/Protestant truce in Northern Ireland or the apartheid resolution in South Africa, and the perpetual crisis in the Middle East.

Practicing a new skill inevitably involves failure, but that failure needs to be part of a series of carefully prescribed steps followed by supportive analysis and encouragement for the next leap. Articulate fingering for the piano player or incisive selection among synonyms for the writer develops through perceptive instruction.

Being a Failure Isn't as Easy as It Looks

Having defined types of failure, the students are now ready to analyze examples from various fields of endeavor. Group students for research into topics such as medicine, science and technology, arts and entertainment, business, history, and sports.

One remarkable resource for this study is the Internet magazine *Failure* (www.failuremag.com), which reports on and categorizes the lack of success in many aspects of society. The magazine is used by many classrooms and requires no registration. As with all Internet sites, care must be taken for the appropriateness of chosen articles. Selected articles can be printed out and offered to the class if the Internet is not available to students. Additional resources for this curriculum are listed at the end of the article.

Using the Internet and print sources, students will isolate particular failures; identify the types and see how they are assessed as failures; find the specific causes, consequences, efforts to ameliorate the effect; and, finally, note any subsequent successes. They should look for patterns and multiple viewpoints within the grouping and any generalizations that can be drawn; for example, warning signs of impending failure are often ignored.

After gathering material, the groups need to prepare methods for whole group presentation using specifics to support their generalizations. PowerPoint slide shows, poster board displays, newscasts, or interviews provide lively means of providing information to a real audience. As the groups report, ask students to note any intergroup relationships and their connections to risks taken as well as particular risk patterns for any given field. A risk/benefit analysis could be included for older students. These insights could become the second part of the students' individual notebooks on failure.

Advanced Mistakes

After students have defined failure in class discussion and extended their understanding with group research reported to the class, they are ready for the third section: individual research examining reactions to failure. This can take the form of character analysis in literature where personal flaws are the source of failure. The inevitable appearance of failure as a component of advancement in a field of endeavor, or some personal understanding where failure was the catalyst for an eventual success offers fertile fields for study.

The final product, of course, is open to the style of your class. General possibilities include:

- an analytic report on a structural or policy failure

- motivational speech to encourage action when the path looks foreboding

- dramatic presentation around the themes of excellence and perfectionism

- an editorial essay responding to a current local impasse where the understanding of failure can restart communication

- a cartoon centered on hiding failure

- a sales talk anticipating and responding to points of resistance

While students are researching their independent projects, talking points for class discussion can be used intermittently to stimulate new approaches and as a forum for raising and answering questions:

- Are society's various plans for dealing with emergencies realistic?

- Is there a way to determine if the risk of a particular action is worth the potential benefit?

- Is assignment of fault worthwhile or do better solutions arise from no-fault laws?

- What is the effect of having errors published regularly?

- What is the effect of pressure to succeed vs. the emotional release when there's nothing to lose?

This series of lessons began with the statement that failure can be a success in the classroom. Failure management should be an integral part of the curriculum—especially for gifted students, whose internal and external pressures to succeed often need a control valve that comes from understanding failure. You can win for losing.

Resources

Dörner, D. (1996). *The logic of failure: Recognizing and avoiding error in complex situations.* Cambridge, MA: Perseus Books. This technical book includes a wide-ranging analysis of disaster—from Chernobyl to AIDS—with strategies for dealing with the negatives in life. Recommended for high school and teacher background.

Goldberg, M. H. (1984). *The blunder book.* New York: Quill/William Morrow. This book contains a collection of colossal errors, minor mistakes, and surprising slip-ups that have changed the course of history. Recommended for upper elementary through high school.

Manz, C. C. (2002). *The power of failure: 27 ways to turn life's setbacks into success.* San Francisco, CA: Berrett-Koehler Publishers, Inc. This motivational book is part of a leadership series with inspiring examples, appropriate epigrams, and a useful index covering people and concepts. Recommended for upper elementary through middle school.

Maxwell, J. C. (2000). *Failing forward: Turning mistakes into stepping stones for success.* Nashville, TN: Thomas Nelson Publishers. This is part of a self-help series dealing with the steps for changing one's attitude from feeling like a failure to being capable of recovery. Recommended for middle school through high school.

Roberts, R. M. (1989). *Serendipity.* New York: John Wiley and Sons. This is a well-researched book of discoveries in science history, from chance observations to accidental discoveries. The technical scientific information is balanced by the lively descriptions of the discoverers and their discoveries. Recommended for high school and teacher background.

Infusing Language Arts Curriculum with Visual and Performing Arts for Gifted Students

Joan Franklin Smutny | FALL 2002

__Joan Franklin Smutny__ is director of the Center for Gifted at National-Louis University, Evanston, Illinois. She also directs special summer programs in the Chicago area for thousands of gifted students including disadvantaged, minority, and bilingual children. Editor and author of thirteen books, her most recent include Acceleration for Gifted Learners, K–5 *and* Differentiating for the Young Child. *In 1996, she received the National Association for Gifted Children (NAGC) Distinguished Service Award for contribution to gifted education.*

Joan Franklin Smutny promotes the integration of visual and performing arts with language arts as a way of stimulating student (1) imagination, (2) divergent and flexible thinking, (3) critical analysis, (4) ability to see multiple points of view, and (5) skill in researching in depth. She presents numerous examples of strategies for using visual and performing arts activities in the subject areas of reading, writing, and speaking.

Most gifted students realize at an early age that books provide a rich and imaginative world where they can always turn for discovery, adventure, and intriguing mystery. While interests and preferences may shift and change from grade to grade, the love for the language arts—be it reading, writing, or speaking—continues and often expands. When I ask children and young people what they like about language arts, they invariably talk about creativity. Here are a few examples:

> I think why kids like Harry Potter is because it's so imaginative and also really funny. I feel like I know Hagrid so well that he could be a friend. Sometimes I imagine meeting him and all his monster pets and it makes me laugh. Then my mom asks, "What are you laughing at Jason?" and I say, "Oh, it's just Hagrid again." It's like Hagrid lives in our house!
>
> —Jason, age 8

> After reading Maya Angelou's *All God's Children Need Traveling Shoes*, I thought, "Okay, Lakesha, if Maya with all her tough experiences can write this, what's your problem?" Her writing is so poetic, but also so real. When I read the book, her whole amazing life in Ghana became my life, too. And it's inspired me to think about what it would be like to create poetic autobiography.
>
> —Lakesha, age 13

> When I write poems, I feel like I'm flying.
>
> —Kira, age 7

Unfortunately, these inspiring encounters with books and language do not always take place in the regular classroom. In the first place, gifted students such as those cited read at a level significantly above their peers and consequently have to fulfill their reading needs outside school. Secondly, most teachers lack the experience and expertise to challenge gifted students who are eager to read more advanced literature and write fiction, plays, biography and autobiography, or poetry.

The following activities are intended to give teachers ideas on how they can meet the learning needs of gifted students in mixed-ability classrooms. They all incorporate the visual and performing arts as a way of enabling gifted students to function at much higher cognitive levels while also challenging other students in the class. A key advantage to the use of the arts in the regular classroom is that it imposes no ceiling on children whose gifts enable them to extend beyond their grade level; yet, it is also accessible to everyone else in the class.

There is a strong rationale for making the arts an essential feature of gifted education. Seeley (1989) argues that all high-ability children—artistically and academically gifted—need the arts to enhance their sensitivity, self-expression, and creative response to complex problems. Goertz (1990; 2002) envisions art instruction as the "fourth R" in education and demonstrates how it increases the skills of observation, abstract thinking, and problem analysis.

Education in art is an invitation to use the reasoning skills of an artist. The artist visualizes and sets goals to find and define the problem, chooses techniques to collect data, and then evaluates and revises the problem solution with imagination in order to create. . . . The artist, in his or her creative process, requires a high-order thought process.

Smutny (1997) found that when the arts are integrated into the regular curriculum, gifted children can explore the complexities of a problem or phenomenon through a variety of learning styles and art media. This significantly advances original thought and expression in every subject area. The following strategies use the visual and performing arts in a wide range of language arts activities in order to stimulate:

- imaginative and creative reasoning

- divergent, flexible thinking

- critical analysis

- multiple points of view

- depth of research and study

Reading

Even gifted students can sometimes become passive readers. The arts sharpen observation and stimulate a more imaginative and analytical way of reading. Examples of activities that have worked well with gifted students include the following:

- Students draw, sketch, or paint characters from a story; then they go back to the text to seek the cues that prompted their visual impressions. They can explore additional details from the text and compare art with their peers.

- Students discuss the environments (interior and exterior) described in the text and where they are in relation to each other. How many details can they remember? What sticks in their minds and why? They spontaneously write their own descriptions of the places as though they are visiting the area. What most strikes them (colors, textures, objects, weather, architecture)?

- Children pick a character from the text and mime it to the class—select a scene or characteristic that would most express the individual in mind. The same can be done with a scene, where students select pivotal moments in the book and mime it.

- Children choose a conflict, issue, or problem raised by the text and stage a debate, with different students assuming the role of specific characters.

Some of these activities work best in small groups. Teachers can cluster the gifted students together so that they can read more challenging literature and benefit from each other's responses.

Writing

Without question, gifted students need more creative approaches to composition. Many students in my creative writing classes complain about the fact that they have no opportunity to "play with words," as one second grader called it. A fifth grader once told me that her teacher scolded her for writing a piece of historical fiction as part of a social studies assignment. "She made me feel like I was trying to get out of work, but I put in more work to get all the facts I needed to create this story!"

When used appropriately, the arts present a wide range of sources for writing (e.g., essays, stories, and poetry). Teachers can:

- Provide visual catalysts (e.g., paintings, photographs, videos) for students to imagine what happened before and/or after the scenes depicted. If they were detectives, what would they conclude from these images? Why?

- Help children compose free verse poems by using paintings and photography as catalysts. If this painting were music what would they hear? What would they feel/see/hear/smell if they were inside the painting? Have students put themselves in the images they see and invent from there.

When starting a class off in free verse poetry, it helps to begin by creating a group poem. Students view and discuss a painting or print and volunteer lines for a poem. The teacher provides guidance and suggestions and facilitates the process.

- Have students listen to music and create a story around it. What does the music suggest to them? An enjoyable way to begin is to demonstrate how much music tells a story in film. For example, teachers could show the class a few scenes from a Hitchcock film without the soundtrack and then with the soundtrack. How much is music telling the story? Have students create different scenarios from a piece of music or movie soundtrack and share with each other.

- Ask children to write a biographical sketch about a famous person based on a text as well as a picture or portrait. Have the children tell their story from a variety of viewpoints: this individual's friend, teacher, mother or father, sister or brother, or the family dog. (I once had a student who told the story of the Declaration of Independence from the standpoint of Jefferson's pen.)

- Some famous paintings have traveled many miles and seen a great deal of historical and social change before they finally landed in a museum. Students can write or create a map of the extraordinary journey of the *Mona Lisa* from King Louis XIV's palace in Versailles to a hiding place during the French Revolution to the trunk of a thief who kept it for three years and was caught trying to smuggle it into Italy, to its permanent home in the Louvre.

- Children explore the changes in values and ideals that brought modern dance to the world. Why did America become a major source for this movement? They could write a short piece as an audience member at a modern dance concert and depict the different modern ballet traditions through various arts media (collage, sculpture, sketches, mime). This activity could also work in the area of music, theater, and visual art.

Using the arts as catalysts for writing can generate an extraordinary amount of original and creative material in any classroom. Gifted children and all children will benefit from the demand to think divergently and by the combination of investigative research, discovery, creative thinking and reasoning, and verbal skill.

Speaking

Like reading and writing, oral expression also benefits from the use of the arts, particularly the performing arts. The process of adapting and interpreting material for performance demands problem-solving visual and staging challenges, a consideration of multiple viewpoints, and enables gifted students to create vivid and original representations of significant events and people. Activities could include some of the following:

Many students in my creative writing classes complain about the fact that they have no opportunity to "play with words," as one second grader called it.

- Students pretend to be an artist of their choice. They can choose an issue in this artist's life that he or she feels passionate about and write a speech as this artist. If they wish, the students can use costumes, lighting, and sound.

- Work with the children to create a chamber theater piece out of a short story. Discuss and select the most important scenes. What scenes do they consider most important and why? Choose students to be narrators and others to speak and act the parts of the characters. Teachers can have students with special talents in visual art and sound and light technology help with set design and explore the most effective use of sound and lights. I have also used gifted writers to help select and adjust the text.

- Children become art detectives. They can read a story of a painting that disappeared and imagine how they—the art detectives—traced it down. They can become "experts" on certain artists, detect forgeries, and present a "60 Minutes" piece on how they discovered a painting and exposed the forgeries. What gave it away?

- Artists have to sell their work. In this activity, students can explore the role of the art dealer in freeing artists from the power of academic authorities who forced painters to depict historical or religious subjects and who fixed the prices of their work. Children can dramatize how things changed when these middlemen began selling artists' works to the private market. They can interview contemporary art dealers, explore the professional art world today, and create a contemporary art gallery for student work in the classroom.

- Students act as reporters who travel back in time to cover important events in artistic and other movements. They review current features on the arts, write a newspaper article on the event, and create a performance (it could involve text, movement, and chamber theater techniques).

- Students can stage an imaginary interview with their favorite musicians. They can work in pairs and explore questions about musical styles, and social, cultural, and political influences on music, as well as the unique contributions of individual artists.

In Conclusion

The strategies described here open the door to a new kind of learning experience for gifted students. Integrating the arts into the curriculum significantly extends the insights and discoveries that occur when teachers integrate different media, material, and content. The result is a curriculum where children can advance beyond the artificial boundaries that a conventional curriculum erects between subjects. Through these strategies, gifted students can find ways to increase flexible thinking, gain practice in innovative projects, and pursue the burning interests that have consumed their imagination for years.

References

Gallagher, J. J., & Gallagher, S. A. (1994). *Teaching the gifted child.* 4th ed. Boston: Allyn and Bacon.

Goertz, J. (1990). The role of art in cognition: A problem solving approach. In S. Bailey, E. Braggett, & M. Robinson (Eds.), *The challenge of excellence: "A vision splendid."* New South Wales, Australia.

————. (2002). Searching for talent through the visual arts. In J. F. Smutny (Ed.), *Underserved gifted populations.* Cresskill, NJ: Hampton Press.

Locker, T., & Christensen, C. (1995). *Sky tree portfolio.* Stuyvesant, NY: Sky Tree Press. (Available at the Center for Gifted, National-Louis University, 847-251-2661.)

Locker, T. (1997). *Water dance.* San Diego: Harcourt Brace & Co.

————. (2000). *Cloud dance.* San Diego: Silver Whistle Harcourt, Inc.

Seeley, K. (1989). Arts curriculum for the gifted. In J. VanTassel-Baska, J. F. Feldhusen, K. Seeley, G. Wheatly, L. Silverman, & W. Foster (Eds.), *Comprehensive curriculum for gifted learners.* Boston: Allyn & Bacon.

Smutny, J. F., Walker, S. Y., & Meckstroth, E. A. (1997). *Teaching young gifted children in the regular classroom.* Minneapolis: Free Spirit Publishing.

Think Like a Historian: Sleuthing Family History

James E. McAleney Jr. | FALL 2006

James E. McAleney Jr. teaches Gifted and Talented Education (GATE) U.S. History and Leadership classes at Cabrillo Middle School in Ventura, California. He has been an educator for thirty-four years, teaching middle, junior high, and senior high school social studies with a brief assignment in high school substance abuse counseling and curriculum administration. He earned a master's degree in education with an emphasis in history by creating curriculum to investigate California gold rush history. He has been using this project off and on for thirty years.

Authentic problem solving and presenting results to real audiences are key ingredients in effective differentiated curriculum. James McAleney demonstrates both in detailed instructions for a family history project aimed at teenagers. Project components include (1) family history booklets, (2) genealogy charts, (3) family interviews, and (4) a family history night display. The project involves both language arts and history classes, and teachers work as a team to develop appropriate skills and share the assessment responsibilities.

Teenagers! Aren't they wonderfully self-centered? The entire world revolves around them. So, how can language arts and social studies teachers tap into this egocentricity and create a meaningful assignment? The answer is simple. Have students research, write about, and produce final products dealing with their families.

Pedagogical Benefits

One of the hallmarks of effective differentiated curriculum is that of engaging students in authentic problem-solving activities and presenting their results to real audiences. This family history project does both in that students learn to use the tools that practicing historians use on a regular basis and then present results, when complete, to family and friends who have a direct interest in their findings. Family history research, of course, can be used with all students, but the open-endedness and the opportunity to dig as deep as they wish is particularly appropriate and appealing to gifted learners.

In this project, students learn history, geography, listening skills, and interviewing skills. They will improve their writing skills and produce a project that may become a family heirloom. The project brings generations together, asks students to improve their interviewing and writing skills, requires students to do some research, and taps into student creativity all at the same time. They come away with a better understanding of their families and make some important connections with members of their families.

The interdisciplinary approach validates both disciplines. It shows students the necessity of writing clearly in both language arts and social studies. It includes several California state standards for both subject areas. Students can use technology to research family names and history. Writing standards, as well as listening and speaking standards, are addressed through the interview assignment. Social studies skills in geography, spatial thinking, and research, as well as content standards related to migration and immigration, are stressed with the Family History booklet and the Family History display assignments. And finally, the project allows students to use their creativity with two authentic assessment projects: a summary of an interview and a display of their choice.

General Guidelines

It is very important that families understand from the beginning of this assignment that their privacy will be respected. At no time should students feel obligated to include things in the project that make them or their families feel uncomfortable. Emphasize to students to share only those things they wish to share.

This assignment works best over winter break when families traditionally get together for holiday celebrations and older relatives are more easily available for interviews.

Begin the assignment by asking students questions such as: "Have you ever thought that you may be related to someone who fought with George Washington in the American Revolution? Maybe you are related to a pioneer who traveled across America to settle in the Old West." It is my experience that many gifted students have some idea of their family history, and these questions will generate stories and interest in the project.

Students come to realize that every one of us is related to people who lived and worked and contributed in some manner to the history of our country. Some students may be fortunate enough to have available a family tree or a published family history that someone has already researched. Others may be literally starting from scratch in looking for ancestors. And for the ones who claim to be related to a famous person, I tell them that this is the time to find out just how.

Project Components

The project has four parts that are graded in the student's U.S. history and language arts classes. Sharing the responsibility of the project between two subjects allows the teachers to focus on specific parts of the assignment without feeling overwhelmed.

PART 1: THE FAMILY HISTORY BOOKLET

The best place to begin family history research is with those family members closest to the student—their parents. We have created a booklet with questions to ask parents about their likes, dislikes, and stories of their childhood. Students also ask parents the same questions about their parents—the students' grandparents. This gives them information about two generations of their family. The cover of the booklet must be decorated with a clever title and a picture of the student. We used ideas from several published booklets available at a local children's bookstore to make up our booklet and had it printed at minimal cost by our district publications department. *Family Fill-In Book: Discovering Your*

Roots written by Dian Buchman and published by Scholastic is a good guide. This assignment is introduced and graded in language arts.

PART 2: A GENEALOGY CHART

Students are asked to become genealogists and trace their family ancestry back as far as they can, using official genealogical charts and genealogical notations. Forms can be downloaded from Ancestry.com or the Web site of the Church of Jesus Christ of Latter Day Saints (one of the best genealogy resources out there for *all* researchers, not just Mormons). The requirements for this part of the assignment include neatness and accuracy in following genealogical notation. Length of lineage cannot be a criterion for scoring. This assignment is introduced and graded in U.S. history class, and the final product is pasted into the back of the Family History Booklet.

PART 3: FAMILY INTERVIEW

Students are to talk with and interview the two oldest relatives (at least sixty years old), one male and one female, that they will visit over winter break. One class period is spent generating three to five open-ended questions in each of the following topic areas.

work	clothing	politics
school	houses	funniest moment
family life	religion/holidays	events in U.S. history

This exercise allows the teacher to explain the difference between open and closed questions—questions that generate lots of information versus questions that elicit one- or two-word answers. Students then select three or four topic areas to emphasize in their interviews.

Students write out their chosen questions ahead of time, leaving space to take notes as they listen to the answers.

Students need to be taught how to conduct a good interview—an interview that will elicit the information necessary to write a good summary report of their ancestor. Items that should be included are shown in Figure 1.

Figure 1: Guidelines for Good Interviews

- Make an appointment for the interview. (If done properly, the interview will take more time than students imagine, and setting aside a specific amount of time is critical for the student and the interviewee.)
- Write down questions ahead of time.
- Prepare follow-up questions to use if a particular question renders little response.
- Allow for spontaneity. If people want to share things not on the list of questions, let them. It might be particularly interesting to ask grandparents about the student's parents when they were in middle school.
- Pace the interview. If the interview goes long and the person is getting tired, stop and ask to talk to them another time. Also, don't rush the interview.
- Show appreciation. Thank the interviewee for the time given to talk to you and promise to give them a copy of your written report.

Once you have established the "rules," you can now stage a practice interview in class. By working with another teacher, you can combine two classes, and one teacher can interview the other. Be sure to ask closed questions, and have the interviewee be reluctant to answer something. The interviewee may go on and on about a particular topic that doesn't interest the class which forces the interviewer to refocus the conversation. All of this is good practice. Evaluate the interview process at the end of the period.

The final interview product can be a neat transcript of the questions and answers, usually a minimum of four pages long (two pages on each person). It might also be a three- to four-page written summary of the interview, including student comments about what was learned. A third option would be a three- to four-page compare and contrast essay about both people. In each case, the emphasis should be on the history these people have witnessed. It should be well written and graded in language arts class.

PART 4: FAMILY HISTORY NIGHT DISPLAY

Now that students have done all their research and interviewed relatives, it is time to put the information together in a creative way to share the information. Students have a choice of display projects including:

- a family mobility map showing where ancestors lived and how they moved to their present location

- a family artifact display, sharing stories about things important to their family

- an illustrated timeline with important family dates on one side of the line and major U.S. historical events on the other side

- a family recipe album

The displays are presented and graded at the Family History Night event and given credit in students' U.S. history class.

Mobility map. The mobility map display consists of a student-created map of the United States, the western hemisphere, Europe and the United States, Asia and the United States, or Africa and the United States—whatever is appropriate to show migration patterns of both sides of the family. Using clear and distinct symbols, students show the movement of their father's family as contrasted with the movement of their mother's family, as far back in time as possible. A legend explaining the symbols must accompany the map. Each place listed should have a brief explanation of what the family did there. Old family pictures, especially scanned photographs, can be used to add flavor to the map. By completing this assignment, students will appreciate the immigration and migration paths of their family.

Artifact display. The artifact display consists of a "science fair board" set up on a three-foot section of a cafeteria table. Students drape the board with fabric, lace, old clothing (something to cover up the cardboard), and then label fifteen to twenty family heirlooms stating the source for each, what it was used for and by whom, the student's relationship to that person, the date the item was made or used, how the family acquired it, and why it is important to the family today. This assignment allows students to learn a variety of information about their family history.

Illustrated timeline. The illustrated timeline display uses a large piece of chart paper, divided in half vertically; it shows family dates and explanations on one side and important U.S. history dates and explanations on the other side. It should include illustrations or pictures for all the dates and events listed. The family side should explain how the historical event impacted the student's family.

I always use the JFK assassination as an example in class, but with the age of parents these days, you may have to use the Challenger disaster or the attacks on 9/11. By completing this assignment, students see a correlation between their family's history and U.S. history.

Family recipe album. The family recipe album requires a one-inch binder in which students put the following items:

- title page with their name and class periods

- table of contents page

- dedication page

- family genealogy chart (yes, a second copy!)

- at least five family recipes that have special meaning, written out completely

- an explanation paragraph of why each recipe is important to the family

- a picture or illustration of each completed recipe

- biographical sketches of the originators of the recipes

This assignment can be great fun if completed with a parent or grandparent during the holiday. For Family History Night, the student will present the recipe book and make a recipe to share. Students gain an appreciation of their culture with this assignment.

For some reason, many of the students choose option four, the recipe book. Initially they think it is the least academic and the easiest to produce. They are later surprised at the amount of work they put into it.

Family History Night

All of the assignments are displayed at an evening celebration we call Family History Night. Students set up their displays in the school cafeteria and parents, grandparents, and friends are invited to examine what essentially is a "one-night-only museum." Students are proud of their displays because they have been created by and about them. Students spend part of the evening explaining their displays to parents and classmates and another part of the evening looking at other student displays and asking them questions about their artifacts, maps, recipes, or timelines.

One evening, a grandparent of a student saw a high school graduation picture in a display from another student and recognized herself. Two grandparents who went to high school together but had not seen each other for forty years were reunited. Last year a student displayed a *Life* magazine picture of people at the JFK funeral. Her grandmother was in the picture; she was the nanny for JFK's children. The uncle of another student witnessed the flag raising on Iwo Jima. We have seen Emmys and Oscars, wedding dresses from the 1920s, christening gowns from the turn of the nineteenth century, purple hearts and colonial muskets, autographed pictures of Mickey Mantle, and daguerreotypes from the Civil War. It is amazing what families have to share.

Evaluation

During the school day after Family History Night, students write an evaluation that includes a variety of questions, from knowledge and comprehension questions to analysis and reflection questions. Some suggestions are shown in Figure 2.

Figure 2: Family History Project Evaluation

1. What was the best thing about your project?
2. What would you do differently if you were to do this assignment again? What ideas did you get from looking at other projects?
3. How is your life similar to that of the people you interviewed?
4. How is your life different from the people you interviewed?
5. What are some things you learned while talking with students about their projects?
6. Explain why you admire the people you interviewed.

One student's response from last year's evaluation summed up the value of the project when she wrote:

> The only piece of advice I really have is to really appreciate your family. Looking back through my ancestors, I found no famous singers, no famous football players, no presidents, no witches, no actors or models, no big-shot CEOs, no inventors. I didn't find anyone that was famous. I just found ordinary people. Just people living through the hardships, nothing special. So my advice is to appreciate who you have, not what you wish you have.

Students come away from this project with a better sense of who they are and how they and their family fit into U.S. history. It is amazing what they learn about their heritage and what you as a teacher learn about your students.

STUDENT COMMENTS

Something I took for granted was actually my grandparents. I have been around them my whole life and I didn't realize all of the stuff that they had experienced.

The best thing was getting the pumpkin recipe from my great grandma written in her own handwriting.

I think the best thing about my recipe book was having to talk to my grandmother and how she gave me a lot of information about my great grandmother.

The best part of the project for me was learning how much of an impact my dad had on Vietnamese kids.

The best thing about my project is that it let me learn more about my family.

Identifying and Developing Technological Giftedness: Exploring Another Way to Be Gifted in the 21st Century

Del Siegle | SPRING 2007

Del Siegle, Ph.D., *is an associate professor of educational psychology and a teaching fellow in the Neag School of Education at the University of Connecticut. Previously, Del worked as a gifted and talented coordinator in Montana. He is president-elect of the National Association of Gifted Children and serves on the board of directors of The Association for the Gifted (CEC-TAG). He is coeditor of the* Journal of Advanced Academics *and the author of a technology column for* Gifted Child Today.

The technology and information age in which we live requires that we update our identification systems in gifted education to include those children who are technologically gifted. Del Siegle identifies three types of such gifted learners: programmers, interfacers, and fixers. Siegle discusses the various traits and abilities of each type and shares an assessment instrument he devised.

Labels are part of life. They help us communicate and share meaning through agreed upon terms. The label "gifted" is used to describe young people or adults with an outstanding skill in some talent area. While some skills are highly valued, others are not. A skill that is considered important in one society, or at one point in time, may not be valued in another. Giftedness is fluid and changes over time.

> If we were a hunting and gathering society, the gifted individual would be one who could stalk game well and shoot with accuracy. Maybe she would be the one who could locate tasty roots easily. If one had special penchant for meat, one might refer to the hunter as highly gifted and the root gatherer as moderately gifted. (Siegle, 1990, p. 5)

We have advanced considerably from a hunting and gathering society. We are a society embedded in technology within an information age. As has occurred in the past, the definitions of who are gifted need to be modified and expanded to reflect the time in which we live.

> When personal computers first appeared just thirty years ago, few imagined the extent to which they would become part of our daily lives. To most young adults, the future will likely bring an even greater breadth of complex information and communication technologies, including those that are not yet imaged. (Tyler, 2006, p. 1)

Schools not only need to prepare students to be effective users of technology, they also need to begin recognizing students with strengths in technology. This involves recognizing and developing gifts beyond those that have been traditionally identified for gifted and talented programs. In the twenty-first century, the classifications for gifted students should include technologically gifted students. Society requires the skills that technologically gifted students possess; educators have an obligation to identify technologically gifted students and help develop their technological gifts to their fullest. Formal identification of technologically gifted students is necessary because the first step in developing any talent is to recognize it.

Technological giftedness appears to manifest itself in three distinct ways. O'Brien, Friedman-Nimz, Lacey, and Denson (2005) identified two distinct groups of gifted technology students: programmers and interfacers. Friedman-Nimz (2006) has since suggested that a third group—those who like to work with hardware and fix computers—probably also exists. Students who excel in each of these categories could be considered technologically gifted. In addition to demonstrating expertise, these young people tend to exhibit passion toward one or more technology related activity.

Programmers

The talent to write computer code appears to be one type of technological giftedness. I have known gifted students who, as early as first grade, were exploring how to write computer code. While this is unusual, all of the academically gifted students with whom I have worked were able to create simple computer programs by fourth grade. Some of those students demonstrated a special talent with programming; others did not. Many were able to conceptually break down programming tasks and see the relationships among them that involved a special type of analytic processing. For many of these students, programming appeared to be a natural way of thinking and seeing the world. Such a gift needs to be developed.

One way to identify and develop programming talent is to expose young people to programming at an early age. The early Apple computers with Apple BASIC were a wonderful medium to introduce programming. Seymour Papert's (1980) LOGO is still an effective program to introduce very young children to programming. LOGO provides programming for pre-mathematical children and helps develop their reasoning and problem-solving skills. Although the program was created for young children, some of the more advanced functions prove challenging for older students as well. Various free versions of the LOGO program are available on the Internet. One popular version is available from softronix.com/logo. html. This site not only includes a working version of LOGO that can be downloaded (see Figure 1), it also includes free manuals to assist those who are not familiar with LOGO programming.

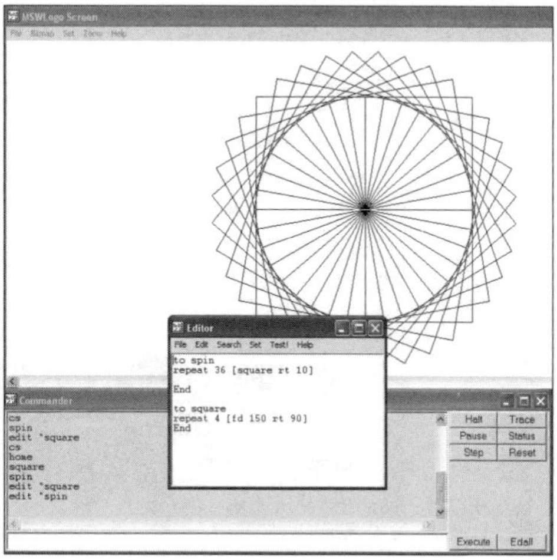

Figure 1: Simple LOGO procedure created with MSW LOGO

A starting place for upper elementary students can be Visual BASIC that can be easily learned. Most educators are not aware that Microsoft has built an abridged, yet still powerful, version of Visual BASIC into the Office products. It can be accessed through Tools→ Macros→ Visual BASIC Editor (see Figure 2) with any of the Microsoft Office products. Once in the program, most of the Visual BASIC commands

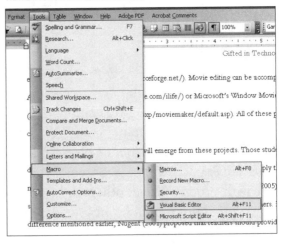

Figure 2: Exploring Visual BASIC programming via macros built into Microsoft Office

and tools are available (see Figure 3). Experiencing Visual BASIC can provide a bridge to more advanced programming that technologically gifted programming students will eventually want to pursue.

O'Brien et al. (2005) found that programmers often liked to work alone with computer language and spent hours deciphering code. In addition to their facility with programming languages, these students reported strengths in logic and problem solving. They typically began using the computer as a toy or education tool, advanced to creating simple Web pages, and ultimately learned more advanced code. They learned code quickly and were often frustrated by the slow pace of formal computer instruction. Because most programmers quickly outgrow the computer programming options provided in their high schools (or find that high school programming courses progress too slowly), these students may benefit from mentoring

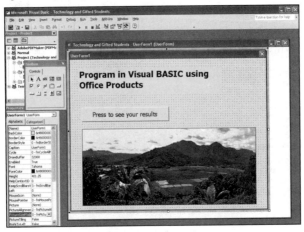

Figure 3: Sample program written in Visual BASIC within PowerPoint

opportunities with professional programmers or may be good candidates for early enrollment in university computer courses.

A second area of exposure can be creating Web pages. This is a great entry point to programming; however, technologically gifted programmers will quickly become discontented creating pages with simple Web editing programs and will need to begin exploring html, Java, and XML. Those students who show an interest and talent for programming can advance to more sophisticated programming such as Visual BASIC, C++, or more advanced Java.

Interfacers

A second area of giftedness involves the application of technology. These students excel in using software. They may or may not be able to program computers, but they apply technology in effective and creative ways.

> Because technologically gifted students usually experiment and often teach themselves how to use new technologies, they show remarkable initiative. Not only are they interested in technology, they have the initiative to satisfy and extend their interests. This is evident when they learn new software programs without formal training. While many use the "guess and check" problem-solving strategy and simply experiment with what a piece of technology or software program can do, others teach themselves by devouring the instruction manual. (Siegle, 2004, p. 31)

Their interest and skills are not necessarily limited to computers. They often focus their interest on audio and video technology as well. These students are adept at using the technology to produce products. O'Brien et al. (2005) found that interfacers were less interested in exploring the computer hardware and more into the social interactions that result from helping others use technology. Technologically gifted interfacers may exhibit the following behaviors:

- They demonstrate a wide range of technology skills. They are attracted to a variety of different types of technology.

- They often learn new software without formal training. This is often because they are able to apply what they learned with one type of software to another type.

- They spend their free time developing their technological skills. There is nothing they enjoy more than "playing with technology."

- They often assist others with technological problems. Because of this trait, students can easily identify who among them has this type of technological giftedness.

- They are able to incorporate a variety of technologies into the products they produce. For example, at an early age, their PowerPoint presentations may include unique graphic images or custom sounds that they have created or edited.

- They eagerly pursue opportunities to use technology. When a new piece of technology appears, they cannot wait to experience it.

- Finally, they demonstrate more advanced technology skills than others their age. This reveals itself in the sophistication of the products they produce.

(Siegle, 2005)

Since technologically gifted interfacers can often be identified by the products they create, the ways they assist others with technology, and the technology-related questions they ask, one possible way to identify them is through a rating scale. The Scales for Rating the Behavioral Characteristics of Superior Students (SRBCSS; Renzulli et al., 2004) includes a seven-item technology rating scale (see Figure 4).

Preliminary studies with the technology scale indicate that teachers identify more males than females with it. In an unrelated study, Schulz (1999) reported different personality traits predict between 20 and 25 percent of students' willingness to embrace new technologies. Males who rated themselves as adventurous, refined, and less jealous were more willing to embrace technology. Conversely, females who embrace technology rated themselves as composed, frank, responsible, and less steady. Male students were also much more likely to embrace new technologies. Based on these preliminary findings, males may be more likely than females to show initiative in using new technology and more likely to experiment with unknown technologies, which are factors measured by the SRBCSS Technology Scale.

Figure 4

SCALES FOR RATING THE BEHAVIORAL CHARACTERISTICS OF SUPERIOR STUDENTS

Technology Characteristics © 2003 Del Siegle

The student . . .	Never	Very Rarely	Rarely	Occasionally	Frequently	Always
1. demonstrates a wide range of technology skills.	☐	☐	☐	☐	☐	☐
2. learns new software without formal training.	☐	☐	☐	☐	☐	☐
3. spends free time developing technology skills.	☐	☐	☐	☐	☐	☐
4. assists others with technology related problems.	☐	☐	☐	☐	☐	☐
5. incorporates technology in developing creative products/assignments/presentations.	☐	☐	☐	☐	☐	☐
6. eagerly pursues opportunities to use technology.	☐	☐	☐	☐	☐	☐
7. demonstrates more advanced technology skills than other students his or her age.	☐	☐	☐	☐	☐	☐
Add Column Total:	☐	☐	☐	☐	☐	☐
Multiply by Weight:	x1	x2	x3	x4	x5	x6
Add Weighted Column Totals:	☐ +	☐ +	☐ +	☐ +	☐ +	☐ +

Scale Total: _____

Technology characteristics subscale of *Scales for Rating the Behavioral Characteristics of Superior Students* is available in print and online from Creative Learning Press (www.creativelearningpress.com)

In 2001, Educational Testing Service (ETS) convened a panel of experts from government, education, and the private sector to define what it meant to be information and communication technology (ICT) literate. Based on its work, ETS has developed two ICT literacy assessments: one for students transitioning to college and a more advanced one for rising college juniors (www.ets.org). Both assessments are Internet-based and require seventy-five minutes to complete. The testing fee, which is about $30, is based on the number of students completing the test. O'Brien and Friedman-Nimz (2006) proposed that the ICT literacy assessment developed by ETS might be used at an earlier age to identify technologically gifted students.

Exposing students to the technologies related to their interests can also be an effective way to identify technologically gifted interfacers. A student who is interested in photography will enjoy working with a digital camera and a photo editing program. Students who are interested in music may enjoy composing music on an inexpensive music composition program such as Music Masterworks (musicmasterworks.com) or editing sound with the free Audacity sound editing programs (audacity.sourceforge.net). Movie editing can be accomplished with Apple's iMovie HD (apple.com/ilife) or Microsoft's Window Movie Maker 2 (microsoft.com/windowsxp/downloads/updates/moviemaker2.mspx). All of these programs are free or are available at minimal cost.

Recognition of technologically gifted interfacers will emerge from these projects. Those students who demonstrate special talent in this area will need additional opportunities to apply their skills with more advanced projects. Based on personality characteristics that O'Brien et al. (2005) found, these students may also benefit from opportunities to share their expertise with others. Due to the gender difference mentioned earlier, Nugent (2001) proposed that teachers should provide girls with opportunities for play and open-ended exploration on the computer (e.g., girls' computer clubs, girls-only lunch, and after-school periods for computer usage). She suggested that such activities help girls gain confidence and comfort with technology. Additional effort may be needed to find and encourage technologically gifted females.

Fixers

The third area of technological giftedness involves those who enjoy working with technology equipment. While the first two types involve creating products with technology, these students enjoy maintaining or even creating the technology for others to use. They may enjoy creating a computer from spare parts, fixing a broken calculator, maintaining a classroom server, or fixing a car stereo.

In 2001, 9-year-old Jacob Komar noticed unused, outdated computers in his sister's school. With the aid of his family, he started Computers for Communities (CFC), a 501(c)(3) nonprofit organization. CFC accepts old computers, printers, and other peripherals from individuals, schools, and businesses. The group refurbishes and redistributes the equipment back to the underprivileged in the community. To date, CFC has distributed over 1,500 computers to individuals and organizations.

> First I acquired computers that were being discarded from a local school. Then I refurbished and distributed them to individuals in my community who could not afford to have a computer at home. What a great feeling to see the smiles on those kids' faces. I felt like I was Santa Claus! Since then, I have created a nonprofit organization that helps other groups do the same thing: locate discarded computers, refurbish them, and distribute them to those in need. (Komar, p.1)

Komar is an example of how a technologically gifted fixer can have a positive impact on the lives of others. By locating technologically gifted fixers and providing them with positive opportunities to apply and develop their special talent, not only do others benefit, but the students develop a sense of prestige and accomplishment while advancing their giftedness. One possible way to develop this talent is to form after-school clubs.

Closing Thoughts

No one knows what technology lies in the future. Technologies that seemed impossible a few years ago are commonplace today. The technologically gifted students of today have the potential to be the creators and implementers of the technology in our future. The possibilities are limited only by their imagination. It is time to identify and encourage students with special interest and skills in technology.

References

Komar, J. (n.d.). *Computers for Communities*. Retrieved January 2, 2007, from computers4communities.org.

Nugent, S. A. (2001). Technology and the gifted: Focus, facets, and the future. *Gifted Child Today* 24(4): 38–45.

O'Brien, B., & Friedman-Nimz, R. (2006, November). *Timing is everything: The emergence of technology talent*. Paper presented at the 53rd Annual Convention of the National Association for Gifted Children, Charlotte, NC.

O'Brien, B., Friedman-Nimz, R., Lacey, J., & Denson, D. (2005). From bits and bytes to C++ and Web sites: What is computer talent made of? *Gifted Child Today* 28(3): 56–63.

Papert, S. (1980). *Mindstorms: Children, computers, and powerful ideas*. New York: Basic Books.

Renzulli, J. S., Smith, L. H., White, A. J., Callahan, C. M., Hartman, R. K., Westberg, K. L., et al. (2004). *Scales for Rating the Behavioral Characteristics of Superior Students: Technical and administration manual* (Rev. ed). Mansfield Center, CT: Creative Learning Press.

Schultz, N. W. (1999, April/May). *Personality traits and willingness to try educational technology*. Paper presented at the annual meeting of the Western Psychological Association, Irvine, CA.

Siegle, D. (1990). *Educating the gifted is a community affair*. Billings, MT: Montana Association for Gifted Education.

———. (2004). Identifying students with gifts and talents in technology. *Gifted Child Today* 27(4): 30–33, 64.

———. (2005, Fall). Gifted students and technology: An interview with Del Siegle. *Northwestern University's Center for Talent Development Talent*, pp. 1, 3–5.

Tyler, L. (2006). *ICT literacy: Equipping students to succeed in an information-rich technology-based society: An issue paper from ETS*. Retrieved December 29, 2006, from ets.org/Media/Tests/ICT_Literacy/pdf/ICT_Equipping_Students_to_Succeed.pdf.

The "Spillover" Effect:
The Power of Gifted Teaching
Strategies for an Entire Staff

Maryanna Gray | SPRING 2004

Maryanna Gray, M.A., is a recently retired teacher and coordinator of gifted programs for the Santa Barbara High School District in Santa Barbara, California. She also serves as the membership chair for the Board of Directors of the California Association for the Gifted. She is the copresident of the Tri-County GATE Council, supervises student teachers at the University of California, Santa Barbara, and works as an educational consultant.

With a principal who "firmly believed that training in proven teaching techniques for gifted learners would have a positive 'spillover effect' for his entire school," Maryanna Gray served as the leader/trainer for a series of professional development days at her school. Gray details logistic issues, guiding principles, in-service activities, and the need for flexibility. Not only were the goals achieved, the shared experiences led to increased collegiality among the staff.

The standards used by the California Department of Education to guide and shape district programs for gifted students require professional development activities to support and improve opportunities for gifted students. However, providing quality in-service training for teachers of the gifted as well as for all staff is a challenge in times of economic uncertainty and widespread budget cuts.

David Ortiz, principal of La Colina Junior High School in Santa Barbara, California, met this challenge head on. La Colina was fortunate to have a core of teachers who had already attended one or more of the summer training institutes sponsored by the California Association for the Gifted under the leadership of Dr. Sandra Kaplan. Their enthusiasm for the concepts and strategies learned during the institutes prompted Mr. Ortiz to look for a cost-effective way to bring these methodologies to his entire staff. He firmly believed that training in proven teaching techniques for gifted learners would have a positive "spillover effect" for his entire school and that student achievement would rise for all students if they were challenged with curriculum using the concepts of depth and complexity coupled with proper scaffolding.

Positive Effects

Staff training focusing on differentiation of curriculum and instruction proved to have many positive effects. One was the recognition by all staff of the different learning requirements of gifted students and the absolute necessity of recognizing these in all subject areas. Furthermore, since students in the school participate in designated classes for gifted learners for only a portion of each day, it is imperative that all teachers be able to accommodate gifted students when they are members of heterogeneously grouped classes.

It also led to new understanding of the daily challenges faced by teachers of gifted classes as they work to create curriculum characterized by depth, complexity, acceleration, and novelty. This increased understanding of the demands faced by the teachers of gifted classes was one element in developing increased collegiality among the staff.

Time Considerations

To accomplish his objectives, Mr. Ortiz used the one full-day provided by the district for professional development prior to the beginning of school, along with five minimum-day sessions. With this model, he was able to provide his entire staff—teachers, instructional aides, counselors, and administrators—with twenty-two hours of training in differentiated instruction. The author as a member of the La Colina staff was fortunate to have the opportunity to develop and conduct this training.

Guiding Principles

Beginning with the full-day teacher in-service prior to the opening of school, the entire staff gathered and was introduced to its yearlong theme: Working Together to Create Powerful Standards-Based Instruction for All Learners.

The objectives for the series of workshops included:

- recognizing the importance of student differences

- understanding the strategies that might be used to meet these differences

- understanding the manipulation of content, process, and product to meet the needs of a diverse student population

- developing a sense in students that they are a community of scholars

- recognizing the critical importance of building a sense of community in the classroom thereby establishing a safe learning environment

- understanding the necessity for pre-assessment, as well as assessment during and at the end of any unit of study

- building an acceptance of the need for flexibility in the classroom

- committing to respectful assignments for all learners as well as assignments that require high levels of thought, demand intellectual rigor, encourage creativity, and call for the application of skills and knowledge to authentic products

The anticipated outcome of the year's training was that participants would understand that change would be necessary if the objectives were to become reality. Change of any kind requires support. In August, a committed staff and administration at La Colina Junior High School began a year of focused in-service training determined to make proposed changes a reality.

In-Service Activities

The staff was organized into ten interdisciplinary teams founded on the idea that each staff member and department had a key role to play. The in-service activities included presentation of information and ideas followed by staff interaction and sharing. The "hands-on" activities were designed to involve each individual actively as he or she investigated students, teaching, and learning. The work of Sandra Kaplan of the University of Southern California and that of Carol Ann Tomlinson of the University of Virginia provided the content foundation for the in-service training.

The in-service began with two lessons modeled after Kaplan's use of graphic prompts (icons), key questions, and a universal theme. The lessons illustrated how these can be used to focus learning and increase the depth and complexity of any lesson.

The objective of the first lesson was to have each person focus on the idea of powerful teaching. Before discussion began, the universal theme of systems was introduced to the group. The participants came to understand that they were indeed a system having parts that functioned together to accomplish a common goal. The second part of the lesson required discussion and sharing of what each group considered powerful teaching. The graphic organizers used for this lesson were kept and used throughout the twenty-two hours of training.

An additional lesson modeled the use of Kaplan's depth and complexity icons to frame a topic that used language arts as a setting (see Figure 1). The activity also served as a community-building activity. The concept of metaphor was introduced much

Figure 1: Dimensions of Depth & Complexity

Language of the Disciplines

Details

Patterns

Rules

Trends

Unanswered Questions

Ethics

Big Idea

Relate Across Time

Multiple Perspectives

Across Disciplines

Acknowledgments: Definitions of dimensions of depth and complexity are from "Differentiating the Core Curriculum and Instruction to Provide Advanced Learning Opportunities," California Department of Education and California Association for the Gifted, 1994. Symbols for dimensions of depth and complexity developed under the auspices of OERI, Javits Curriculum Project T.W.O., 1996 as it would be in a language arts classroom. Teachers then selected one of four musical instruments that created the best metaphor for themselves as teachers. Musical instruments were placed around the room and individuals moved to the instruments that best represented themselves as teachers. Teachers then shared in pairs, fours, and finally, collaboratively as a whole group before they returned to their original groups.

The next activities also modeled Kaplan's work in depth and complexity. The facilitator played two roles. After giving directions, she stepped aside and explained the methodology being used. Joan Bauer's *Sticks* and Patricia Polacco's *Thank You, Mr. Falker* became the content used in lessons designed to help participants focus on what makes for powerful teaching. Using one of Kaplan's strategies, each story was framed with a combination of icons and content imperatives combined with key questions. Using the two pieces of children's literature, participants looked for patterns, rules, and points of view that would clarify the components of powerful teaching. With each activity, groups tackled their assignment, worked collaboratively, and reported to the group as a whole.

Melissa Ewart, teacher at La Colina and teacher trainer at the summer institutes, led the group in a study of America in the 1960s, using the universal theme of convergence. Working with primary documents and the icons of depth and complexity, each group was given a question to explore. As the day progressed, participants became more comfortable with the strategies they might employ to extend the curriculum for all learners.

Yearlong Structure

The structure of each component during the yearlong training combined input with group activities and sharing. The collaborative, collegial work built staff cohesiveness and fostered understanding of the conceptual basis of curriculum differentiation. Each segment ended with an assignment, the sharing of which began the subsequent session.

At the end of the full-day training session, each group received a sample differentiated lesson. The assignment was to study the example to determine what was being differentiated, how it was being differentiated, and why. The what was usually content, the how was quite often process, and the why corresponded to learner differences in readiness, interest, and style. The teachers were asked to analyze the example. They then replicated the example of differentiation in their own classrooms and returned to the next minimum day ready to share. During the discussion that followed the presentations, teachers explored methods of adjusting content, process, and product to meet diversified student needs in their own classrooms.

Each minimum-day session focused on the overall theme that all students deserve respectful assignments that challenge them to achieve more than they believed they could. Strategies were presented and participants practiced these strategies with their colleagues before exploring their potential in their own classrooms. Each in-service involved both group work and group presentations.

Flexibility Counts

The March minimum day unfortunately fell on the day that the first flurry of pink slips arrived for new teachers. With some teachers unsure of whether they would be rehired for the following school year, the situation demanded a quick change in the content of the minimum-day activities. It could not be business as usual; differentiation was called for. Using the text of the story, *God Bless the Gargoyles,* participants were asked to find the parallels between the angels in the story and educators. Using the icons for the content imperatives: Parallels, Origin, and Contribution, groups used the text of the story to explore the contributions all educators make to the lives of children. A second children's story, *Gettin' Through Thursday,* was also used. Groups used this text to examine the parallels of the plot to the current situation in education and to develop a generalization based on the story. The importance of creative problem solving and optimism as keys to survival in any situation dominated the discussions. Although the plans for this minimum day had changed due to circumstance, these changes served as a further example of the need to be flexible to accommodate the specific needs of a given learning environment.

As the year progressed, there was a noticeable increase in staff collegiality. The year's focus on differentiation could be heard being discussed at lunch. Teachers across disciplines collaborated in new ways. There was a common vocabulary being used among staff members, and the sharing of successes and insights were common topics. Graphics produced by groups during the staff in-service days were posted in the lounge. There was universal appreciation of the opportunity to share in a formalized collegial way. As new, open-ended, and challenging assignments were developed, they were shared with pride. The climate of the school—the prevailing temper, outlook, set of attitudes, and environmental conditions that characterize a group—had changed in a positive way.

"Spillover" Value

From the end of the very first day of training, the "spillover" value of gifted education methodologies was clearly evident. La Colina's focused staff development dramatically supported the potential of concepts and strategies from gifted education in increasing staff as well as student effectiveness. It also forged a vital working environment for the entire staff.

Resources

Bauer, J. (2002). *Sticks*. Horatio, NY: Puffin Books.

Cooper, M. (2000). *Gettin' through Thursday*. New York: Lee & Low Books.

Kaplan, S. N., Gould, B., & Siegel, V. (1995). *The flip book*. Calabasas, CA: Educator to Educator.

Kaplan, S. N., & Gould, B. (1998). *Frames: Differentiating the core curriculum*. Calabasas, CA: Educator to Educator.

Pilkey, D. (1996). *God bless the gargoyles*. New York: Harcourt.

Polacco, P. (1998). *Thank you, Mr. Falker*. New York: Philomel Books.

Tomlinson, C. (1999). *The differentiated classroom: Responding to the needs of all students*. Washington, DC: Association for Supervision & Curriculum Development.

PART 3

SEEKING AND SERVING SPECIAL POPULATIONS

Many educators and parents object strongly to the way general education seems to marginalize gifted education. Administrators often view gifted students as such a small part of student enrollment—and the money available to serve them so limited (sometimes nonexistent)—that they feel little urgency to support and provide for gifted education programs. After all, "If they're really gifted, they'll get it on their own," is an all-too-common belief of some. Such statements make us cringe and gear up to do battle for gifted education.

Sometimes, however, those of us in gifted education are guilty of marginalizing subpopulations of gifted students. For various reasons, the gifts and talents of many learners can be hidden or masked, and these students may slip through the cracks without receiving the education they deserve. We, of all segments of the education picture, must do our best to prevent that from happening.

Authors in Part 3 focus on identifying and serving specific groups of gifted learners who often are not adequately served, including: children in poverty; visual-spatial learners; underrepresented minority and racial groups; English language learners; inner-city youth; twice exceptional students; and gay and lesbian gifted youngsters. Authors share ways to find and serve these gifted learners as well as to affirm their existence and needs.

Issues of Identification and Underrepresentation

Barbara Clark | SPRING 2007

Barbara Clark, Ed.D., is a professor emeritus in the Charter College of Education at California State University, Los Angeles. She is the author of the widely used text, Growing Up Gifted, *now in its seventh edition (2007). Dr. Clark is a past president of the World Council for Gifted and Talented Children and the National Association for Gifted Children, and is on the Board of Directors and is a past president of the California Association for the Gifted. She is a recognized scholar and has presented major addresses and workshops throughout the United States and the world.*

Barbara Clark outlines two current theories used to explain underrepresentation of Hispanic Americans, African Americans, and Native Americans in gifted programs: the discrimination theory and the distribution theory. Clark acknowledges the existence of discrimination and the need to address it, but suggests that the greater causes are poverty and economics. Poverty results in uneven distribution of the cultural resources and support systems needed to do well in school. She makes suggestions to alleviate both discrimination and limited resources.

It is true that giftedness at the highest level can be found in every cultural group. It is also true that the incidence of participation in gifted programs by some of the racial, ethnic, and socioeconomic groups in society varies from group to group; it is far lower among some of the culturally and linguistically diverse (C&LD) groups such as the Hispanic-American, African-American, and the

American Indian than participation by Anglo-American and Asian-American groups. A number of factors have often been cited as contributors to this underrepresentation. Primary among them are the:

- method of identification for gifted programs

- definition of intelligence and giftedness

- bias and prejudice of educators

An extraordinary amount of writing, research, and concern has been focused on these factors. But are these the issues that are most responsible for the very real problem of underrepresentation obvious in gifted programs in schools today? Do these issues provide the best framework to use in planning research and seeking solutions? How do culture and linguistic differences impact intelligence and the incidence of giftedness? Is the issue of underrepresentation even about racial and ethnic diversity?

The Discrimination Theory

There are currently at least two theories that are in use to explain the unequal representation of racially and ethnically diverse groups in gifted education. The discrimination theory is supported by those who believe that underrepresentation is created by inappropriate identification procedures, limited definitions of intelligence and giftedness, and prejudice on the part of members of the educational community. This group believes that there would be equal representation of all diverse groups in gifted programs in direct proportion to the demographics of the district if the educational community took the following action.

Change biased identification practices. The advocates for this view believe that traditional tests are unfair to anyone outside of the mainstream culture, because they are too limiting in the type of information sought and often normed on quite different populations than those that are underrepresented. These advocates believe that the standards set by the schools of what must be known do not include the type of information, abilities, and skills developed by these populations, making it impossible for them to test well. Nonverbal tests are suggested as better at finding these abilities and skills. From this belief, a new cadre of such tests has been developed to fill this gap. In addition there is concern among advocates of the discrimination theory that in the identification process too much emphasis is placed on checklists used by teachers that list only behaviors atypical of students in underrepresented groups. They are concerned by the use of low-test scores and additional criteria such as school attendance and class behavior to eliminate students.

Change the definitions of intelligence and of giftedness, the term used to label a high level of intelligence. The current definitions are seen as too narrow and skewed toward Anglo-American and Asian-American groups. In addition to the intellectual thinking skills it is believed that emotional, social, kinesthetic, and interpersonal skills should be included in the definitions and characteristics used to define giftedness. The manifestation of creativity should be considered important even in the absence of more rational skills and abilities. Standards for what needs to be learned and what represents intelligence need to be changed to better fit the values, attitudes, and opportunities of the underrepresented students.

Prevent bias and prejudice among members of the educational community from blocking the entry of the underrepresented students into the gifted programs. While teachers are often the gatekeepers determining who will be selected for gifted programs, many teachers lack knowledge in regard to the characteristics, values, and differing abilities of students from underrepresented groups. Research has shown that teachers often have low expectations for diverse students. Advocates of this point of view refer to such expectations as deficit thinking. They find that such thinking causes diverse students to doubt their ability and to sabotage their own achievement.

In summary, advocates of the discrimination theory believe that giftedness is evenly distributed across all demographic groups, but the traditional methods of identifying students for gifted programs are culturally biased preventing equity in the identification process and limiting access to gifted programs. In this view, adoption of a quota system to ensure that all cultural groups—usually defined by these advocates by race—are equally represented in the same proportion in the classroom that they are found in the community is justified. If we were to look with more openness and willingness to change the standards of what information must be known and what skills must be learned, discrimination theorists believe we would find equal numbers of gifted learners in every racial and ethnic group. All other points of view are regarded as deficit thinking and dismissed as racially biased. Much of the current writing, thinking, discussion, and activity in the field of gifted education is based on the discrimination theory as the only possible explanation for underrepresentation.

The Distribution Theory

Although much of what has been discussed about underrepresentation from the discrimination theory point of view certainly needs our attention, there is a second theory that suggests that giftedness actually *is* unequally distributed across demographic groups. Advocates of the distribution theory of underrepresentation are concerned about how this unequal development is caused and how it can be prevented. A significant body of information has shown that there are real differences in the level of important intellectual skills and achievement ability among racial and ethnic groups and that these IQ/achievement gaps and what caused them are real and important. These advocates point out that cultural groups differ on availability of support systems, provision of resources, priority given to certain kinds of talent, individual initiative, and leadership, among other factors. What is valued by the culture is produced by the culture.

From decades of research from the neurosciences it is known that the development of intelligence is an interactive process. The growth of intelligence depends on the interaction between the inherited neurological patterns of the individual and the environment in which the individual is developing. A high level of growth of intelligence requires a variety of intellectually challenging experiences in a responsive, stimulating environment from the earliest years of the child's life. Therefore, the following conditions must be considered as important reasons for underrepresentation among cultural groups:

- Low socioeconomic status (SES) homes tend to have restricted environments both in terms of learning materials and opportunities available and in practices of child rearing.

- Larger percentages of African-Americans, Hispanic-Americans, and American Indians grow up in low SES circumstances than do Anglo-Americans and Asian-Americans.

- Low SES students are generally much less likely to be high academic achievers than high SES students. This is true in all industrialized nations.

Advocates of the distribution theory believe that the larger issues in underrepresentation are not about race or discrimination; they are about economics. It has been found to be easier to identify gifted students from middle-class homes, regardless of their racial or cultural group, than to identify giftedness in homes in poverty. Underrepresentation of gifted children from poverty crosses all racial and ethnic groups.

Poverty is not just about money. Rather, it is important to understand that poverty involves the extent to which an individual does without resources. Not only financial resources but emotional, intellectual, and physical resources; relationships and role models; and innumerable external support systems. The major difference between children from poverty and other children, say researchers in this area, is in the type and quantity of opportunities inherent in the child's environment.

Here is the dilemma of excellence versus equity. Why shouldn't we strive for both?

Regarding the use of quota systems in the identification process, it is significant that limited experience in the early environment provides limited skills. A child raised in these environments needs opportunities for development of such skills, not for the more advanced or complex work found in gifted programs. If there is no match between the experiences needed by the child and the goals and curriculum of the gifted program, placing the child in the program will only lead to frustration and further damage intellectually and academically. In regard to testing, it should be noted, that those in the field of psychometrics continue to publish data showing that the gifted students in underrepresented groups actually do better on standardized testing than on nonverbal testing and confirm that two quite different groups are formed from the results of these two testing formats. Terms like underrepresentation and quota requirements are less applicable when the limitations of opportunity the student has previously experienced are considered.

Here is the dilemma of excellence versus equity. Why shouldn't we strive for both? It will take a long-term effort requiring systemic change in the belief systems and cultural practices that shape early learning and child rearing necessary to optimize brain development. Disparity cannot be satisfactorily alleviated through changes in either the definition of giftedness or the identification process.

Actions to Alleviate Underrepresentation

From both theories comes knowledge of the following conditions that can appropriately be said to create underrepresentation and that we must work to alleviate:

- Biased beliefs about the diverse populations. The appropriate action would be to work to change these beliefs.

- Lack of opportunity for early learning. Act to make sure the parents from all cultures are given information on the essential experiences a child needs to develop intellectually and knowledge of activities that provide such experiences.

- Lack of opportunity to learn school skills and testing skills. The appropriate action would be to provide opportunities for learning basic skills that may be missing. Use of dynamic assessment or the "test-learn-test" framework would be of benefit.

- Fear the students have of rejection by their culture and peer group if they participate in school-related learning and/or intellectual skill building, especially if they are successful. There is evidence that many outstanding African-American students are performing less well than they are able to avoid the threat of being viewed by members of their culture as a negative stereotype. This is one of the most difficult problems to remedy. Having the student examine the consequences, both short term and long term, of participation and nonparticipation, may be of help in removing this self-defeating block.

It is clear that opportunities for growth must be provided for culturally diverse students, but in so doing, we must guard against changing cultural and family patterns just because they are different. Diversity is the cornerstone of developing potential and only patterns that inhibit the development of that potential need modification. Potential for giftedness may be found regardless of the cultural background in the manner in which abilities are expressed, such as:

- a strong desire to learn

- intense, sometimes unusual interests

- unusual ability to communicate with words, numbers, or symbols

- effective, often inventive strategies for recognizing and solving problems

- exceptional ability to retain and retrieve information, resulting in a large storehouse of information

- extensive and unusual questions, experiments, and explorations

- a quick grasp of new concepts, connections; a sense of deeper meanings

- logical approaches to figuring out solutions

- an ability to produce many highly original ideas

- a keen, often unusual sense of humor

Needed is the development of enriched learning opportunities through which youngsters can actually demonstrate their potential by their performance and products, making self-identification an integral part of the assessment process.

Those who work in gifted programs should continue to search out the extraordinarily talented in all social groups by using the soundest techniques at their disposal. The problems of identifying and nurturing talent potential are not resolved by formulating constructs of giftedness solely for minority and economically disadvantaged students that differ from those for the majority populations, by lowering the criteria or standards for excellence or outstanding performance, or by seeking different areas of talent in various populations. The challenge is one of creating opportunities that take culture and context into account to enhance the possibilities for identifying potential of many kinds in all populations. Appropriate opportunities and conditions must be provided to nurture potential into giftedness. Underrepresentation is a far more complex problem than a change of testing can solve. We should not trade excellence for equity. We must aim for increasing both.

Gifted education programs should continue to do what they do best and what no other education program attempts to do: provide a variety of educational opportunities for exceptionally able children so that they may realize their potential. Finding ways to change the IQ/achievement gap between cultures at the level of causation instead of the level of its symptoms should be an important part of the mission for programs in gifted education and talent development. If we could help *all* families in *all* cultural groups in culturally sensitive ways to understand what experiences are essential to develop the child's intelligence at the beginning of their lives, the current waste of human potential would change and discussion of theories of underrepresentation would be unnecessary.

References

Ford, D. Y. (2003). Equity and excellence: Culturally diverse students in gifted education. In N. Colangelo, & G. A. Davis (Eds.), *Handbook of gifted education* (3rd ed., pp. 506–520). Boston: Allyn and Bacon.

————. (2006). Creating culturally responsive classrooms for gifted students. *Understanding Our Gifted* 19(1): 10–14.

Frasier, M., Garcia, J. H., & Passow, A. H. (1995). *A review of assessment issues in gifted education and their implications for identifying gifted minority students.* Research Monograph 95204. Storrs, CT: National Research Center on the Gifted and Talented.

Gottfredson, L. S. (2004). Realities in desegregating gifted education. In D. Boothe, & J. C. Stanley (Eds.), *In the eyes of the beholder: Critical issues for diversity in gifted education* (pp. 139–155). Waco, TX: Prufrock Press.

Miller, L. S. (2004). *Promoting sustained growth in the representation of African Americans, Latinos, and Native Americans among top students in the United States at all levels of the educational system.* Storrs, CT: The National Research Center on the Gifted and Talented.

Slocumb, P. D. (2001). Giftedness in poverty. *Gifted Education Communicator* 32(4): 6–11.

Slocumb, P. D., & Payne, R. K. (2000). *Removing the mask: Giftedness in poverty.* Highlands, TX: aha! Process, Inc.

Giftedness in Poverty

Paul D. Slocumb | WINTER 2001

Paul D. Slocumb, Ed.D., *is an author and consultant for aha! Process, Inc. He is the coauthor of* Removing the Mask: Giftedness in Poverty *and the author of* Hear Our Cry: Boys in Crisis. *He presents widely at conferences and for school district professional development training.*

"The larger issue [of underrepresentation] is not one of race or cultures, but one of economics." So states Paul Slocumb in laying the groundwork for proposing a shift in identification practices and services for underrepresented populations in our programs for gifted learners. He discusses factors such as (1) language development at home, (2) lack of support resources at home, (3) need for nontraditional identification measures, and (4) different responses of children of poverty versus middle-class students.

The lack of racial and cultural diversity in programs for the gifted has become a major concern in many school districts and states. While some have made great progress in this area, efforts to identify gifted children who come from low socioeconomic backgrounds have not fared as well. Frequently, a lack of diversity in gifted programs is often viewed as too few students from different racial or ethnic groups. The larger issue is not one of race or cultures, but one of economics. Identifying gifted students from middle-class homes, regardless of their racial or cultural group, is easier than identifying giftedness in poverty. It is underrepresentation of gifted children from poverty that crosses all racial and cultural groups and that presents the greatest challenge.

Frank Frankfurter, former U.S. Supreme Court Justice, said, "There is nothing so unequal as the equal treatment of unequals." Potentially gifted students who come from poverty, however, are frequently expected to meet the same criteria as students from middle income families even though their life experiences are far less rich than those of middle-class students. As a result, they all too often go unidentified and unserved.

Most identification processes are based upon the notion that all students must be treated alike. Consequently, gifted and talented identification processes are frequently based upon absolute cut-off scores for performance on achievement tests, ability tests, teacher recommendations, grades, or a myriad of other data sources. The expectation that "one size fits all" is defended as "fair." Systems adopt such procedures because they want to rely on hard data if they are called upon to defend their choices. In the process of developing systems of fairness in which all students are treated equally, equity is lost.

Parents want their children to have what they perceive to be the best program, with the best curriculum, for the best students, with the best teachers the school district has to offer. This environment sets the stage for a system that is based upon equality rather than equity. Students who come from backgrounds that are different from middle-class America do not fare well on traditional assessments. Thus, they go unidentified and unserved. Why? They don't meet the standard—the cut-off score(s).

This discrepancy is apparent in gifted programs throughout this country. Though districts have made efforts to eliminate this disparity by using standardized tests that purport to be more culturally fair, disparity remains. Until school personnel address existing factors that continue to perpetuate this disparity, school districts will continue to have minimal success in identifying and serving this subpopulation effectively and efficiently.

Point #1: Reframing the Purposes of Gifted Education

Gifted education is a special program. Special programs exist to address special needs that are not typically met by the mainstream program and the regular classroom teacher. Thus, special programs for the gifted should be created and staffed with teachers who have been trained in meeting the needs of this special population. While this is certainly appropriate, students identified and served are typically those who meet criteria that align with school systems' middle-class norms to the exclusion of students who look and behave differently. One of the largest groups of students who look and behave differently consists of those who come from poverty.

The use of IQ scores, standardized achievement scores, and teacher rating scales that look at giftedness from a middle-class perspective will generally yield a gifted population that achieves academically. There is nothing wrong with identifying students who should be identified and served. When the result, however, is a gifted population that does not reflect the demographics of the larger school population, then the identification process needs to be re-examined.

While the identification process is critical, the right teacher is even more critical. A master dentist is not shocked to see a patient in need of major dental work. Though the dentist might be appalled that someone has become so negligent about oral hygiene, it would not deter the master dentist from working on the patient. Master dentists know that their skills can produce beautiful smiles. Master dentists see beyond what is to what can be, given the appropriate treatment over time.

Such is often the case with potentially gifted students from poverty. It takes a master teacher who can see the potential behind the mask of poverty. Gifted students already achieving do not need "fixing." They usually need a little polishing, requiring the skills of a good dental hygienist, not necessarily those of a master dentist; but for the gifted from poverty it is absolutely essential.

All students have the right to master teachers. Potentially gifted students from poverty, however, *must* have the services of master teachers. Gifted students who are not from poverty typically have master parents who can offer the many opportunities that come with money. Master teachers are the ones who must become advocates for students from poverty once those students have been placed in programs. They must be the ones who can visualize the potential of these students. They must know that because of their interventions, the beautiful smile can become a reality.

Gifted programs must be more than just polishing bright, able learners. They must provide the intervention that helps all gifted students realize their potential. For students from poverty to reap the benefits of such a program, schools must revisit the means used to identify this population. They must also abandon practices that increase the likelihood that these students will drop out of their traditional, middle-class gifted programs. Those practices include expecting that all gifted students must:

- make high grades consistently

- display good behavior, be model students

- have parents who are actively involved in their child's academic program

- be able to work independently outside of the school day

- be able to produce products that require resources outside the school

- be eager to learn

- be able to work productively with other gifted students

Such practices, such mindsets, almost certainly eliminate many potentially gifted students from poverty. Systemically, districts must design gifted and talented programs with curriculum and master teachers that produce results that would not be produced if the intervention were not provided.

Point #2: Recognizing the Disparity and Significance of Environmental Opportunities in the Identification Process

Students who come from poverty do not come to school with the same experiences as those from middle class. Affluence buys opportunities not usually afforded students from poverty. Educated parents typically provide their children with a quality and range of experiences that have a positive impact on things measured in school. In addition to vacations, books, quality childcare programs, computers, and a host of other goods and services, educated parents almost always provide their children with daily interactions that develop facility with language, a skill critical to success in school. Standardized testing, textbooks, and social interactions within the school require vocabularies and sentence structures that are well developed in standard, formal English.

In a longitudinal study of forty-two families with preschool-age children, Hart and Risely (1995) identified many of these disparities. The forty-two families were divided into four groups including:

- parents who were professional and managerial workers

- parents who worked in offices and hospitals

- parents who were in construction, factories, and service jobs

- families on welfare

The findings include the following:

- Between the ages of 11 and 18 months, the average number of parent utterances per hour was 642 for the professional group, of which 482 were addressed to the baby. In the office and hospital group, parents averaged 535 utterances per hour, of which 321 were addressed to the baby. In the construction and factory worker group, parents averaged 521 utterances per hour, of which 283 were addressed to the baby. In the welfare group, parents averaged 394 utterances per hour, of which 197 were addressed to the baby.

    Finding: The major difference among the four groups was in the number of verbal exchanges that occurred, and this difference was strongly associated with the socioeconomic status of the families.

- The utterances of professional parents were not only greater in number but also richer in the use of nouns, modifiers, past tense verbs, declarative sentences, and affirmative feedback. In the welfare families, the utterances were both fewer in quantity and less rich in nouns, modifiers, verbs, past tense verbs, and clauses. After initiating or responding to their children, welfare parents continued talking to their children less than half as often as did working-class parents.

    Finding: In each hour of their lives, welfare children received less than half the language experience of working-class children.

- Professional parents gave their children an average of five prohibitions per hour whereas the welfare parents gave their children an average of eleven prohibitions per hour. Additionally, the welfare parents gave more negative imperatives ("Don't," "Stop," "Quit") than professional families.

- Professional parents gave their children affirmative feedback every other minute, more than thirty times per hour. This was twice as often as that of working-class parents, and more than five times as often as that of parents in welfare families.

     Finding: Children in welfare families heard a prohibition twice as often as they heard affirmative feedback.

The language experiences of children during preschool years significantly affect their performance in school. Schools are middle-class institutions. As such there is an expectation that when children enter school they:

- can speak in complete sentences

- ask questions

- use declarative sentences to express wants, needs, and feelings

- sequence, and work cooperatively with other children by displaying socially acceptable behaviors

- understand cause and effect relationships

Students who come from poverty typically do not have preschool experiences that put these things in place. Therefore, without factoring in the environmental circumstances, chances are slight that the student from poverty will be perceived as "bright." Ironically, such students are much more likely to be referred for testing for a disability.

Point #3: Recognizing the Disparity in Early Childhood Experiences and Factoring That into the Identification Process

When school personnel use traditional measures such as IQ and achievement scores to identify giftedness, most of those identified as gifted will be those who come from families who have enriched language experiences in their home environments. In *Removing the Mask: Giftedness in Poverty*, Slocumb and

Payne (2000) purport that in educated households children have environmental opportunities that push their skills and performance higher. These opportunities outside the school environment result in higher measured test performance in school. In poor, uneducated households, children have limited access to environmental opportunities that have a positive impact on skill and performance levels. They don't get identified as gifted because their skills are lower than the expectations, not because of their intellectual potential. The less opportunity in the environment, the lower the test scores will be as measured by the school. When gifted children are identified on the basis of traditional measures without factoring in the impact of the environment, what gets identified is opportunity and not giftedness (Slocumb & Payne, 2000).

To identify gifted students from poverty, their environment must be a component in the identification process. *The Environmental Opportunities Profile* (EOP) (Slocumb & Payne, 2000) achieves this. EOP is designed as an interview instrument to account for the lack of resources within the environment that inhibit or delay the learning process. Poverty is more than just not having money. "Poverty is the extent to which an individual does without resources" (Payne, 1998, p. 16). The availability or lack of resources yields very different results. Students from poverty, middle class, and even from wealth may lack some of these resources. It is the degree to which a student lacks these resources that determines the extent of a student's impoverishment. Table 1 illustrates the impact these resources have on the home environment of children.

Identifying elements within the environment that inhibit a child's development allows school personnel to calculate a "handicapping score" much as one might have for a game of golf. Use of the EOP results in a numerical score that can be juxtaposed against scores based on a student's performance on standardized tests. The following diagram illustrates this paradigm.

Resources affect student performance. Judging all students as though they have access to the same resources may be treating them equally but it is not equitable. In 1993, the U.S. Department of Education defined gifted and talented students as "Children and youth of outstanding talent who perform at remarkably high levels of accomplishment when compared with others of their age, experience, or environment." In practice, environment and experience are rarely considered and the comparative factor typically used is that of age (grade level). Students who come from poverty are in fact not compared with their

Table 1 : Differences in Environmental Opportunities

Resources	Result of sufficient resources	Result of insufficient resources
Financial	Health care, books, toys, computers, vacations, transportation, food, shelter	Lack of prenatal care; poor nutrition; lack of physical space for adequate motor development; lack of experiences through toys and play for children; unemployment; basic necessities lacking
Emotional	Task commitment; persistence; ability to reason through and verbalize situations and solve problems, articulate feelings; ability to control anger and behavior	Impulsive behavior; lack of causal reasoning; lack of language to express feelings; physical punishment of children for misbehavior; may curse at children when scolding them; models aggression to resolve conflict
Mental	Ability to read, write, and compute; presence of books, magazines, puzzles, and games; ability to function with day-to-day tasks, learning new things as needed; can problem solve	Absence of books, puzzles; parents unable to read to children; dependence on television for entertainment and information; limited job possibilities; poor problem-solving skills; little experience with abstract reasoning; decisions made on basis of likes and dislikes
Spiritual	Environment of hope, empowerment, inner strength, self-worth, purposefulness	Personal efforts perceived to be insignificant; feelings of hopelessness; dependence on fate and luck
Physical	Healthy; able to perform daily routines; ability to work; alert; energized	Poor health; diets high in sugar and fats; poorly developed sensory motor and ocular motor systems; adults miss work and have no sick leave benefits
Support systems	Friends and relatives available to help in times of need; ability to hire help when needed; can find answers when needed; physical and emotional support available from others	Quality childcare unavailable; older children caring for younger children; high stress levels because there is no help; feelings acted out rather than verbalized and dealt with logically and rationally; lack of knowledge about how to deal with institutions
Relationships/ role models	Presence of nurturing adults; feelings of love, caring, safety; knows help available in times of need; trusts others; attitude of "I can"	Feelings of being isolated; unable to find answers; feelings of abandonment and victimization; unable to show affection toward others; distrust of others
Hidden rules	Adheres to rules of social class; is accepted by social class to which he/ she belongs; can adapt and survive in social situations; knows expectations of group	Unable to understand rules in workplace; loses jobs; difficulty in communicating with social-service organizations because of lack of understanding of "rules"; distrust of institutions

From Slocumb & Payne, 2000

peer group. They are compared with their grade-level peers, regardless of the differences that exist between their home environments and subsequent life experiences.

Point #4: Using Nontraditional Measures to Identify Nontraditional Students

Lacking resources within their environment, students from poverty typically do not perform as well on standardized tests as do students from middle-class backgrounds. Using more nontraditional measures, however, can reveal strengths within students from poverty. To discover these strengths, it is helpful to assess them on activities and performances in which language is not the driving force. Most standardized tests require a facility with language that most students from poverty simply do not have. Problem-solving activities using manipulatives are helpful. Portfolios that show a student's abilities in the areas of critical and creative thinking are also useful. Teacher rating scales, such as the Slocumb-Payne Teacher Perception Inventory (Slocumb & Payne, 2000), that have teachers look at the concomitant attributes of giftedness are essential because gifted students from poverty frequently manifest their gifted attributes in socially unacceptable ways.

The identification process needs to look at a preponderance of evidence rather than establishing cut-off scores. Looking at a variety and a wide range of student performances over time, and looking at that performance in relationship to the student's environmental opportunities can reveal strengths that would otherwise go undetected in processes steeped in middle-class values and behaviors.

Point #5: Detecting the Strengths of Students Hidden Behind the Mask of Poverty

Systems must look beyond the mask of poverty to see the strengths and talents that students from poverty bring to the system. For example, a 5-year-old student who comes to school and has a storehouse of knowledge about dinosaurs or the NASA space program would probably be perceived as a very bright student.

The 5-year-old who comes to school and knows all the words to a variety of rap songs by a popular rap artist, or the names and statistics of all the players on a national basketball team, might not be perceived as bright, especially if the student does not display an interest in the content the school presents.

Educators must be trained to focus on identifying students who have the ability to store knowledge rather than focusing on judging the merits of the knowledge the students have stored. The young student from poverty is going to reflect a knowledge base of those things that are valued in the culture of poverty. Entertainment is one of those values. The degree to which students from poverty have such information stored when compared to their peers who come from poverty is what needs to be considered. It is the job of the program to provide such students with opportunities and motivation to want to store other kinds of information.

Middle-class educators tend to recognize the creativity inherent in a cleverly written story created by a child as part of a language arts activity. However, when the student from poverty spins an original, clever tale to convince the teacher that someone else committed an offense, the creativity is not acknowledged and the behavior is admonished.

Gifted students from poverty are not going to look like middle-class gifted students in a multitude of ways. It is the job of the program, however, to identify these students and then to channel their gifts and talents in a manner that allows them to be successful in a middle-class system. Students who are survivors in poverty develop many skills and talents. It is their creativity, their problem solving, and their perseverance that has allowed them to survive—in some cases under extreme circumstances. That does not mean that they will do well on standard creativity worksheets. Could the middle-class gifted student survive in the student's neighborhood of poverty for three days?

Point #6: Differentiating the Differentiated Curriculum for Gifted Children in Poverty

Top-end teaching yields top-end results; bottom-end teaching yields bottom-end learning. Students from poverty are frequently perceived as deficient learners because of their lack of experience. Poverty is a world based on concreteness not abstraction. When survival is a driving force, dealing with abstract ideas does not generally have concrete payoffs. For example, doing well in school so one can go to college appears very abstract to someone in poverty because it is in the future and does not help one survive in daily life. To a middle-class person who is future oriented, this does not appear logical. Middle-class families recognize that education is a critical component in one's success in the future job market as an adult.

Much of schooling is abstract, studying things that happened long ago, labeling words and phrases so language can be dissected and manipulated, and trying to understand things like cells and chemical reactions that cannot be seen. Not seeing the relevancy of school learning to daily survival in the neighborhood, and lacking essential life experiences in the environment produces students who come to school with skill gaps. These skill gaps become a major focus for educators. How can students be gifted when they do not know the basics? Programs focusing on what students are missing, all but guarantee that students from poverty will never "catch up" with the other middle-class gifted students.

Could the middle-class gifted student survive in the student's neighborhood of poverty for three days?

Students from poverty must be afforded the same high-level learning as gifted students from middle class. The challenge is to fill in the learning gaps while teaching to the higher end of learning. Commenting on the instructional needs of gifted students who are limited English language learners, Kaplan (1999, p. 20), states "fill-in-the-gaps activities must be identified as inherent features of an exemplary differentiated gifted curriculum and not just as good teaching practices. Too often, limited English language learners who are gifted are either excluded from the differentiated gifted curriculum because of limited experience, or the experience is given to students in a limited manner." The same is true of gifted students from poverty.

To get students to the higher end of learning requires that teachers understand the culture of poverty and help students tap into their life experiences as a source of energy to move to higher levels of learning. Understanding concepts and generalizations related to systems may require that teachers understand systems that are integral parts of poverty, such as bartering, food stamps, and hidden communication systems. When these are used as referents for students, they can be brought forward to understand more complex, abstract systems that are part of the differentiated curriculum for the gifted. What is part of the students' concrete world of poverty must be used as the bridge to get to the higher learning.

Point #7: Districts Must Deal with Political Realities While Being Responsive to the Needs of a More Diverse Gifted Population

As school districts move toward a more inclusionary, diverse gifted program, they must face some realities. Programs that have served middle-class gifted students for many years cannot be changed quickly. Redefining the purpose of the gifted program and developing an identification process that includes more diversity may not be popular among the school's constituents. School personnel should never refrain from identifying and serving a gifted student from poverty when found at any grade level. Systemically, however, a district needs to transition into its new model slowly and methodically. A new generation of gifted programming must be created.

Districts need to begin at the primary grade levels and then move that more diverse group of gifted students up through the system. Training teachers along the way in effective teaching practices for this more diverse gifted population must be done as the program expands to subsequent grade levels. This grade-by-grade expansion is not only politically smart—it is the way to build successful programs. Parents have an image of what their school district's gifted program is and is not. When that image begins to shift, parents will have to be reeducated. Some will be very reluctant to embrace a program that includes a more diverse population, especially one that includes students from poverty. Because those from the middle class do not understand the culture of poverty any more than people from poverty understand the middle class, there will be those who say, "I don't want my child in the same class with those kids." Having a diverse gifted population begin together in the early grades and then move through the system, allows those involved time to learn and appreciate one another. School personnel must be willing to shift the paradigm for gifted education, and they must be willing to fight the political fight.

Conclusion

Gifted students come from all segments of the student population. When one population is served disproportionately in comparison to other subgroups in the student population, equity is compromised. Gifted students from all segments of the population must have the same access to the gifted program. To achieve equity and excellence for all gifted students, school personnel must begin the process of examining current practices in identification and in instruction. This will bring about change. School personnel must be willing to accept the challenges that come with this change. The system must advocate for those students who have no advocate. Gifted students in poverty must be given a voice and that voice begins with educators who are committed to equity and excellence in gifted programming for all students.

References

Hart, B., & Risley T. R. (1995). *Meaningful differences in the everyday experience of young American children.* Baltimore, MD: Paul H. Brookes Publishing Co.

Kaplan, S. (1999). Teaching up to needs of the gifted English language learner. *Tempo* 19(2): 1, 20–21.

Payne, R. (1998). *A framework for understanding poverty* (Rev. ed.). Highlands, TX: aha! Process Inc.

Slocumb, P., & Payne, R. (2000). *Removing the mask: Giftedness in poverty.* Highlands, TX: aha! Process Inc.

Gifts of Language Diversity: Building Educational Aspirations with Latino Students in Middle School

Todd Kettler, Alexandra Shiu, and Susan K. Johnsen | WINTER 2006

Todd Kettler, M.Ed., is director of advanced academics for the Coppell Independent School District in Coppell, Texas. He is also a doctoral student in the department of Educational Psychology at Baylor University. He taught middle school and high school English and worked for an educational service center as a gifted education specialist. His research interests include social constructivist learning theory, conceptual foundations of gifted education, and creative writing.

Alexandra Shiu, M.S., is a doctoral student and a graduate assistant in the Department of Educational Psychology at Baylor University in Waco, Texas. She taught college-level economics as an adjunct faculty for two years. Her research interests include social capital, resilience, and gifted minority students from lower socioeconomic backgrounds.

Susan K. Johnsen, Ph.D., is a professor in the Department of Educational Psychology at Baylor University, Waco, Texas. She directs the Ph.D. program and programs related to gifted and talented education at both the graduate and undergraduate levels. She has published widely, and works include her recent book, Identifying Gifted/Talented Students: A Practical Guide, *and three tests that are used in identifying gifted students. She is a frequent presenter at international, national, and state conferences. She is editor of* Gifted Child Today.

Rapid acquisition of language is becoming recognized as a mark of giftedness; there is also evidence citing the middle school years as key in developing students' long-term educational aspirations. The Waco Texas school district placed Hispanic middle school students with advanced Spanish language skills in an experimental Advanced Placement Spanish class. Results were so positive the program was expanded. The authors include assessment and analysis in their article.

Edgar entered seventh grade in a central Texas middle school speaking very little English. He had recently moved from southern Mexico to the central Texas area and now found himself in a school where English was the language of instruction. Fortunately, the school had a newcomer center for students like Edgar. He had an opportunity to learn English through an intensive language instruction program, but more importantly, Edgar found a group of friends with whom he could relate. The year progressed as did Edgar's use of English. He was spending half his days in English language classes by midterm, and his teachers assured his parents that he was on his way to full participation in the regular English language curriculum. Edgar's year ended with six weeks of full inclusion in English-speaking classes. He was on the verge of leaving the English language learner program at the school. The English-speaking classes were by no means easy for Edgar, but they were manageable. He made mostly Cs, and grew closer to his fellow newcomer friends when his obvious language barrier separated him from his English-speaking peers.

Summer vacation was a welcome relief for Edgar. He returned to Mexico with his mother and three younger siblings. He enjoyed the comfort of familiar surroundings, family, and his native language. He played soccer with old friends, went to work with his grandfather, and read several books from his uncle's collection. But August arrived and so did the long bus ride back to central Texas.

When Edgar and his family arrived at their house in central Texas, they had a message from the school. The Spanish teacher at the school left the message asking for Edgar and his parents to meet with her and the principal to consider Edgar's participation in a special program for students with advanced Spanish skills. Edgar called the school and said he and his mother could come right away to discuss the special program. Within a week, Edgar was registered to take Advanced Placement (AP) Spanish Language. No one in Edgar's family knew what AP meant; no one had ever heard of the College Board. But when Mrs. Flote said, "We believe that your advanced skill in Spanish is a gift that needs to be nurtured," Edgar was sold. When Principal Ingram told Edgar and his mother that the special program would give Edgar and students like him a jump start on college, Edgar's mother fought through her emotions and encouraged her son to participate. Prior to that day, college seemed an unattainable goal; it was rarely talked about for fear of expectation. More pointedly, it was rarely talked about because no one in the family knew anything about how to get there.

Middle school is a crucial time in the lives of students. These years lay the foundation for students to learn more about themselves, select close friends, and form educational aspirations for the future. A sense of belonging, or how connected and accepted students feel in terms of relationships with peers and school personnel, plays a role in school engagement as measured by their attendance, participation in school activities, and effort in the learning process. The middle school years are a sensitive period when this sense of belonging at school is formed, or in some cases not formed (Osterman, 2000). By the time students reach ninth grade, they feel most vulnerable to risky behavior (Boyd & Tashakkori, 1994). Therefore, intervention programs in middle school can have significant influence on a student's sense of belonging at school and ultimately long-term educational aspirations. The impact of middle school interventions for students like Edgar is even more important because of the natural barriers that are formed due to his language diversity. Latino students make up the most rapidly growing minority group of students in American schools, and their achievement continues to fall short of the achievement levels of peers in other racial or ethnic groups. Latino students who are English language learners are particularly susceptible to achievement gaps and lower graduation rates, and are among the least likely students in American schools to go to post-secondary education (Gándara, O'Hara, & Gutiérrez, 2004).

Latino students are often underrepresented in gifted education programs as well (Worrell, Szarko, & Gabelko, 2001). They frequently lack knowledge about college as a post-secondary option, and students from Mexico have the lowest college aspirations among the Latino population living in the United States (Kao & Tienda, 1998). Furthermore, for Latino students who do decide to pursue higher education, the majority do not achieve their aspirations of a college degree and enter the job marketplace undereducated and unskilled (Gándara, 1995).

The AP Spanish for Middle School program is an intervention designed to increase a sense of belonging and educational aspirations for middle school students whose home language is Spanish. *The program is founded upon the idea that language diversity can be considered a strength on which to build rather than a risk factor on which to remediate.* The Waco Independent School District (WISD) in Waco, Texas, began its program in 2002 and became part of a Texas statewide AP incentive grant in 2003. More than 150 Latino students in WISD have participated in the program by taking AP Spanish during the eighth-grade year. The following provides an overview of the program, results from the program evaluation, and suggestions for program replication.

AP Spanish in a Middle School Program

What if we could change the way students and educators think about language diversity? What if our middle school treated advanced skills in Spanish similar to advanced skills in mathematics: students who are really good at it get a cool label and then get placed together in advanced courses to further achieve in the subject. Wait a minute; could a student in eighth grade really be successful on the AP Spanish examination? Those are the questions that were tossed around the curriculum department when AP Spanish in middle school surfaced as a possibility. When the initial brainstorming excitement wore down, the educators in the room had a somber realization: perhaps answers to these questions could have implications beyond earning college credits on the AP exam. What if a program like this could fundamentally change a middle school student's belief about himself and his ability to excel through high school and earn a college degree?

The program began with ten students at one middle school. There was no budget. There were no textbooks. The Spanish teacher had never had a day of College Board training for Advanced Placement curriculum and instruction. The AP program director and the principal gave her a copy of the College Board's course description for AP Spanish (apcentral.collegeboard.com), and a brief description of the vision. The teacher and her ten students were off and running. The class was difficult and the pace was faster than any other class in middle school. The teacher's only conception of Advanced Placement included "college level instruction," and as nebulous as it sounded, that is what she tried.

Had any of the ten students understood the practice of schedule changes, the exodus may have begun. At the first follow-up with administrators, the teacher very calmly said, "These students are smart. I believe they can do it."

All ten students were still there in May when AP examinations rolled around. The middle school had never administered AP exams or even applied for a College Board campus number, so the students had to walk to the high school on the morning of the AP exam. Seven out of the ten students earned scores of three or higher on the exam, including four students who earned scores of four. No student scored a one on the exam. That answered one question. Yes, eighth-grade students can be successful on an AP Spanish examination. In this case, they were successful in spite of the lack of instructional resources and teacher training.

Years two and three included grant money and training from the Texas Education Agency. The principal at a neighboring middle school asked to have the program at her school also, and by year three, so had two other middle school principals. By the fall of 2004, four of the district's seven middle schools were offering AP Spanish to eighth-grade Latino students who demonstrated moderate competency in the language. The annual program enrollment numbers had grown to approximately seventy-five students per year. Since the program's inception in WISD, every student enrolled in the program has taken the AP exam for Spanish language, and 79 percent of the students taking the exam earned scores of three or higher. Approximately 10 percent of the eighth-grade students in the program have earned College Board's highest possible score of five on the exam.

Building Aspirations

Success on the AP exam is only part of the story. This program was founded upon a vision of building educational aspirations for Latino middle school students who are native Spanish speakers. The goal of the statewide initiative was to promote student success, develop self-confidence, and support academic aspirations among an at-risk student population (Fierro-Treviño, Pérez, & Kettler, 2005). A detailed program evaluation study (Kettler, Shiu, & Johnsen, 2006a) examined progress toward these goals and the overall vision of giving students tools to succeed.

The Kettler, Shiu, and Johnsen study focused on two factors that had an impact on Latino students' school aspirations and self-efficacy: sense of belonging at school and composition of the students' peer group. Students who participated in the AP Spanish program held higher college aspirations and were more involved in academic activities than a similar comparison group. Additionally, students who participated in the program were more likely to have friends who felt that good grades were important than students in a comparable comparison group. The study also found that Latino students taking part in the AP Spanish Middle School program not only held higher educational aspirations but also expressed confidence in their future academic involvement (Kettler, Shiu, & Johnsen, 2006a).

In a second evaluation study, Kettler, Shiu, and Johnsen (2006b) examined the course-taking patterns of program participants after they reached high school. Course-taking patterns were studied for a group of fifty-five program participants attending WISD high schools as freshmen. Of the fifty-five ninth graders in the study, fifty-four of them were taking at least one pre-AP or "college preparatory" class (98.2 percent). Of that group of fifty-four students, thirty-seven (67.3 percent) were taking three or more pre-AP or "college preparatory classes" during the freshman year in high school. In addition to the pre-AP courses, eighteen of the fifty-five students in the study (32.7 percent) were taking Advanced Placement Human Geography. That class is the only AP course offered to freshmen in WISD. While 14.6 percent of the total freshman class enrolled in this course (162 out of 1,110 total freshman), 32.7 percent of the students from the AP Spanish Middle School program enrolled in the AP course that was available. Thus, the students in the AP Spanish intervention group were more likely than the general freshman population to take the AP Human Geography course (Kettler, Shiu, & Johnsen, 2006b).

At the first follow-up with administrators, the teacher very calmly said, "These students are smart. I believe they can do it."

These two evaluation studies provide answers to some of the other questions that formed the vision of the program. Yes, participation in an AP Spanish Middle School program can raise educational aspirations as evidenced by student responses about their sense of belonging at school, educational aspirations, and selection of a peer group (Kettler, Shiu, & Johnsen, 2006a). Yes, the results are sustainable into high school as evidenced by course-taking patterns of students in the program (Kettler, Shiu, & Johnsen, 2006b). Perhaps the biggest questions are yet to be answered about the students' long-term success in post-secondary education; the original ten students are currently in their senior year.

Implementation Suggestions

WISD did not originate the idea for this program, and neither did they perfect it. They did, however, act on the belief that middle school is the critical time to intervene for Latino students whose most obvious gifts may be their native language skills. Language diversity can be a benefit or a risk factor, and the critical difference rests in the school climate and practices that embed such labels, whether consciously or unconsciously. Anecdotal stories abound of ways these students were honored for their gifts of diversity. They founded and participated in Spanish clubs, and they partnered with a local university chapter of international students for tutorials. They took field trips to visit college campuses, and they provided translation services for a local nonprofit organization. Their pictures were displayed on school bulletin boards because they were a new wave of gifted students despite the fact that they were also among the most at-risk.

After that initial year, AP teacher training through College Board summer institutes has been a critical component of success. Additionally, the middle school teachers in the Waco program work closely with the high school AP Spanish teachers to plan and align curriculum and share resources.

Identifying qualified students for the program occasionally seemed like a concern. Teachers and program directors in Waco began with the list of students whose home language was on record as Spanish. From that list they examined scores for sources such as state tests (Texas Assessment of Knowledge and Skill) and testing done through the English language learner program. Ideal and potential candidates were invited to informational meetings. There was no magic formula used to determine who could or could not participate, and program records reveal that no student who asked to participate and spoke Spanish as a first language was ever turned away.

The results of this project taking place during the critical middle school years in the lives of Latino English language learners offers a pathway for success. Students' sense of belonging at school matters. Students' beliefs about their chances at school success matter. Facilitating positive peer groups to build on these two ideas can work, and the AP Spanish program for middle school is an example of a successful intervention.

Edgar completed the middle school program for AP Spanish, and he received a five on the AP exam. He enrolled in AP Human Geography as a high school freshman, AP World History as a sophomore, and he even dared to take pre-AP English, even though he was only one full year removed from the newcomers' center. He is still in high school today and stands to be the first person from his family to attend college. He hopes to be a doctor someday. Technically, Edgar never met the school's definition of gifted and talented, but in his interview that was never brought up.

References

Boyd, R. R., & Tashakkori, A. (1994). *A comparison of the Latino dropout and non-dropout between the 8th and 10th grades.* Paper presented at the Annual Meeting of the Midsouth Educational Research Association, retrieved September 23, 2004, from ERIC (ERIC Document Reproduction Service No. ED. 382910).

Fierro-Treviño, M. J., Pérez, R., & Kettler, T. (2005). *Middle school AP Spanish: Are you crazy?* Paper presented at the annual conference of The Southwest Conference on Language Teaching, Irving, TX.

Gándara, P. (1995). *Over the ivy walls: The educational mobility of low-income Chicanos.* Albany: State University of New York Press.

Gándara, P., O'Hara, S., & Gutiérrez, D. (2004). The changing shape of aspirations: Peer influence on achievement behavior. In M. A. Gibson, P. Gándara, & J. P. Koyoma (Eds.), *School connections: U.S. Mexican youth, peers, and school achievement* (pp. 39–62). New York: Teachers College Press.

Kao, G., & Tienda, M. (1998). Educational aspirations of minority youth. *American Journal of Education* 106(3): 349–384.

Kettler, T., Shiu, A., & Johnsen, S. K. (2006a). AP as an intervention for Hispanic middle school students. *Gifted Child Today* 29(1): 39–46.

———. (2006b, April). *Identifying and serving gifted Hispanic students in middle school.* Paper presented at the 2006 Annual Convention and Expo of the Council for Exceptional Children, Salt Lake City, UT.

Osterman, K. F. (2000). Students' need for belonging in the school community. *Review of Educational Research* 70(3): 323–367.

Worrell, F. C., Szarko, J. E., & Gabelko, N. H. (2001). Multiyear persistence of nontraditional students in an academic talent development program. *The Journal of Secondary Gifted Education* 12: 80–89.

Black English and Academic Excellence: Emerging Practices for Student Success

Saundra Scott Sparling | FALL 2007

Saundra Scott Sparling, Ph.D., is a retired associate professor from California State University (CSU), Northridge, and was director of Elementary Education at CSU, Bakersfield. She is a founder and member of the Board of Directors of the Mar Vista Family Center in Culver City, California. Dr. Sparling created the first gifted magnet school for the Los Angeles Unified School District, an inner-city parent participation program that served African-American and Hispanic students. She specializes in the identification and education of gifted minority and low socioeconomic status populations.

Discussions of the merits of Black English often degenerate into polemics with people lining up on opposing sides of the issue with no middle ground. Saundra Sparling, an African American and a retired university teacher, discusses a positive approach. She presents recent research confirming the positive results of using Black English as both a catalyst and a bridge in leading students to mastery of Standard English. Sparling details successful strategies to make this happen.

Recently, I was asked two questions: "Why do African-American gifted students insist on using Black English (BE), also known as African-American Vernacular English (AAVE), even though they know it's a barrier to their success? And, how can teachers of gifted education get them to use Standard English (SE), sometimes called edited American English, to promote excellence in their performance in gifted programs?" As an African American and a retired professor whose field of study is giftedness in underrepresented populations, a group that includes BE speakers, I am heartened by what recent research has to say.

The question of students' insistence on using BE in their classes concerns what the research identifies as the mismatch between the language of home and community and the language of instruction in the classroom (Lee, 2006). There is a significant body of research addressing this mismatch and the quest to improve the academic performance of students who use BE. Lee analyzed the cultural underpinnings of classroom talk and found that:

> An emerging body of research now moves beyond the mismatch problem to document and develop new ways of proactively leveraging everyday language as a resource for subject matter specific learning. (p. 308)

Some of this research looks specifically at BE, focusing not on causes and remedies for gifted BE speakers' failure to achieve, but alternatively, on BE speakers who are achieving academic excellence and classroom practices that promote their doing so. In these classrooms, BE is seen as a rich resource by which teachers simultaneously draw students into high-level classroom participation and SE usage (Perry, Steele, & Hilliard, 2003). It is important to add that teachers from a variety of racial and ethnic backgrounds, not just African Americans, effectively employ these practices.

This growing body of research provides background for this article in three areas:

- students' insistence on using BE in the classroom.

- practices teachers and administrators are using in programs to successfully promote academic excellence with BE speakers.

- exposure to and learning from the research that is focused on the achievement excellence of African-American students.

Why Do Students Insist on Using Black English?

On this issue, reasons vary from student to student. A reason that is often cited is opposition identity (Worrell, 2007; Perry, Steele, & Hilliard, 2003). Worrell explains that African-American, American Indian, and Hispanic students often develop an identity in opposition to mainstream society, including in academic achievement. This practice may lead to failure to fully engage in academic enterprises and, at worst, to actively resist achievement because to them it represents "acting white."

Another reason may be the perception of insistence. Many teachers perceive BE to be a substandard dialect indicative of lower intellectual capacity than that of SE speakers. They also see it as urgently requiring replacement with SE, and feel that SE mastery must occur before other advanced skills in subject matter content can be taught or learned. Perry (Perry, Steele, & Hilliard, 2003) argues that, while developing fluency in the language of the dominant culture is an appropriate goal for schools, such fluency should not be a prerequisite for skill acquisition. Belief in such a prerequisite is "very different from the philosophy and practice that were prevalent in many historically black southern segregated schools where developing academic competencies and fluency in mainstream culture were pursued as simultaneous rather than sequential processes" (p. 67).

Instruction based on these beliefs is often characterized by classroom interaction patterns that devalue a BE speakers' classroom participation and achievements. Students struggling to perform under such constraining conditions can appear unresponsive or even resistant to instruction. Godley, Sweetland, Wheeler, Minnici and Carpenter (2006) suggest that teachers' negative beliefs about BE contribute to the oppositional stance of African-American students toward school culture. It can also contribute stress that is sufficient to inhibit students' learning, thereby preventing black students from mastering the very English usage skills teachers seek to promote. "Such pedagogical responses to stigmatized dialects are damaging and counterproductive."

In a similar vein, Clark (2007) states:

> Research has shown that teachers often have low expectations for diverse students. Advocates of this point of view refer to such expectations as deficit thinking. They

find that such thinking causes diverse students to doubt their ability and to sabotage their own achievement. (p. 23)

Wynn (2002) offers the following example:

It was over twenty years ago, but it could have happened yesterday. I had taken a group of African-American high school newspaper staff to a university journalism workshop and awards ceremony. There were about eight students with me that day to learn more about print journalism, and, more importantly, to receive an award for being one of the ten best high school newspapers in the metropolitan area.

We were sitting together, in a sea of white faces, listening to one of the media experts talk about ways to improve school newspapers. After he had spoken, he opened the session to questions. My students had several they wanted to ask in the effort to discover new ways of writing creatively for their peers back at school. One of my editors leaned over to me and whispered, "Here is a list of questions we want you to ask him."

I said, "No, you ask him," surprised that my student and his cohort were suddenly shy.

"We don't talk right. You ask him."

No amount of encouragement from me would prompt them to speak. What I now know is that until that moment, I did not understand how psychologically damaging language biases are. I watched eight students, who happened to be some of the brightest young people I have ever taught, shrink from their brilliance. Here they sat, knowing they had competed with other journalism staffs for the best newspaper—and won—yet, at the same time, they felt inferior. (p. 205)

Teachers can help BE speakers prepare for and even overcome both real and perceived threats posed in scenarios like the one above. One approach would be for the teacher to create opportunities for students to practice in advance. Examples of this strategy will be discussed later in this article.

In truth, most African-American students do enter school speaking BE (Craig, Thompson, Washington, & Potter, 2003). Among these are gifted students. They use BE because it is what is used in the home, the community, or with peers. It is their language of intimacy and comfort. It is simply what they know. However, an increasing number of teachers are harnessing the power of their language as a bridge to the successful learning of SE and to academic excellence.

How Are Teachers Supporting Academic Excellence for Black English Speakers?

At least five practices have been found to be successful in promoting academic excellence with BE speakers:

- providing contrastive analysis experiences

- employing culturally responsive teaching

- building cultural capital

- involving students in challenging real-world activities

- creating opportunities for advance practice

The first four are used to legitimize students' BE usage and draw them into high-level classroom participation and SE usage. The fifth helps student overcome their fear of contributing ideas in public setting.

Providing contrastive analysis experiences. Contrastive analysis is a compare and contrast strategy. Hilliard (Perry, Steele, & Hilliard, 2003) offers an example of contrastive analysis from the work of Carry Secret, a teacher in Oakland, California:

> For Carrie Secret, helping African-American children acquire fluency in the standard code is not about helping them correct their home language. Rather, it is about helping them acquire fluency in another language. Using contrastive analysis with her students, she uses her knowledge of Black English to help her students understand how their home language differs systematically from edited American English [Standard English]. Sometimes this means helping her students hear differences in pronunciation that they don't automatically hear, and even over-enunciating endings that they might ordinarily drop. (p. 56)

Perry (Perry, Steele, & Hilliard, 2003) offers a personal example, stating, "Even today it is difficult for me, having been born and reared in Birmingham, Alabama, to hear when I have produced the black-inflected pronunciation of 'ask.' And if I don't consciously think about it, I will inevitably pronounce the word 'ask' as 'ax'" (p. 56).

Continuing with her contrast analysis example, Perry further describes Carrie Secret's strategy:

> She routinely exposes her students to models of black literary excellence, individuals who, in their writings—sometimes in the same text, and other times in different texts—write in both Black English and edited American English [Standard English]. In her practice, she affirms that these two modes of linguistic expression are not only not in contradiction with each other but ultimately compatible, and more to the point, evidence of literary excellence. (p. 57)

Employing culturally responsive teaching. Culturally responsive teaching is the result of linking classroom teaching with successful minority student performance (Rex, 2006). Such methods develop SE and mastery of advanced subject matter simultaneously by using the "stuff" of the students' cultures, communities, and daily lives as a basis for classroom instruction. Familiar literature or music, community source materials, references to daily life, artifacts, and guest speakers are the tools of culturally responsive teaching. In this example, Perry (Perry, Steele, & Hilliard, 2003) shares more of the work of teacher Carrie Secret:

> Understanding the role of music in black culture, Secret uses music—black popular and classical music and European classical music—to help her students center and calm themselves and to help them focus. Carrie Secret understands that what makes students powerful is not simply their acquisition of the standard code, but their fluency in content knowledge and their familiarity with many literatures and the language of many disciplines. Perhaps most important, she does not see this broad knowledge as oppositional to language and culture of African Americans. For her classroom, she readily draws upon and uses the cultural characteristics that have been identified as central to African-American culture to ground her educational practice.
>
> She also creates multiple speech events in her classroom, events in which students are expected to practice speaking and presenting in edited American English [Standard English]. She frames these events as "formal locations," some of which are construed as formal locations or events within the black community, and others as formal events in society at large. For example, she sometimes asks her students to imagine that they are students at Spelman or Morehouse College and to think how they would be required to speak in edited American English [Standard English] when they have visitors and when they make reports to the class on their group work. Using culturally responsive practices deeply engages Secrets' largely African-American student body and they achieve at high levels. (p. 57)

Building cultural capital. Perry (Perry, Steele, & Hilliard, 2003) identifies SE as a kind of cultural capital through which the mainstream culture, and consequently the school culture, traditionally distributes educational opportunity, such as exposure to advanced skills. She suggests that gifted students are among those who have the intellectual capacity for taking advantage of educational opportunities even though they lack the cultural capital for accessing them. Some causes for this low level of cultural capital include: SE is not spoken in the home; students have had limited exposure to certain books and works of art; and they have never been to a museum or a concert. She points out that the school culture can be modified so that access is given simultaneously to cultural capital and the advanced skills. The following is an example provided by a kindergarten–first-grade teacher:

> **In many classrooms across the United States, BE speakers are achieving academic excellence.**

> In order to prepare for teaching a unit about Greek architecture, this young kindergarten teacher, unbeknownst to her children, took pictures of every one of their homes. She then put all of the pictures on slides. When she actually began to teach about Greek architecture, she would point to the columns, gables, and other features of the architecture that were present in their homes, as well as in Greek architecture. The vocabulary that emerged from this unit was meaningful, not only in the context of the unit on Greek architecture, but also in the context of descriptions of the children's homes, homes of their peers, and the architecture of their community.
>
> The same teacher has arranged monthly visits to the Museum of Fine Arts for her kindergarten and first-grade pupils. By February of the academic year, her students were more comfortable in the museum and knew more about what is in the museum than the average college student. Monthly visits to the museum had become an accepted ritual, "a practice." In both these instances, the teacher has explicitly passed on to her students' cultural capital. And she had also organized instruction such that a prior level of cultural capital was not necessary for her students to access, to fully benefit from, her instruction. (p. 69)

Involving students in challenging real-world activities. Challenging real-world activities involve having students prepare for and participate in highly engaging and challenging campus, district, or community competitions, performances, and projects in the real world. Producing a school-wide creative writing journal or newspaper, entering young author events, joining debate teams, or participating in mock trial programs are examples.

Hilliard (Perry, Steele, & Hilliard, 2003) discusses a mock trial program:

> A recent *New York Times* story charted the rise over the past few years of a new group of dominant schools in the world of competitive high school "Mock Trials" (McDougall, 1999, as cited in Perry, Steele, & Hilliard, 2003). In this intellectual sport, traditionally dominated by elite schools, where participants take the roles of attorneys in arguing cases based in real law, "schools with poor academic achievement have consistently risen through the championship ranks." In New York and Philadelphia a tradition of high achievement has emerged.

Hillard goes on to quote the following remarkable results:

> • Philadelphia's inner-city schools have finished first or second in the last three Pennsylvania championships, beating elite suburban schools.
> • Overlook High School [in Philadelphia] jumped from its spot on the city's academic warning list into the No. 1 spot on the state's Mock Trials teams . . . finishing eleventh in the nation. . . . Every member of the team was a rookie, recruited and trained by a history teacher who also doubled as a baseball coach.
> • Carver High School, from North Philadelphia's notorious Badlands, won the city championship and defeated dozens of prep and private schools to finish second in the state finals.
> • In Manhattan, the team to beat is Louise D. Brandeis High School, which has nearly as many dropouts as graduates.
>
>   Expert observers note that the pace and culture of national Mock Trials have changed, as the new champions make their distinctive mark and presumably inspire each other to new levels of performance. The nature of the courtroom arguments has changed—"more hotly contested," with "rapid-fire objections." And the new style has raised levels of performance across the board. Deborah Lesser, coordinator of the New York City Mock Trials, says that "students are sharper, more nimble on their feet, more in command of rules and strategies and presentation." (p. 145)

Creating opportunities for advance practice. Through such techniques as role-playing and visualization, students can practice handling themselves in a mock or imaginary event before participating in the real event. In role-playing, students brainstorm a list of past reactions they have had when speaking in

SE-dominate settings. Then, while their classmates react in the ways listed during the brainstorm, they each practice sharing their ideas or asking their questions just as they would at the real event. The goal is to practice confidently expressing ideas in a context of varied reactions.

The goal in visualization is to have students picture themselves responding effectively during the event. Ask the students to close their eyes and guide them through hearing the sounds and seeing the faces of the other people who might attend. They are then guided to experience themselves staying calm and feeling confident, speaking effectively, and if they do falter, persisting in giving their input.

Summary

Excellent instruction is the primary tool teachers can use to help students develop academically (Roscoe & Atwater, 2005). In many classrooms across the United States, BE speakers are achieving academic excellence. BE is being valued as a rich resource by which teachers simultaneously draw students into high-level classroom participation and SE usage. The instructional practices of these teachers have major implications for gifted education teachers working with BE speakers. Creating opportunities for advance practice, providing contrastive analysis experiences, employing culturally responsive teaching, building cultural capital, promoting cultural fluency, and involving students in challenging real-world activities are only some samples of what can be done to promote academic excellence in gifted Black English speakers.

References

Clark, B. (2007). Issues of identification and underrepresentation. *Gifted Education Communicator* 38(1): 22–25.

Craig, H. K., Thompson, C. A., Washington, J. A., & Potter, S. L. (2003). Phonological features of child African American English. *Journal of Speech, Language, and Hearing Research* 4: 623–635.

Godley, A. J., Sweetland, J., Wheeler, R. S., Minnici, A., & Carpenter, B. D. (2006). Preparing teachers for dialectally diverse classrooms. *Educational Research* 35(8): 30–37.

Lee, C. D. (2006). Every good-bye ain't gone: Analyzing the cultural underpinnings of classroom talk. *International Journal of Qualitative Studies in Education* 19(3): 305–327.

Perry, T., Steele, C., & Hilliard, A. G. (2003). *Young, gifted, and Black: Promoting high achievement among African-American students.* Boston: Beacon Press.

Rex, L. A. (2006). Acting "cool" and "appropriate": Toward a framework for considering literacy classroom interactions when race is a factor. *Journal of Literacy Research* 38(3): 275–325.

Roscoe, B., & Atwater, M. M. (2005). Black males' self-perceptions of academic ability and gifted potential in advanced science classes. *Journal of Research in Science Teaching* 42(8): 888–911.

Worrell, F. C. (2007). Ethnic identity, academic achievement, and global self-concept in four groups of academically talented adolescents. *Gifted Child Quarterly* 51(1): 23–38.

Wynn, J. (2002). We don't talk right. You ask him. In L. Delpit & J. K. Dowdy (Eds.), *The skin that we speak.* New York: The New Press.

Bumps Along the Road

Susan Baum | FALL/WINTER 2005

Susan Baum, Ph.D., is professor of Education at the Graduate School of the College of New Rochelle in New York where she teaches courses in elementary education and the education of gifted and talented students. She consults internationally and is cofounder of AEGUS, the Association for the Education of Gifted Underachievers.

Susan Baum discusses the obstacles (bumps) faced by students who are both gifted and have one or more learning disabilities. Chief of these are: (1) appropriate identification of both exceptionalities, (2) balanced services, (3) identity, and (4) acceptance. For each obstacle she provides numerous strategies (tips) to assist twice-exceptional learners in becoming successful.

The road to success for students who are twice exceptional is far from smooth. The journey is long but well worth it as these special youngsters develop their talents and become productive and satisfied adults. Along the way, however, twice-exceptional students experience very predictable bumps in the road that may derail and delay them for a while. Unfortunately, these bumps may reoccur many times over the course of the journey as these individuals reach new stages of development and face new challenges. If we become aware of these perils and understand the issues, we can offer necessary support to help twice-exceptional students get back on track. Specifically, bumps occur when the issues pertaining to identification, balanced services, identity, and acceptance are not addressed with positive resolution.

Identification

The first bump in the road is failure to identify a child as twice exceptional. The gift may mask the disability or the disability may obscure the gift or both. We must make sure that both are appropriately identified. Identification of the gift should be talent-specific rather than reliant on a full-scale score on an intelligence test; any learning problem can depress IQ scores as well as compromise classroom performance. In such cases the gift is rarely noticed. Likewise the gift may mask the disability. The advanced abilities these students possess often allow them to compensate for problematic weaknesses. It may be years before these students fall below grade level.

Therefore, identification of the problem (ADHD, Asperger's syndrome, or a learning disability) may require careful observation of how a student stays on grade level. Noticing how the student engages in a task and how much time and support is needed for successful completion of the task can provide essential information about the struggle underlying his seeming success.

Finally, we must be vigilant lest we misdiagnose gifted students as twice exceptional. Diagnosis must follow only after evaluating the appropriateness of the learning environment. Often these students act quite gifted when appropriately challenged; attention and behavior issues seem to disappear. Likewise, intensities and focus in areas of passion should not be confused with ADHD or autism. Understanding the different learning profiles of gifted youngsters can help to distinguish gifted behaviors from those associated with other areas of exceptionality.

TIPS

- Become knowledgeable about how characteristics of giftedness affect and interact with learning, behavior, and attention.

- Keep careful records of the types of support the student needs to complete homework, stay on task, and memorize information.

- Make sure professionals on the team evaluating the youngster are also knowledgeable about the issues facing twice-exceptional students.

- Persist until the appropriate diagnoses are made. Assure that the team uses information that details when the student is at his personal best as well as those times when he is struggling.

- When all fails, hire an advocate to secure the appropriate diagnosis.

Balanced Services

The second bump is an ongoing struggle for these students to receive the services they need and deserve. Twice-exceptional students require opportunities for talent development that may include entrance into a gifted program, acceleration, mentorship, experiences with professionals, or interaction with interest peers. They may also need targeted remediation to learn skills not mastered. And finally, these students need specific strategies to compensate for problematic weaknesses and accommodations, such as access to technology or more time on task to help erase the effects of learning and attention difficulties.

TIPS

- Assure that the student is being taught skills and concepts appropriately at the student's instructional level. This may mean that a student gifted in math is receiving instruction several years ahead, while this same student may be in a remedial writing class.

- Insist on appropriate accommodations and be sensitive to how they are implemented. The student should be part of the discussions about necessary accommodations and how they will be put in place.

- Provide talent development opportunities as part of the school curriculum and outside of school. The one singular way to improve a student's sense of self and academic self-efficacy is through talent development.

- Provide school breaks that may be called "mental health days." Sometimes the best learning occurs in authentic settings where there is no pressure. Substituting a trip to the museum or to a soup kitchen may be more meaningful than the weekly spelling test.

Identity

The third bump—identity—looms large especially during adolescence. "Who am I? How can I compete with my intellectual peers? I don't want to be in a class with dummies. I must be dumb." Such comments reflect the confusion these students experience with identity. One youngster described her feelings when searching for her identity:

> I left sixth grade feeling good about myself and my ability to be successful in school but seventh and eighth grade were turbulent times. Not only was I in the heart of adolescence, but I was also in with the popular crowd at school and did not want to have anything wrong with me. I was extremely embarrassed about my learning disability and would go to great lengths to hide it from my peers. Fearing that they would not understand, I decided it was better to avoid talking about it than to explain it. Although I received accommodations for my disabilities, I was reluctant to use them or discuss them. I did not want to be different. (Baum, Rizza, & Renzulli, 2005)

TIPS

- Focus on talents, strengths, and interests. Students find identity through their talents.

- Find environments where students are with like-minded peers in both interests and abilities rather than simply those who are age mates.

- Seek out small group settings where the focus is on the individual as well as the content. Teachers who focus on who the student is rather than what she knows can help students believe in themselves.

- Find teachers who differentiate the curriculum for all students and value all talents. In such cases no student feels uncomfortably different; instead they celebrate their uniqueness.

Acceptance

Finally, the biggest bump of all is acceptance. It may take years for students who are twice exceptional to understand their gifts and talents as well as their areas of challenge. Seeing themselves as unique individuals who are a mixture of strengths and weaknesses will allow them to choose appropriate environments, seek help when needed, and develop appropriate advocacy skills. The youngster mentioned above clearly had not yet dealt with accepting who she was and chose to hide her disability from her gifted peers.

Samantha Abeel, a twice-exceptional adult, describes her journey to acceptance in her book entitled *My Thirteenth Winter* (2003). Only when Samantha was able to accept the fact that, even though she was a talented writer, she would forever be confused with details, numbers, and social situations, did her depression dissipate. Only when she understood that the dichotomy of her traits made her unique and special did she have the courage to live her life fully and stop hiding behind her fears. In a biographical poem she concludes,

> . . . Now I've written out their shadows
> like the wind collects its secrets
> to whisper into receptive ears, and I
> will leave them at your doorstep,
> A reminder of what others cannot see,
> A reminder of what I can and cannot be.
> (Abeel, 2001)

TIPS

- Make sure twice-exceptional students see the value of their talents and what doors are opened because of what they can do.

- Seek out counseling. Most twice-exceptional students have periods of depression and anxiety. Professional help will allow them to develop self-understanding and to learn coping strategies.

- Find appropriate medication for depression and anxiety when necessary. Students often find that the proper dosage of medication helps them to deal with their angst and fears.

- Allow for failure as motivation comes from within. Help students realize that failure is a temporary result of their ongoing research study focusing on what avenues will lead to fulfilling paths. Failure may help students come to grips with their goals and learn how to achieve them. It is important to support twice-exceptional students in both their successes and failures.

- Be patient. Remember that it takes time to find oneself.

These four issues of identification, balanced services, identity, and acceptance can reappear throughout one's life journey. New settings, new careers, and new friendships may require identification of issues that accompany the changes and the need for support or the learning of new skills. As roles change in life, identities change along with responsibilities. How successfully twice-exceptional individuals manage change and make appropriate decisions will depend on their acceptance of who they are and what is needed for them to perform at their personal best. Creating environments based on this self-knowledge will enhance the likelihood that they will lead successful and happy lives.

Recommended Readings

Abeel, S. (2003). *My thirteenth winter: A memoir.* NY: Orchard Books.

Baum, S., & Owen, S. (2003). *To be gifted and learning disabled: Strategies for helping bright students with LD, ADHD, and more.* Mansfield Center, CT: Creative Learning Press.

Lovecky, D. V. (2004). *Different minds.* Philadelphia: Jessica Kingsley.

Neihart, M., Reis, S., Robinson, N., & Moon, S. (Eds.) (2001). *The social and emotional development of gifted students: What do we know?* Washington, DC: National Association for Gifted Students.

Mooney, J., & Cole, D. (2000). *Learning outside the lines.* NY: Simon and Schuster.

Webb, J. T., Amend, E. R., Webb, N. E., Goerrs, J., Beljan, P., & Olenchak, F. R. (2005). *Misdiagnosis and dual diagnosis of gifted children and adults.* Scottsdale, AZ: Great Potential Press.

West, T. (1997). *In the mind's eye: Visual thinkers, gifted people with dyslexia and other learning difficulties, computer images and the ironies of creativity.* Updated Edition. New York: Prometheus Books.

References

Abeel, S., & Murphy, C. (2001). *Reach for the moon.* New York: Orchard Books.

Baum, S., Rizza, M., & Renzulli, S. (2005). Twice-Exceptional Adolescents: Who are they? What do they need? In F. A. Dixon & S. M. Moon (Eds.) *The Handbook of Secondary Gifted Education.* Waco, TX: Prufrock Press.

The Irony of "Twice Exceptional"

Sara Renzulli | FALL/WINTER 2005

Sara Renzulli graduated from Union College in Schenectady, New York, in June with a degree in European history. In her senior year, Sara completed an advanced history thesis on the education of Charles I, and its subsequent impact on his reign. After writing this thesis, Sara decided to pursue a career in historical documentaries; she hopes to one day work for the History Channel.

Sara Renzulli is an example of a twice-exceptional learner—a bright gifted child who is also dyslexic and ADD. She experienced many learning obstacles at the hands of inexperienced, unknowledgeable, or uncaring educators—especially during her first years in high school. Her story provides insights for educators in knowing what *not* to do as well as what to do in working with twice-exceptional students.

"Twice exceptional" is an ironic way to describe gifted students with learning disabilities. As one of those students, I never felt exceptional in any way. In fact, throughout most of my educational experiences, I felt stupid and inferior compared to every other student sitting in the classroom around me. It has taken me a long time to realize that there are exceptional things about me and the way I learn. The path to that realization has not been a particularly enjoyable one for me, but it has taught me to be tough and resilient and has been instrumental in the development of many aspects of my character.

A little background about my learning disability will help me tell my story. I was formally identified as having a learning disability in fifth grade when my math teacher realized I was getting all the problems wrong because I was copying them incorrectly off the board. And after several weeks of this repeated behavior, she suggested that I be formally tested. My parents had suspected something was wrong many years earlier, however, when I just could not learn to read. I talked early and was grade skipped in kindergarten because of my advanced verbal skills, and each year my teachers would assure my parents that I would be reading by the end of the year. Although my mother had asked about learning problems for years, my abilities seemed to mask my disabilities, and finally, in fifth grade, I was identified as having dyslexia: information processing and auditory processing disorders. I was also diagnosed with ADD.

At that point in my life, those labels meant little to me, but they would later accentuate the differences between the rest of the "normal" students and myself. Like most teenagers, all I wanted at that age was to be "normal." My middle school experience was a warm and happy one, and my special education teachers who specialized in learning disabilities were supportive of me and helped me learn to compensate for my learning differences. My family was always there for me and my parents and sister spent hours helping me to learn to read and reading to me.

I wanted to be just like everyone else when I entered high school. For me, high school was the worst part of my educational experience. The high school I attended was a big regional high school with too many students. The teachers were spread too thin and had a general absence of any awareness about kids with learning differences. Advanced placement biology was my first class on my first day of high school. I went in and took a seat in the back of the room because that is where all the cool kids sat. The teacher walked in and began lecturing immediately, using language that was more suited to a graduate-level biology course. I was intimidated by the lecture and frantically began trying to take notes. But by the time I could write down half of one note, he would be onto a different topic, and the previous notes would be completely lost; my notebook was full of half thoughts that made no sense and could not be read because I had so many misspellings.

Not surprisingly, I failed my first biology test. I was in shock. I had never failed anything in my life. Several meetings took place between my special-ed teacher and my biology teacher, after which it was agreed that an alternative test would be given to me. The second test came around a few weeks later, and I took the alternative one which was all essays. However, I failed again because I could not read the words in the essay assignment. The questions appeared to be phrased in language that Stephen Hawking might have written. When I failed this test, the teacher assured my parents that I was not smart enough for honors biology; I was depressed, deflated, and did not feel like trying anymore. I moved down to regular-level biology, which was significantly easier, but I got nothing out of it and hate science to this day.

Keyboarding was my next class after biology. I had to copy from a textbook that had small print and type in paragraph after paragraph of meaningless text with a wooden box over my hands. Unfortunately I could not spell most of the words to begin with, so surprisingly enough, I was not the star student in that class either. After failing numerous assignments, my special-ed teacher met with the keyboarding teacher who had steadfastly refused to allow me to use spell check. She insisted that spelling was a critical part of keyboarding and despite my IEP, she insisted that she would grade me on spelling.

After several other meetings with my parents and my special education teacher, an agreement was reached that I would carry all my finished typed assignments upstairs and across the building to have the assistant edit them in the resource room; then I would run back to the keyboarding classroom to make the changes and hand them in. It was clear that the teacher was not a fan of me doing this; she called it "special treatment."

After several weeks of going through the "hand-editing" process, one day I asked if I could go upstairs to the resource room to have them look at my work. The teacher screamed at me, "Edit your own work here!" I was humiliated, mortified, angry, and most of all embarrassed. When I went back to my seat, people were staring at me and asking me what the teacher was talking about. When that class was over, I walked out and never went back.

My resource room for students with learning disabilities was the only part of my day in which I was not tense, and my resource teacher was the only adult I felt cared about me or students with special needs at the school. I had a double block of time with about five other students in there. We would do work or talk about how much we hated school, play card games, study for exams together, and so on and so forth. Being in the resource room was an escape for the students with learning disabilities from the otherwise painful experiences of school. No one else in the school (and it often felt like in the world) seemed to understand how unnecessarily separated we felt. We were all smart, we had all always been told that we were smart, and yet when we came to high school, we were placed in lower-level classes and encountered problem after problem.

Unfortunately, the administrators in the special education department were not as spectacular as my special-ed teacher. I had a parent-teacher conference each semester; usually only one or two of my teachers would attend and I stopped going after leaving the first two in tears. The focus of these meetings was always on my deficits and how I would never be good at this or never be able to do that, and I would most definitely not be able to attend competitive colleges. My high school teachers made me feel as if having a learning disability was equivalent to being stupid. This negative aspect of me took over my identity as a student in the school. Instead of calling out "Sara Renzulli" for attendance, I felt that they should have called out "dyslexic girl who wants a lot of accommodations."

After one more year at this school I was depressed, had stopped seeing the few friends that I had, and thought my life was miserable. I took the opportunity myself to file an application to attend Miss Porter's School in Farmington, Connecticut, an independent school where I could have a new chance. When I was accepted at this new school, I found that I did not have to make a big deal out of my learning disability because the teachers taught me as if everyone had a similar problem. They did not care if every student needed extra time on the tests, and they did everything they could to help all of us who wanted to work and experience academic success. My teachers took a personal interest in me, and because of that I wanted to succeed. It was at Miss Porter's that I learned to work and learned that I was smart and that I could be a leader. It was at Miss Porter's that I learned to debate, love history and art history, and focus on what I could do well.

When looking back at my high school experience now, I feel exhausted just remembering what I went through for those first two years, but it was those experiences that made me tough and resilient. I know that I can handle a lot of stress, rejection, and other hardships because of what I already went through then. I also know that if I did not have the support I experienced at Miss Porter's and the constant support of my family, I would not be in college now and would not feel as if I could be a success in life.

My Gifted Teenager
Is Gay . . . Now What?

Judith J. Roseberry and Martha Flournoy | WINTER 2002

Judith J. Roseberry is past president of the California Association for the Gifted (CAG). The social and emotional well-being of gifted young people has long been a major emphasis for her in writing and speaking around the country. She was an educator for forty years in the Garden Grove Unified School District in Garden Grove, California.

Martha Flournoy is the mother of two gifted adult daughters. She has served on the CAG Board of Directors as parent regional representative, president, past president, and is currently chair of the Legislation Committee. She is Gifted and Talented Education (GATE) coordinator in the Oxnard Elementary School District in Oxnard, California.

A little-addressed issue in gifted education is service and support for gay and lesbian gifted youths. Judith Roseberry and Martha Flournoy explore the topics most relevant to learners who are both gifted and gay or lesbian; they suggest ways parents can provide support for their children and also address their own needs in adjusting to this newly expressed character of their child.

When a gifted youngster makes the decision to tell parents and/or teachers about his or her sexual orientation, the world can wobble on its axis. What can parents, family, and friends do to support and nurture this young person during a time of change and challenge?

We need to look at the very nature of the gifted young person before we try to meet all the challenges presented with this new information about this youngster.

In the early 1970s, May Seagoe and Jeanne Delp identified "Twenty-Six Demands of Giftedness." Their premise was that having a high level of intelligence made certain demands upon the gifted person. These demands resulted in behaviors. We might also call these twenty-six demands *characteristics* of the gifted.

Three of the twenty-six demands speak especially to our topic.

To crave knowledge. To crave knowledge requires that a youngster satisfy the need to feel progress in what he or she is learning. This can be a need to know and to be known. These young people have the craving for knowledge but also have the desire or need to be known for who they are, and who they can become. To hide an essential part of their personality is very difficult and frustrating as their high-level intelligence says to them they must find out, learn, and know. How can they invest their lives in learning and knowing and still keep a part of their selves unknown and hidden?

To be sensitive and empathetic while having high standards for themselves and others. This is a complex and serious demand of giftedness. As parents and educators we encourage, even insist, that our children become people who have very high standards for themselves, people who expect top performance from themselves and others, as well. We also want, in the same young person, one who will be sensitive to the needs of others and who will be understanding of those who are not the same, who are in some way different from the norm.

To seek out mental peers. This is perhaps the characteristic of gifted people that we must give closest attention. Gifted individuals of any age seek out others like themselves intellectually. We know as parents and educators that the gifted learner needs to be with others who understand the thoughts, actions, opinions, and behaviors of a gifted person. This is no less true for a gifted youngster who also happens to be gay.

We must remember that our young people are who they are first and foremost. They are human beings deserving to be accepted, loved, and protected. We all promise to do that for our children. Secondly, they happen to be people who need to make observations and see relationships. They may need to be creative and inventive. They may question authority often and sometimes without the social maturity to do this questioning in a polite and productive manner.

These youngsters may have a wide variety of interests, may resist routine, and may have the ability to understand abstract cause and effect relationships. They will surely be people who need time to think and ponder.

The fact that they are gay is just one more piece of information about who they are as people. As parents we raise our children to be honest. Children pay a wonderful compliment of faith, love, and trust by sharing this information with us. That child has been trying to be something that he is not. There is great stress in worrying about being found out or having to lead a double life. He or she has not changed, but rather has shared an essential part of self. There is no difference between the child now and the child you knew before the information was shared. They need our support, not condemnation or avoidance of the issue. Keeping communication avenues open is crucial. The fear of rejection may be present, so we need to be reassuring and supportive.

Upon learning that a child is gay, parents must start their own process of coming out. How will they tell other family members and friends? How can they accept this new realization of their child? This process may not be easy or comfortable. Parents should realize that they are not the first or only parents to be in this situation. You can't do this alone and your child cannot do it for you. You can't change attitudes or unlock firmly closed minds. There is no magic formula. It may have taken your child a long time to discover that he or she is gay. It may take parents a long time to adjust as well. Information is essential in this process. Learning to understand your child as a gay individual by sharing experiences, finding someone to talk to, or joining a group such as PFLAG (Parents, Families and Friends of Lesbians and Gays) can be helpful. There are wonderful resources, books, articles, Web sites, as well as supports in place to assist with this process. Not going through that process leaves parents and children in isolation and distress.

In summary, parents of gay gifted youth can be most effective if they:

- understand the demands of giftedness

- accept and support their child as he or she is

- seek resources to assist in understanding their child's needs as a gay gifted youngster

Suggested Reading

Bass, E., & Kauffman, K. (1996). *Free your mind: The book for gay, lesbian and bisexual youth and their allies.* New York: Harper Perennial.

Blumfield, W. (1992). *Homophobia: How we all pay the price.* Boston: Beacon Press.

Cohen, S., & Cohen, D. (1992). *When someone you know is gay.* New York: Laurel Leaf.

Fairchild, B., & Hayward, N. (1989). *Now that you know: What every parent should know about homosexuality.* San Diego: Harcourt Brace Jovanovich.

Harbeck, K. (1992). *Coming out of the classroom closet: Gay & lesbian students, teachers, & curricula.* Binghamton, NY: Harrington Park Press.

Huegel, K. (2003). *GLBTQ: The survival guide for queer & questioning teens.* Minneapolis: Free Spirit Publishing.

Marcus, E. (1993). *Is it a choice? Answers to 300 of the most frequently asked questions about gays and lesbians.* San Francisco: Harper.

Rafkin, L., ed. (1987). *Different daughters: A book by mothers of lesbians.* San Francisco: Cleis Press, Inc.

Singer, B., ed. (1993). *Growing up gay: A literary anthology.* New York: The New Press.

Sutton, R. (1994). *Hearing us out: Voices from the gay and lesbian community.* Boston: Little, Brown & Company.

Witt, L., Thomas, S., & Marcus, E., eds. (1995). *Out in all directions: A treasury of gay and lesbian America.* New York: Warner Books, Inc.

Looking Back

Heather Flournoy | WINTER 2002

Heather Flournoy is a linguist, author, musician, and avid lover of musical theater, so the dream of a "real job" in her field is more than a little far off. She is an award-winning playwright whose work has been performed in Missouri and California. She has two short stories published in lesbian-oriented anthologies, and is currently working on a novel. She resides in Portland, Oregon, with her partner of many years in their house of never-ending do-it-themselves projects.

Now a college graduate and successful adult, Heather Flournoy recounts her doubts and fears as a teenage lesbian. She describes the negative impact of verbal abuse and exclusion she experienced in school hallways and classrooms. She encourages teachers to use gender-neutral language as a starting point in reaching toward a goal where the school is truly an "all-inclusive environment" wherein gay and lesbian youths no longer feel that they are "invisible or being marginalized."

I recently attended my ten-year high school reunion. The event brought up many memories from that time in my life, several of which I would rather forget if I had a choice in the matter. In the retrospective atmosphere of the evening, what affected me most was how much I had changed as a person since my high school years. I looked back and asked the person I was then, "Why were you so scared?"

I am certain that everyone goes through something similar when we marvel at the power of time to transform ourselves from the people we were at that incredibly awkward time. I might have had one additional facet that compli-cated adolescence more than most. Not only was I part of the gifted/honors/AP programs at my high school, but I was also struggling to make sense of my sexuality.

I came out to myself as a lesbian when I was 15, which luckily coincided with meeting my first girlfriend, and we were able to work through some of the questions together. I didn't come out to my parents until I was 17, a month before I left for college. But far before that, back to vague memories I had in kindergarten, I had a feeling I was different. I hid this unnamable identity as best I could, terrified that the mainstream societal prejudices and their subliminal and blatant messages were right; that there was something wrong with me, that I was sick, that I was a mistake. I felt there was no one I could talk to about what I was experiencing; there was no safe place to go where I could be myself.

Throughout my high school years, but before I came out to other people, I was subjected to all sorts of verbal abuse and exclusion that made me feel invisible and completely devalued. There is a part of me that will always be upset about the arrogant and casual way that people dismissed me as a person without even knowing they were doing so. High school vernacular is not particularly kind to begin with, but phrases like "That's so gay," and "What a fag," hit me with more impact than their intended effect. Not only did my peers not know I was a lesbian, but it probably didn't occur to them that they were saying anything insulting or exclusionary.

> Unfortunately, it doesn't take blatant language to have profound effects on people, and I believe that too often we do not take those linguistic implications seriously.

There is a visibility problem that comes with being gay, lesbian, bisexual, or transgendered (GLBT); unlike issues of race or gender, it is not a state that is easily seen on the surface, and therefore lends itself to being hidden, especially in an unfriendly environment. The same people who avoided making sexist jokes in front of women had no issue with telling a gay joke in front of me, and were equally ignorant that they had just attacked one of their listeners. Unfortunately, it doesn't take blatant language to have profound effects on people, and I believe that too often we do not take those linguistic implications seriously. There are things that teachers can do within their own classrooms to make sure that they do not alienate their GLBT students, but at the same time not stigmatize themselves or their students in a detrimental or even dangerous manner. One very powerful strategy is to refrain from using heterosexist language.

Teachers should strive to use gender-neutral language whenever possible. The impact of using words like "fireman" or "policeman" on female students is well-documented, and training to heighten awareness about these effects is more and more prevalent. Educators need to incorporate that same vein of awareness and sensitivity to the unconscious heterosexist language that we use every day. In health classes, for example, it is not more difficult to refer to a love interest as just that, or even "partner," as opposed to "member of the opposite sex."

Every time teachers mentioned something about growing up and meeting a man and getting married, I felt they certainly weren't talking to me. These instances add up and have a large psychological impact on GLBT youth. Since I didn't feel included in these discussions, I had a tendency to tune out the classroom and the lesson, which led to boredom and a lack of interest—it did not apply to me. It was a double blow; not only did I feel personally excluded from what the teacher was presenting, but it also hindered my learning process.

The goal is to create an all-inclusive environment where GLBT students do not feel that they are invisible or being marginalized. This is harder to do than it sounds; even with a degree in linguistics, I find myself on occasion using phrases in everyday conversation that are inappropriate. The sexist and heterosexist language norm is so ingrained that we often do not catch the offenders before they slip from our lips. What teachers do not say in the classroom is just as important as what they do say; not hearing heterosexist language can be a very powerful thing to a struggling GLBT student. The first step is recognizing and being aware of those things that can alienate GLBT students, and avoiding their use. It would be fantastic for teachers to talk openly about homosexuality as something that exists and even try to normalize the idea through discussion; but even altering speech patterns to be more inclusive would be a progressive step forward.

Although I admired many teachers in high school, none stand out as having made an effort to make their classrooms safe and accepting places for GLBT students. I had several teachers who professed their distaste for things like racism and sexism, but none that included GLBT issues among discussions about societal mores or civil rights or social injustice. They demonstrated their liberal stance by displaying books banned in other states or those that put forth more progressive opinions, but none of the books mentioned GLBT people, and certainly none had GLBT themes. I couldn't even find anything at the local library to answer my questions.

My teachers and the library, however, did have bulletin boards whose fly-ers rotated with the "history" theme of the month—Women's History—Black History—Latino History. But October came and there was no Gay and Les-bian History. I didn't even know there was gay and lesbian history until I turned 16 and was able to drive into Los Angeles and tap the resources of a GLBT bookstore. In a society where we are striving to put the celebration of diversity at the forefront, I believe it is essential for educators to recognize and acknowledge the fact that regardless of the racial, ethnic, socioeconomic, and cultural compo-sitions of their schools, chances are that 9 percent of their student population is lesbian or gay (2000, U.S. Census Bureau).

GLBT youth have very few positive role models in mainstream society. Those that we do have are often undermined by the tendency of people to hide, ignore, or omit issues that would recognize their sexuality. Where heterosexual teens are bombarded with images that present and model their lifestyle in almost every aspect, GLBT teens have to search much harder to find anything at all. With the vast majority of GLBT adolescents questioning or hiding their sexu-ality, any mention of homosexuality in a positive sense has tremendous impact. As a teenager just beginning to put a name to what I was going through, I was starving for any information I could get about homosexuality. It was as though my ears and eyes were supersensitive to any mention or presentation of non-heterosexual people, searching for something to be able to identify with. Even the negative images, which made me feel that I was patently "less" than my heterosexual counterparts, were at least slight affirmations that I in fact existed within a larger community. It seems that the silence about sexuality in general can be quite detrimental when questioning teens are searching for something to relate to, or something that makes sense to them. Left to find these answers on their own, GLBT youth are subjected to misinformation, no information, and even cruel or harmful behaviors by others. One step in making schools safe for GLBT students can take place in the classroom. Dispelling myths, challenging prejudices, and talking about facts openly can help not only bolster the self-esteem of GLBT students, but also educate heterosexual students.

In terms of gifted GLBT students, I believe that there are a few factors that make the gifted GLBT experience unique. Gifted kids may be more sensitive in general, and this sensitivity could make the feelings of "differentness" more intense. Since gifted students often feel different to begin with, adding a sexuality issue on top of that serves to increase that feeling. Gifted kids may also be harder on themselves. I know that I struggled with the idea that I was smart enough to be able to think my way out of the emotional issues I was dealing with, and that because I was smart, I shouldn't be having such a difficult time. It was the first challenge that I couldn't resolve easily, and that did affect my conception of self-worth.

I am not entirely sure what might have made my school experience a better one. However, I do know in terms of my sexuality that I felt completely alone and isolated, with no one to talk to about these issues. Why was I so scared? I was scared because there was no information available, no discussion about anything but heterosexuality, no safe place for me to go to figure it all out. It wasn't until college that I finally discovered that there were other people like me, and that it was okay to be who I was. The silent and hidden minority of GLBT people suddenly revealed itself, and a whole new world opened up for me. I wish I had been able to see it sooner, to know during those times of hateful speech and ignorant opinions that I wasn't alone, that even if the teacher didn't talk about a lifestyle I could relate to I was still a valid person. I do believe that teachers can have a tremendous impact on GLBT students if they simply monitor their language and actions to be sure they are being inclusive. This inclusiveness is what GLBT students will be looking for to make them feel safe. And even if they do not come out in high school, I can guarantee that feeling included will affect them positively for the rest of their lives.

The Power of Images:
Visual-Spatial Learners

Linda Kreger Silverman | SPRING 2003

Linda Kreger Silverman, Ph.D., is a licensed psychologist. She directs the Institute for the study of Advanced Development and its subsidiaries, The Gifted Development Center and Visual-Spatial Resource. Her life has been devoted to the study and development of giftedness in all of its forms. Among her three hundred publications are Counseling the Gifted and Talented *and* Upside-Down Brilliance: The Visual-Spatial Learner.

For centuries, school systems have been structured in favor of learning in a verbal and sequential mode. Through her research, however, Linda Silverman concludes that at least 30 percent of learners think and respond best in images and whole-idea patterns. She calls these students visual-spatial learners, a group whose learning needs are not effectively met in most schools. She presents specific recommendations and strategies to serve visual-spatial learners more effectively.

Once upon a time, students sat in rows of straight-backed chairs facing the teacher. Teachers talked; students listened, and recited prose, poetry, facts, and numerical properties that had been committed to memory. The three Rs—Readin', 'Ritin', and 'Rithmetic—were the undisputed curriculum designed to prepare children to enter the work force in their adult lives. Teachers taught sequentially. Students learned sequentially. The curriculum of each school year built upon the knowledge and skills taught the previous year, in a nice, neat, sequential progression. Since this was viewed as the natural order of things, this system of education prevailed for millennia.

All of this is changing as we move into a new millennium. Reading, writing, and arithmetic are the curriculum of the sequential left hemisphere. They served us well as society evolved from an oral tradition to a written one, but they are insufficient for success in the new age. We are now in the midst of an enormous cultural transformation that began with movies, then television, then computers. The computer is to the Age of Information what the printing press was to the Age of Literacy. As it uses both hands, it invites information from the right hemisphere, and integrates the two hemispheres. It has no time constraints, does not rely on drill and repetition, and it teaches visually. The Internet allows access to any information, out of sequence, regardless of the age of the learner.

Leonard Shlain (1998) suggests that talking pictures marked the closing stages of a 5,000-year reign of our left hemispheres, and the emergence of our right hemispheres. Our left hemispheres have the words, our right hemispheres have the images.

> The printing press disseminates written words. Television projects images. As television sets continue to proliferate around the world, they are redirecting the course of human evolution. The fusing of photography and electromagnetism is proving to be of the same magnitude as the discovery of agriculture, writing, and print. (p. 409)
>
> I am convinced we are entering a new Golden Age—one in which the right-hemispheric values of tolerance, caring, and respect for nature will begin to ameliorate the conditions that have prevailed for the too-long period during which left-hemispheric values were dominant. Images, of any kind, are the balm bringing about this worldwide healing. It will take more time for change to permeate and alter world cultures but there can be no doubt that the wondrous permutations of photography and electromagnetism are transforming the world both physically and psychically. The shift to right-hemispheric values through the perception of images can be expected to increase the sum total awareness of beauty. (p. 432)

In the twenty-first century, images are becoming more salient in our consciousness than words. September 11, 2001, attests to this fact. In the preface of *Upside-Down Brilliance: The Visual-Spatial Learner,* I wrote:

> On September 11, 2001, life as we knew it changed forever. The world became smaller, and our connectedness became apparent. We were all witnesses, we all

suffered. If we had heard the news on the radio or from a family member, it would not have had the same impact. The way many people shared the event with each other was simply to say, "Turn on the TV." For days afterward, I heard, "There are no words; there are no words."

We watched the footage of the first plane crashing into the World Trade Center in stunned disbelief. As we tried to understand what had happened, we witnessed the next plane crash into the second tower as it was happening. We were there—a part of it all. These are images we will never forget. They are indelibly emblazoned on our psyches. (p. ii)

The marriage of photography and electromagnetism is the by-product of visual-spatial thinking, and the new millennium is job-friendly for visual-spatial learners. Success in our technological era depends upon different skills than are currently emphasized in school: visualization, grasping the big picture, three-dimensional perception, pattern-finding, thinking graphically, and creativity. Scientific progress relies heavily on the brilliance of people who think in images. And if we are ever to achieve peaceful co-existence, it will take visionaries to lead us there.

Students who are visually adept will have a much easier time gaining employment in adult life than those who are excellent readers, writers, spellers, calculators, and memorizers, but who do not have well-developed visualization abilities. Unless we begin to recognize the importance of visual-spatial abilities and pay more attention to the development of these capacities in school, we may be grooming students for success in a bygone era and dooming them to unemployment in this one.

What Is a Visual-Spatial Learner?

Visual-spatial learners are individuals who think in images. They have three-dimensional perception, which means that they can transform images in their mind's eye, and see them from many perspectives. It takes more time for visual-spatial learners to translate their mental pictures into words, and word retrieval may be problematic, so they usually have difficulty with timed situations. They learn all at once rather than step by step. Their learning takes place in great intuitive leaps, when, all of a sudden, they see the big picture. Since they do not learn sequentially, they are at a distinct disadvantage on class tests and state achievement tests that require them to show their work. They may have a poor sense of time, but a superb awareness of space. Deadlines may escape them. They learn best by understanding relationships, not by memorization. Complex concepts are easier for them to grasp than simple, sequential skills. They may master calculus before their times tables. They are highly intuitive, but organizationally challenged. It is easy to see why these children suffer in school. They tend to be late bloomers, getting smarter as they get older.

Academically successful students are more often auditory-sequential learners, who learn in a step-by-step manner, the way the teachers teach and the way the curriculum is designed. They think in words, so they can express themselves easily. They have good auditory skills and excellent phonemic awareness, which enables them to master reading phonetically, as it is usually taught. They have a good sense of time, are punctual, and usually turn in their assignments in a timely manner. They are fast processors of information, and often enjoy contests like "Mad Minutes." They are well-organized. They usually have neat handwriting, neat papers, neat desks, and neat attire. They can easily show their work, because they take a series of steps to reach their conclusions. Gifted auditory-sequential learners are more likely than equally capable visual-spatial learners to be high achievers in academic subjects, to be selected for gifted programs, to be recognized by their teachers as having high potential, and to be considered leaders.

Additional differences between auditory-sequential learners and visual-spatial learners can be found in Table 1. Please keep in mind that we all are a combination of both sides, since we all have two hemispheres. However, some individuals fit many more of the visual-spatial characteristics, and these are the ones who feel disenfranchised in school.

Visual-Spatial Learners and Giftedness

I coined the term "visual-spatial learner" in 1981, after observing an interesting phenomenon in testing gifted children. The children with the highest test scores, the ones who went beyond the norms in the manual, achieved these scores by passing visual-spatial items that were designed for children twice their age. They demonstrated excellent auditory-sequential abilities, but their visual-spatial abilities were even more extraordinary. As they tended to be somewhat

Table 1 : Visual-Spatial Learner, Characteristics Comparison

Auditory-Sequential Learner	Visual-Spatial Learner
Thinks primarily in words	Thinks primarily in images
Has auditory strengths	Has visual strengths
Relates well to time	Relates well to space
Is a step-by-step learner	Is a whole-part learner
Learns by trial and error	Learns concepts all at once
Progresses sequentially from easy to difficult material	Learns complex concepts easily; Struggles with easy skills
Is an analytical thinker	Is a good synthesizer
Attends well to details	Sees the big picture; may miss details
Follows oral directions well	Reads maps well
Does well at arithmetic	Is better at math reasoning than computation
Learns phonics easily	Learns whole words easily
Can sound out spelling words	Must visualize words to spell them
Can write quickly and neatly	Much better at keyboarding than handwriting
Is well-organized	Creates unique methods of organization
Can show steps of work easily	Arrives at correct solutions intuitively
Excels at rote memorization	Learns best by seeing relationships
Has good auditory short-term memory	Has good long-term visual memory
May need some repetition to reinforce learning	Learns concepts permanently; does not learn by drill and repetition
Learns well from instructions	Develops own methods of problem solving
Learns in spite of emotional reactions	Is very sensitive to teachers' attitudes
Is comfortable with one right answer	Generates unusual solutions to problems
Develops fairly evenly	Develops quite asynchronously (unevenly)
Usually maintains high grades	May have very uneven grades
Enjoys algebra and chemistry	Enjoys geometry and physics
Masters other languages in classes	Masters other languages through immersion
Is academically talented	Is creatively, technologically, mechanically, emotionally, or spiritually gifted
Is an early bloomer	Is a late bloomer

From Silverman, 2002

shy and cautious, I made the connection between visual-spatial learning style and introversion. Introverts (who gain energy from within themselves rather than from interaction with others) may or may not be visual-spatial, but visual-spatial learners are very often introverted (Dixon, 1983; Lohman, 1994). Soon I began to notice that not only were the highest scorers visual-spatial, so were the lowest scorers. These were children who fit most of the descriptors on our Characteristics of Giftedness Scale (Silverman, 1990), but fell short of the gifted range on the IQ tests and bombed in school. The main difference between the two groups was that the students who took the top off the IQ tests had advanced auditory-sequential skills as well as advanced visual-spatial abilities, whereas the underachievers had exceptional visual-spatial abilities combined with weak auditory-sequential skills. For example, they could copy extremely complicated block designs and tell how many blocks were in an array with some of them hidden, but they could not repeat five random digits.

As I spent more time observing visual-spatial children, I realized that they saw the world differently, multidimensionally. They saw through artists' eyes, and some demonstrated artistic talent. Some were scientists and mathematicians, able to see the complex interrelationships of systems. Some were computer junkies. Some were dancers, actors, musicians, imaginative writers. Some were highly emotional, extremely empathic. Some were spiritually aware and psychically attuned. Most were pattern-seekers and pattern-finders, excited with each new discovery. They pursued their interests passionately, sometimes to the exclusion of everything else. They definitely marched to a different drummer.

Children who are strong in right-hemispheric abilities, but weak in left-hemispheric skills, are more likely to become underachievers and dropouts. They are more often counted among gifted children with learning disabilities (for example, dyslexia, dysgraphia—difficulties with handwriting—central auditory processing disorder, ADHD); bright children from culturally diverse backgrounds; left-handed children; children who had difficult births; and children who suffered chronic ear infections in the first few years of life. Unless they're taught to their learning style, they are also at risk for delinquency (Seeley, 2003). Their learning differences are perceived as deficiencies, and most of the attention paid to these children is for the purpose of ameliorating their deficits. Rarely are their visual-spatial gifts recognized and developed in school. Ironically, the most effective way to reach these students is to teach to their strengths.

Everyone has two hemispheres, but no one uses both hemispheres equally. Just as each person prefers one hand over the other, auditory-sequential learners use their left hemispheres much more than their right, while visual-spatial learners use their right hemispheres more often than their left. We have to honor hemispheric preference, just as we honor hand preference. We would no more expect children to be equally proficient with each hemisphere than we would expect them to be equally proficient with either hand. The problem, as I see it, is that left-hemispheric proficiency has been emphasized in school for eons at the expense of right-hemispheric development.

Visual-Spatial Learners and School

The right hemisphere is our mental video camera. It enables us to see the "big picture" rather than just a series of details. It gives us the context in which to place our experience (Ornstein, 1997). It is essential to art, music, dance, drama, sports, mechanics, geometry, physics, calculus, technology, invention, metaphor, intuition, emotional responsiveness, and spirituality. Art is born in images. Scientific breakthroughs and visionary leadership originate with images. Beauty, love, and peace are the promise of the right hemisphere (Shlain, 1998).

For thousands of years, school has been primarily dedicated to the education of the left hemisphere. Children enter school with more balance between their left and right hemispheres than when they graduate. They begin kindergarten with vivid imagination that expresses itself in their block play, their pretend games, and their dress-up corner. By first grade, they are taught that playing is something they do at recess in organized games, and school is where they work. Children with good phonemic awareness, who learn to read on schedule by the phonetic approach employed in most primary grades, are considered good students. Children who struggle with reading often develop poor self-esteem.

For some visual-spatial learners, reading is "Flatland." It is a two-dimensional experience that is difficult for their three-dimensional minds to grasp. If you see the world in three dimensions, you live in a world of moving forms—of dynamic shapes. You may be able to build a space station with Legos or create a magnificent horse out of clay, but b, d, p, and q all look alike. They are all the same shape—flipped and rotated. Imagine trying to learn to read when the letters turn upside-down, flip backwards, and even trade places—moving around the page! Visual-spatial learners learn best whatever they can see in their minds. In some countries, children first learn to read words like "mountain," and "lake," that they can visualize, and when they have established a large enough reading vocabulary of these words, then they begin to learn the smaller words, such as "the," and "is," that are not as amenable to visualization.

Writing can be even more discouraging. The fine motor skills needed for writing with one's right hand are controlled by the left hemisphere (Springer & Deutsch, 1998). Letters that flip and rotate in one's field of vision will end up upside-down or backward on the paper. Spelling is a nightmare. It is purely sequential. Many visual-spatial children (and adults) speak at one level, and write at a much lower level, because there are so many words that they cannot remember how to spell. They may overuse the same words, because each word is a label for a picture in their minds, and they would no more dream of using a synonym than they would consider changing all the names of the pictures in an art gallery (Grow, 1990). While their ideas may be superb, they cannot express them well because of mechanical difficulties: handwriting, spelling, punctuation, capitalization, grammar, syntax, organization—all the left-hemispheric skills that educators cherish.

Memorizing math facts is yet another roadblock for visual-spatial learners. They are natural mathematicians and scientists, excellent pattern-finders, but they cannot do rote memorization. They understand a concept by forming a visual image in their minds, and seeing the underlying structure. This allows them to arrive at answers to math problems intuitively. When commanded to show their work, they go completely blank, because they did not take a series of steps to arrive at their answers. Show your work may be an appropriate request for an auditory-sequential learner, but it simply cannot be done by someone who uses a visual-spatial thought process. For this reason, state achievement measures are prejudicial against visual-spatial students.

Time is an anathema to the visual-spatial learner. School is all about time. You must arrive on time, take timed tests, complete your work in class on time, move on to other subjects on time, and turn in your homework on time. According to Leonard Shlain (1998), our time sense originated in the left hemisphere. "Time is the quintessential attribute of the left brain. All of the functions of this hemisphere proceed temporally" (p. 220). Time is essential for linear speech. "A conversation can be understood only when one person speaks at a time. In contrast, one's right brain can listen to the sounds of a seventy-piece orchestra and hear them holistically" (pp. 22–23).

As it is currently structured, school is an unfriendly place for visual-spatial learners, and they do not demonstrate their full potential during the school day. It is a much better match for auditory-sequential learners. But I predict that in the near future, schools will become more welcoming to visual-spatial students. Every day there are more and more computers in schools. At the college level, notes are taken on laptops, and homework is turned in and corrected via email. It is only a matter of time before every student has a computer. A computer is as indispensable to the visual-spatial child as a book is to an auditory-sequential child. It is visual, graphic, unconcerned with time, highly motivating, responsive to the inquisitive mind of the visual-spatial learner, and accesses the right hemisphere. It is the skating rink where a visual-spatial mind can perform dazzling feats.

How Many Visual-Spatial Learners Are There?

We have been conducting studies using the Visual-Spatial Identifier (Haas, 2001), which was developed over a ten-year period by a multidisciplinary team. The Identifier has been validated with 750 fourth-, fifth-, and sixth-grade students (the entire student body in these grades) in urban and rural school districts. Nearly 50 percent of each school was Hispanic. Following are some sample statements from the self-report form of the Visual-Spatial Identifier:

1. I have a wild imagination.
2. I think mainly in pictures instead of words.
3. I solve problems in unusual ways.
4. I have a hard time explaining how I came up with my answers.

    (Silverman, 2002)

Remarkably, one-third of these mixed-ability school samples was strongly visual-spatial (Silverman, 2002). Less than one-fourth (23 percent) was strongly auditory-sequential. The remainder (45 percent) was a mixture of both. However, 30 percent of this middle group showed a slight preference for the visual-spatial learning style, whereas only 15 percent showed a slight preference for the auditory-sequential learning style. In these schools, the student body was clearly more visual-spatial than auditory-sequential.

We plan to validate the Visual-Spatial Identifier with third- and seventh-graders and gradually extend the age range, as well as test its usefulness with different ethnic groups. The Identifier is available on our Web site: www.gifteddevelopment.com, and we can assess individuals as well as groups.

It appears that at least one-third of the student population is visual-spatial. This is a substantial number of students whose needs are not being met. And their numbers are growing. According to studies conducted by John Flynn (1999), intelligence is increasing all over the planet at the rate of one-third of an IQ point per year, and the greatest gains have been in spatial visualization and verbal problem solving, not in areas related to school-based learning. Children from different ethnic backgrounds appear to be more visual-spatial than auditory-sequential, and there is greater ethnic diversity in the schools in the twenty-first century than there was in the twentieth century. Gifted children are also more likely to be visual-spatial, particularly those in the highly gifted range (Silverman, 2002).

How Can We Recognize Visual-Spatial Learners?

Preschool-age visual-spatial learners are attracted to puzzles, building, and art projects. We've found children who could do four to six puzzles at once—with all the pieces mixed up—at 18 months! We've heard of 3-year-olds doing 300-piece puzzles. Some toddlers prefer to do all the puzzles brown-side-up. It's always a red flag to me when a visual-spatial learner doesn't like puzzles. I send these children to optometrists to see if there is some slight visual processing glitch that can be corrected with six months of vision therapy.

Visual-spatial learners are natural builders. They may toss aside their presents and build something interesting out of the boxes and ribbons. So many of them are Legomaniacs that I sound like a Legos commercial. K'nex, Construx, Tinkertoys, Zome, and any other building materials are likely to engage them for hours on end. They also like to unbuild—or take apart—everything within reach, just to see how it works. They love anything with gears. Here are some anecdotes from parents:

He thinks in three dimensions, and his first "art" project, at about 9 months, was a mountain made of tiny pieces of masking tape piled on the coffee table. I carried tape with me all of the time and he piled it on anything he could. (Mirrors were a favorite.)

[At 2 years] Clocks and gears entered our life around this time. He got clocks for gifts and we'd sit on the bed watching them. He wanted to know about gears and had to see the engine of the car. We'd be riding and he'd be listening for the gears operating. The summer when he was 2, we'd go to the amusement park, and the kids loved the rides but I was a nervous wreck. He would lean way over to see how the ride operated. On the merry-go-round his head was always up watching the poles to see how they operated or else he was leaning into the center of the ride to see the gears. On one of the little car rides, he started crawling under one of the cars. We ran with the attendant and when we got there he looked up and asked, "What makes this thing run, anyway?"

Vivid imagination and creativity can be seen before school age. Visual-spatial children are always transforming ordinary things into something else. Instead of using her spoon to shovel soup into her mouth, the visual-spatial child is as likely to turn the spoon into a microphone for her TV interview, a baton to be twirled, a catapult for ice cubes, a metal dancing figurine, or a large earring. Art projects abound, using everything in sight. Never throw anything out that can be recycled into a work of art or a construction project or an invention.

We have a joke in our home, every time someone tries to throw something in the garbage we say, "Don't throw that out! 'J' can make something out of it!"

He can make anything just looking at a picture or creating out of his imagination. He also builds things out of odds and ends around the house. Many rolls of Scotch tape have been sacrificed in the name of science. One time my husband had some little scraps of wood left over from an outdoor project and he asked "J" (then age 4) if he would like them to build with. Enthusiastically, "J" ran for his shoes to head out to the garage. "What are you going to make?" I asked. "J" stopped and looked at me like I was crazy. "I don't know that yet," he replied, "I have to see the wood first!"

Visual-spatial children are often drawn to animals and seem to commune with them. Remarkably tuned in, they appear to apprehend the emotional state of everyone with whom they come in contact. They instinctively discern friend from foe, true from false, authenticity from pretense. They love movement, all kinds of music, dance, drama, art—beauty in all of its forms. They come to uncanny conclusions, and when you ask them how they know what they know, they just shrug their shoulders. They can't tell you. They just know. Their intuition is extremely well developed.

There sometimes is an other-worldly quality to visual-spatial learners. It's as if they are only partially paying attention to what we are saying, while another part of them is on a magic carpet sweeping over beautiful landscapes on the way to more inviting adventures. They have vivid recollections of movies, which they enjoy describing to you, or even better, acting out, in glorious detail, while you strain to keep your attention focused on what they're saying. Their world is full of wonder, magic, vivid imagination, and crystal-clear pictures that they desperately try to communicate in words. Our world is practical, realistic, and filled with words. They tune out our words, and we have trouble grasping their pictures. We live in two different realities.

> **It appears that at least one-third of the student population is visual-spatial. This is a substantial number of students whose needs are not being met.**

How Can We Serve Their Needs?

There are many techniques teachers already employ that activate the right hemisphere, and engage visual-spatial learners. The techniques simply need to be used more frequently and more pervasively. Auditory-sequential learners will also benefit from these strategies, finding school more stimulating, as they develop more of their right-hemispheric abilities. Jerre Levy, a prominent brain researcher at the University of Chicago, warns that unless the right hemisphere is activated, little learning can occur.

> When tasks are so easy that they fail to challenge mental capacities, communication between the two hemispheres declines and one hemisphere dominates processing with little participation from the other. Under these conditions, the attentional level is low and cognitive performance is poor. In contrast, in response to challenging tasks, the left and right hemispheres become tightly integrated into a unified brain system, which increases attentional resources and cognitive power. The right hemisphere is especially important in regulating attentional functions

of both sides of the brain. Unless the right hemisphere is activated and engaged, attention is low and learning is poor. (J. Levy, personal communication, June 12, 2001)

Try the following suggestions one at a time, and see which ones reach which students. Use different strokes for different folks.

Have students picture what you are saying. When presenting a new concept, ask students to close their eyes for a moment and picture what you are saying. Have them share their pictures with a partner.

Show them! Use visual presentations as often as possible: overhead projectors, computers, demonstrations, diagrams, videos, pictures, charts, and graphs.

Teach to their strengths. Help them use their imagination, creativity, as well as their abilities to visualize, recognize patterns, see from different perspectives, build, draw, dance, sing, or act to compensate for their weaknesses.

Give students time to think, time to translate their pictures into words or numbers. Word retrieval is difficult for visual-spatial learners, especially under the pressure of time. Support well thought out answers above fast ones.

Give them the big picture. Visual-spatial learners learn best if they understand the goals of instruction. Tell them where the lesson is leading, so that they have an idea of the whole, before they try learning the parts.

Use visualization techniques. Ask them to picture what you are saying. Have them record their images using webbing, mind-mapping, or pictorial notes. Teach the students to visualize spelling words, math problems, "What would happen if . . ." scenarios in reading, science, and social studies. Employ movie, television, and computer techniques to assist them in visualizing: zoom-in, split screen, slow motion, superimposition, fast forward, and instant replay.

If their handwriting is poor, let them use a keyboard. Teach keyboarding as soon as possible. Child-sized keyboards are now available. If they cannot master a keyboard, allow them to use a voice-activated computer.

Make the learning significant to them. Meaningful, relevant material will be remembered, while insignificant information and rote memorization will be quickly forgotten. How does this learning relate to their experience? In what way can they apply it to solving a problem they care about?

Use discovery techniques. Visual-spatial learners are good at discovering rules and principles. Have them discover their own methods of problem solving instead of teaching step by step. Employ inductive reasoning and inquiry training.

Avoid timed tests and contests. Timed tests actually freeze the thought process of visual-spatial learners. Let them take untimed tests, or demonstrate mastery in some other manner, such as creating a PowerPoint slide show, a diorama, a photographic exhibit, a videotape, a series of drawings, or an oral story about the concept.

Use hands-on approaches, such as manipulatives, experiments, real-life experiences, field trips, three-dimensional models.

Remove drill and repetition from their lives. These children do not learn from drill; it simply turns them off. Art begins with an image in one's mind. That image is permanent: it is not improved at all by drill and repetition. Like artists, once visual-spatial learners see concepts in their mind's eye, they learn them permanently. Their images are not improved by drill. Drill and repetition work best with auditory-sequential learners.

Do not require them to show their work. Trust that they got the correct answer in their own way. Respect visual, intuitive methods of knowing.

Give more weight to content of papers than to format. Allow them to use computer software, such as spell check and grammar check, to help them with the mechanics of spelling, capitalization, punctuation, grammar, and syntax. These technological supports provide instant feedback, which is important for visual-spatial learners to acquire skills. Don't penalize students in other subject areas when they haven't mastered these skills.

If they struggle with easy, sequential tasks, give them more advanced, complex work. These upside-down learners surprise us: hard is easy and easy is hard. Acceleration is more beneficial than remediation.

Teach them about their learning style. Help them understand their strengths as well as giving them hints about improving their weaknesses.

Expose them to role models of successful visual-spatial adults. Many of the most celebrated physicists, artists, and statesmen were visual-spatial learners. Biographical sketches of famous visual-spatial learners can be found in *The Spatial Child* (Dixon, 1983) and *In the Mind's Eye* (West, 1991).

Conclusion

The most loving thing anyone can do is to honor the reality of the visual-spatial learner. Our left hemisphere can be rather narrow-minded. It tells us to be on time, and admonishes anyone who does not adhere to that standard. Our left hemisphere is often judgmental. It believes that there is only one right way to do things, and that everyone ought to do them that way. Our left hemisphere processes rapidly, and has little patience with anyone who doesn't think as quickly. Our left hemisphere is highly verbal, and misunderstands people who don't express themselves as well in words. Our left hemisphere is linear, sequential—accruing knowledge through a series of retraceable steps; it invented the requirement to "show your work." Our left hemisphere believes that every effect has a cause, and scoffs at anything that cannot be explained through logic.

Our society has lived for millennia under the domination of our critical, verbally bombarding left hemisphere. Our mute right hemisphere has a difficult time getting a picture in edgewise. It takes quieting of the mind (the left hemisphere), ceasing of the continuous flow of words, for the pictures of the right hemisphere to be received. Tribal societies had rituals to invite their right hemisphere to guide their lives through visions. Today, many go on vision quests, or do daily meditation practices, as a means of gaining intuitive wisdom and clarity. These practices bring more balance to our hemispheres. They are paths to inner peace, which, eventually, may translate into world peace.

Children who come equipped with powerful right hemispheres need to be cherished for their tremendous potential as artists, builders, designers, musicians, inventors, actors, technological wizards, surgeons, innovators, CEOs, visionaries, empaths, and spiritual leaders. Our society needs their gifts. We must stop treating them as defective if they can't read by age 6, if their handwriting is poor, if their spelling is atrocious, if they're hopelessly disorganized, if they can't memorize their math facts, if they don't know when to capitalize and where to put commas, and if they turn in assignments late. These are all left-hemispheric values. Instead, we need to look at what they can do well, what fascinates them, what is deliciously lovable about them. That is how we will reach them. Teach to their delights. Believe in them. Love them and they will blossom.

References

Dixon, J. P. (1983). *The spatial child.* Springfield, IL: Charles C. Thomas.

Flynn, J. R. (1999). Searching for justice: The discovery of IQ gains over time. *American Psychologist* 54: 5–20.

Grow, G. (1990). *The writing problems of visual thinkers.* [Available from the author at Florida A & M University, Tallahassee, FL]

Haas, S. (2001, August 1). *A validated instrument for identifying visual-spatial learners.* Paper presented at the 14th World Conference of the World Council for Gifted and Talented Children, Barcelona, Spain.

Hafenstein, N. L. (1986). *The relationship of intellectual giftedness, information processing style, and reading ability in young gifted children.* Unpublished doctoral dissertation, University of Denver.

Lohman, D. F. (1994). Spatially gifted, verbally inconvenienced. In N. Colangelo, S. S. Assouline, & D. L. Ambroson (eds.). *Talent development: Proceedings from the 1993 Henry B. and Jocelyn Wallace National Research Symposium on Talent Development.* Dayton, OH: Ohio Psychology Press.

Ornstein, R. (1997) *The right mind: Making sense of the hemispheres.* New York: Harcourt Brace.

Seeley, K. R. (2003). High risk gifted learners. In N. Colangelo & G. A. Davis (Eds.) *Handbook of gifted education* (3rd ed.). Boston: Allyn & Bacon.

Shlain, L. (1998). *The alphabet versus the goddess: The conflict between word and image.* New York: Penguin/Arkana.

Silverman, L. K. (1990). *The characteristics of giftedness scale.* Denver: Gifted Development Center.

———. (2002). *Upside-down brilliance: The visual-spatial learner.* Denver: DeLeon Publishing.

Springer, S. P., & Deutsch, G. (1998). *Left brain/right brain: Perspectives from cognitive neuroscience* (5th ed.). New York: W. H. Freeman.

West, T. G. (1991). *In the mind's eye: Visual thinkers, gifted people with learning difficulties, computer images, and the ironies of creativity.* Buffalo, NY: Prometheus Press.

The High School @ Moorpark College: Serving High School Gifted Students at Risk

Victoria Bortolussi | FALL/WINTER 2003

Victoria Bortolussi, Ph.D., has been an educator more than thirty-seven years at the middle school, high school, and college levels. She is a former editor of the Communicator, *and started* PAGE, *a parent advocacy group in Ventura, California, where she resides. A retired dean from Moorpark College, she is the founder of LINC (Learning in Communities) an educational consulting collaborative. Her degrees are from the University of Southern California and the University of California at Santa Barbara.*

The conventional large, comprehensive, American high school is not a good fit for some gifted adolescents. These students become at risk for school drop out and substance abuse. Victoria Bortolussi, as a dean at Moorpark College in southern California, founded a high school for at-risk eleventh and twelfth graders on the college campus. Modeled after the Learning Communities system at Evergreen College in Washington, students can earn both a high school diploma and college credit.

So many reasons exist for having a high school on a college campus devoted to gifted and talented youth, especially those who may be considered at risk. We are not talking about the gifted young people and the high achieving students who flourish in honors programs at comprehensive high schools. Rather, we are talking about often highly gifted and talented young people who struggle with daily life because of their extreme creativity, individualism, rebelliousness, questioning of authority, and other traits, which in themselves are not negative. In a highly structured, competitive environment that is often teacher- and achievement-centered, these students can become alienated and lost.

Where excellent programs exist for gifted children in elementary and middle school, these students may do well. They are nurtured for who they are, and they become friends with true peers who share their interests and abilities. But something can happen when they enter the large, comprehensive high school, where programs for the gifted are also intended for high achievers. These programs work for some gifted students, but not all. Those who do not fit into this traditional environment can be lost—not only to themselves but to society. These may be the leaders, inventors, artists, and problem solvers we need. Instead, they may become dropouts, alienated from the world in which they live. That is, if they survive at all. Many teenagers, including those who are highly gifted and talented, and/or creative, get involved in substance abuse, gangs, suicide, or any number of self-destructive behaviors.

Beginnings

The High School @ Moorpark College is the culmination of a lifetime of many people. It was born out of need, opportunity, innovation—and most of all—identifying educational needs by listening to student voices, those who are the learners. A growing body of research indicates that in order to truly learn and to become lifelong learners, students must play an active role in designing their learning and have a say in how they learn. This can be accomplished while maintaining both requirements and standards; and it activates the learner so that real and deep learning can occur.

This student-centered learning perspective is part of The Learning Community movement, which actually began in the early 1900s. Learning Communities were revitalized in the '60s with schools like the University of California at Santa Cruz and The Evergreen State College in Washington. Evergreen is now at the national forefront of this teaching methodology. The High School @ Moorpark College is based on the Learning Community model.

It was my highly gifted and talented son who actually led me to The Evergreen State College and Learning Communities. He did well in his elementary and middle school gifted classes, as these were ones in which he was able to be the most comfortable and to excel. He was never an "easy" child or a model student. But the open classroom, gifted classes, and outstanding teachers supported him from kindergarten through eighth grade. When he entered high school, however, his struggle was painful and acute. We tried many alternatives, including a residential placement with a strong counseling component along with academics; he then did a stint at another private school. He went on to a community college, dropping in and out, then finishing on what he called the "five-year plan."

At the time he was readying to transfer to a four-year school, he did some research and found The Evergreen State College. He applied, was admitted, and we went to the campus together to attend an Academic Fair; at this fair, teachers, students, clubs, and other activities meet together in a chaotic two hours to "shop around," and students determine which courses they wish to take the following term. Students enroll in one Learning Community each quarter, which is an interdisciplinary thematic blending of courses.

Making Learning Communities a Reality

With Learning Communities, I discovered what I truly believe is the way we must reform education at many levels. I was so excited that I arranged for a group of thirty-five educators—college and high school—and our college president to visit Evergreen. We immersed ourselves for several days in this four-year university model; we also visited Seattle Central Community College.

We returned from this trip inspired to begin Learning Communities at Moorpark College. Moorpark College, being innovative, added two things to the Learning Community model. One is a career/profession path in which students enroll in a Learning Community Institute: Health Science, Media Arts, Business, or Liberal Arts (for future teachers or those who are undecided about their futures and wish to begin with a general education). Field trips, guest speakers, and senior projects also connect student learning with their futures.

The other unique feature Moorpark College added was to extend the Learning Community methodology to our high school connections. High school and college faculty meet each summer to gain greater skills in implementing Learning Community work. A special focus is on seminars, which are a cornerstone of the Learning Community methodology. In seminars, readings are assigned and then students lead discussions, thereby learning how to discourse and write in relation to the text they read.

Making It Work

The High School @ Moorpark College (HS@MC) is now entering its fourth year. We started with fifty high school juniors and seniors and have grown to an enrollment of 120. Along the way we've added faculty, counselors, and office staff as enrollment increases.

The high school is housed on the college campus with an office solely dedicated to the program, and four classrooms used by both the college and the high school. Students take their high school classes in the afternoon, Monday through Thursday (12:00–5:30 p.m.), when there is less demand for use of these classrooms by the college. Mornings, evenings, and Fridays are free for students to take college classes, in many cases earning both high school and college credit. This eliminates the often boring and discouraging repetition that can alienate and discourage young people from continuing their education in conventional high school settings.

All college services, activities, and classes are available to the students; under current California legislation, students do not pay tuition for the college classes while they are still in high school. The program has four high school teachers, one principal, one-and-a-half clerical staff, two part-time counselors (one high school and one college), and a full-time college faculty member (grant funded) who provides the career/professional component. The high school staff is part of the college community and participates in college activities and committees.

Because both the college and the Moorpark Unified School District communities recently sponsored successful bond issues for building, we are in the process of designing a facility to house The High School as part of an Academic Center on campus. We are also seeking grants that will enable us to put more time into development and fundraising as well as to increase the number of students from underrepresented groups such as first-time college students and ethnic minorities.

Additional Possibilities

The HS@MC, with its target population of gifted and talented at-risk students, its Learning Community approach, and its career/profession component, is one of a kind. As one of nine institutions awarded a national grant, we have the opportunity for serious research to be conducted by the University of California at Berkeley. We are actively beginning grant development to expand our efforts, even though the school is institutionalized and self-sustaining. But with its smaller size, its need for continued professional development, its connecting with the business community and the college, as well as the nature of teaching this often "difficult, draining, and demanding" group of students, we are constantly looking for support.

Student Success Stories

The programs at HS@MC offer unique opportunities to students who fail to thrive in a large comprehensive high school. With the smaller Learning Community environment and nurturing atmosphere of HS@MC, there are countless success stories of students who overcame significant obstacles to graduate, to complete college courses prior to graduation, and to gain the confidence to continue their education beyond the secondary level. Some of the barriers to success have included attendance issues; significant emotional, health, and family issues; peer pressure and peer exclusion; poor performance in school; lack of motivation to continue in school; nonparticipation in school life; significant low esteem; and learning disabilities.

With few exceptions, the students who graduate from HS@MC have made significant advances in either their personal or academic growth. Not only do students discover that they can succeed in college-level courses, particularly those that have some direct correlation to their future goals, but they overcome personal obstacles to their future success in both the work and educational world and have begun to enthusiastically make plans for their futures. Parents are so grateful that the HS@MC exists to give their students an opportunity to succeed and move on to post-secondary activities with a future.

Many of the students who have high potential—many identified as gifted and/or talented—but who have demonstrated poor performance and attendance in a comprehensive high school, not only thrive in the environment provided by the HS@MC, but are able to articulate that transformation to the public. Several students presented their Senior Projects, a culminating graduation requirement, to panels of professionals and community members. Briefly, here are a few student success stories, with names changed.

Annie. Annie had done well in previous high schools; but she was in danger of dropping out because of emotional and personal issues. In addition to becoming one of the top students at the HS@MC, she also became an advocate at the state level for special education students, obtained an internship in special education at a local school, and was offered a job by the coordinator of Moorpark College Disabilities Department as a result of her senior project. Her parents credit HS@MC with turning this talented student around and saving her life.

Sally. Sally did a paid internship at a dental office, obtained her X-ray license through the process of completing her senior project, and was offered a job by one of the senior project panel evaluators. She is continuing her studies at Moorpark College and plans to transfer to a dental school.

Jennifer. Unbeknownst to her parents, Jennifer was contemplating suicide before she entered the HS@MC. While at the school, she changed her original plan of teaching high school to explore an alternative career path. She did her senior project with a kindergarten class at Campus Canyon Elementary School and absolutely loved her teaching. She overcame her fear of public speaking and performed a song at the graduation ceremony.

Jon. Jon traded a life of crime for studying about crime. He took a college Learning Community of philosophy and career exploration and now has a college professor as his mentor.

Mike. Mike, a quiet, "social misfit" and a poor student, became more social with peers of similar interests and was instrumental in creating the school Web site. He completed an amazing senior project designing and producing a video game; it led a college professor to try to obtain an internship for him with a local game company. He also obtained an internship with Moorpark College Information Technology Department.

Joe. Joe, a severely visually impaired student, was selected to serve on the Workforce Investment Board Youth Council and other leadership activities. He designed a Web site for a local nonprofit organization for his senior project and will be a lead alumni mentor for the students next year. The schedule he devised for his senior project is being considered as a scheduling model for senior projects next year.

Angelica. Angelica, a teaching assistant at a local elementary school (for her own third-grade teacher), plans to do her senior project on teaching and supervising other students who will do the Junior Achievement teaching program for their senior projects.

Robert. Robert, a very quiet, withdrawn, shy, and timid student, had an excellent academic record, but did not participate in any high school extracurricular activities. Through HS@MC, he developed confidence, excelled in public speaking, obtained an internship with the Health Science Institute, and graduated with over 50 college units. He enrolled at the University of California Davis as a junior when he graduated from the HS@MC.

Matt. Matt did several internships in video production and grew emotionally, socially, and academically. He is working in the video field as a cameraman while completing his studies at Moorpark College.

There are many more stories of students with different obstacles, but the results are always the same. The students who graduate from HS@MC have engaged in the educational process at a personal level and have formulated a plan to continue their education to pursue their career goals. Many of them have overcome significant obstacles, and many have become more motivated to pursue their futures. All of them have gained the confidence that they can do college-level work.

We must listen to our own voices and those of the young people we are dedicated to encourage, whether they are our children or our students. They deserve nothing less, and the world needs their gifts and talents.

Useful Learning Community Web Sites

The Learning Institutes at Moorpark College
www.moorparkcollege.edu/institutes

The High School at Moorpark College
www.moorparkcollege.edu/hs

The Middle College National Consortium
www.MCNC.us

National Learning Community Project (Evergreen)
http://learningcommons.evergreen.edu

Federal Small Learning Community Project
www.ed.gov/programs/slcp/index.html

National Career Academy Coalition
www.ncacinc.org/ncacinc/site/default.asp

PART 4

PARENTS AND EDUCATORS TEAMING TOGETHER

Parents are teachers, too. As such, the essays in this book geared toward educators can provide beneficial information for parents. Likewise, Part 4, which focuses on the concerns and challenges of parenting gifted children, is useful to educators, too—for two reasons:

- Educators provide greater understanding of what parents of gifted children experience at home.

- They serve as a resource that can be shared with parents—especially parents of newly identified gifted children.

Elaine Wiener suggests, "It would be the most valuable piece of information for teachers and parents if they were to trade information and expectations in writing at the beginning of each school year."

This requires that parents and teachers regard themselves as members of a team. In Cherie Drummond's words, "After all, parents and teachers have the same goal: student success." The goal is easier to reach when parents and teachers work together to accomplish it.

GR–ATE Expectations: What Parents Expect of Teachers

Cherie K. Drummond | SUMMER 2003

Cherie K. Drummond, R.N., M.B.A., is an education consultant and Gifted and Talented Education *(GATE) specialist. She served on the board of directors of the California Association for the Gifted for eight years, including four as chair of the Parent Representatives Committee. She is the recipient of several awards, including the GATE Distinguished Service Award, Parent of the Year, and GATE Education Recognition award. She is the mother of two highly gifted adults.*

Cherie Drummond, former leader of the Parent Representatives of the California Association for the Gifted, uses her extensive experience as an advocate for gifted children in voicing the expectations parents have for the teachers they entrust their children to each school day. Topics include (1) gifted literacy, (2) myths about giftedness, (3) personal qualities, (4) professional development, (5) grouping, and (6) communications. She concludes with a call for a partnership between parents and teachers.

It is important to note that the goal for teachers and parents should be to have an effective partnership, one that will benefit not only the parent's child, but the entire school community. Such a partnership takes effort, commitment, and understanding from both parties.

People bring expectations to any relationship. In the basic school-home arena, teachers, parents, and students have expectations of one another, and themselves, whether or not they are aware of them. In order to build positive working relationships, it is important to know and appreciate both the experiences and expectations each has of the other.

There are many "ate" words that can be used to help describe mutual expectations. For example, educate. Parents, students, and teachers all need to be educated about giftedness and gifted education, school policies, and curriculum; and all can educate others in some way. All expect each will communicate well with each other. All need to advocate for the benefit of gifted learners. Communicate, appreciate, motivate, differentiate, educate, participate, cooperate, stimulate, advocate, accelerate, and accommodate are other GR–ATE words that can be used in discussing mutual expectations.

Gifted Literacy

The primary expectation of parents is that teachers are well trained regarding gifted learners and their special needs. It is important that teachers of gifted students and all staff know and recognize the characteristics of gifted learners in order to act and react appropriately to their different behaviors and to teach them appropriately. Gifted children are often inquisitive, question authority, have a heightened sense of justice and fairness, have a sophisticated sense of humor, are very curious, may even march to a different drummer, and are usually immersion learners needing little repetition and drill. Teachers need to know how to channel these behaviors while they differentiate their instruction and content to meet the needs of gifted and other learners in their classrooms; in addition they must have an understanding and appreciation of the extremes of the asynchronous gifted learners. Further, when teachers see behavior problems—and may even suspect ADD or ADHD—the teacher should also consider the possibility that these children may be frustrated gifted learners.

Classroom teachers are often the primary people making recommendations for identification of children for gifted education programs; therefore, it is especially important that they be able to distinguish between those typically thought to be gifted—bright or high achieving children—and those who are gifted in the classic understanding of the term. Janice Szabo's classic, "Bright Child, Gifted Learner," from *Challenge Magazine* (1989) is helpful in making this distinction.

Teachers frequently nominate the bright child for identification not realizing the differences between them and gifted learners.

Social and emotional aspects of gifted children are often overlooked, but are very important for teachers and parents to recognize and understand. Gifted learners often have extreme sensitivities, which Kazimierz Dabrowski (1967) identified as psychomotor, sensual, intellectual, imaginational, and emotional "overexcitabilities." Teachers need to recognize these traits and make appropriate accommodations to benefit student learning. For example, an auditory sensitivity may require headphones so that the students can block out voices and other auditory stimulation; and some children can't stand the tags in shirts or the seams in socks.

Emotional and psychological sensitivities can also be seen when gifted children have extreme reactions to world news such as seeing children wounded in war or starving in a third world country. Age peers typically do not understand and may even ridicule one who seems to be obsessed about such issues; these children may seek out adults with whom they can talk about their concerns or withdraw into their own world. Adults need to help channel these concerns into productive avenues to ease the frustration of not being able to do anything from a long distance. Parents appreciate teachers who understand and accommodate for the sensitive nature of gifted children; teachers' efforts to guide parents and students in dealing with social and emotional needs will also be noticed.

Myths and Giftedness

Myths seem to accompany gifted children like shadows. Administrators, teachers, parents, and community members can be heard saying, "We don't have to worry about the gifted—they will do just fine." Or, "We better not group them, they will be snobbish. It isn't fair to others if we group the gifted students together." Scientific research reveals that for academic gain, and for social and emotional health, gifted learners need to be grouped together with their mind mates. When this is done, others gain academically, and in self-esteem also (Rogers,1991). Some ask, "Why should we fund a gifted program? It only serves the middle-class white students." Great strides have been made, especially over the last decade, to identify gifted children from underrepresented populations. Giftedness is color and culture blind; it occurs in all populations.

Other common myths and realities include: (a) gifted students are equally good at all things—in fact, they may be outstanding in some areas, average in some, and only fair in others; (b) if gifted students are grouped together, they form a homogeneous group—in fact, a class of gifted students still has a broad range of abilities, especially when highly or profoundly gifted are included; (c) a class of gifted students is the easiest to teach—in reality they can be a great challenge to teach. Parents expect teachers of gifted students to be aware of these myths, and to dispel them with reality whenever they appear, and to educate others about the realities of gifted learners.

The most common myth is that all children are gifted. As Ellen Winner (1997) says in her book *Gifted Children: Myths and Realities,* "every child has relative strengths in some area and certainly all children deserve the opportunity to fulfill their individual potential. The gifted are different, however, by virtue of the fact that their strengths in one or more areas are extreme."

Barbara Clark in *Growing Up Gifted* (1997), says, "All students are valuable, all students are important, and all students should be allowed to develop to their highest potential; however, all students are not gifted." The federal definition of gifted students refers to those "who require services or activities not ordinarily provided by the school in order to fully develop such capabilities." The capabilities to which the law refers include advanced levels of intellectual, creative, artistic, leadership, and/or academic abilities. Obviously not all children meet these standards, and yet, in a misguided effort to assert the value of all children, a statement proclaiming that "all children are gifted" is mistakenly made. *The problem is that such a statement can cause the unique educational provisions needed by this group of students to seem unnecessary, and therefore, not be provided.* Parents expect teachers of gifted learners to know and understand these truths and to advocate for appropriate gifted education.

Personal Qualities of GR—ATE Teachers of Gifted Learners

Intuitively, parents know that the most important influence on their child in a given school year is the classroom teacher. Research shows and experts report that teachers' self-concept, high self-esteem, mental attitude, style, expectations, response patterns, and behaviors are the most important factors in student success, even more important than techniques and materials (Clark, 1997).

Qualities parents would like to see in teachers include a passion for teaching gifted learners and for their students; acceptance and understanding of themselves, students, and parents; flexibility, spontaneity, creativity, and authenticity including the ability to admit fallibility and lack of knowledge; enthusiasm for learning and teaching; and the ability to stimulate and motivate students. Parents would like teachers to be facilitators of learning, to offer an appropriately challenging curriculum regardless of grade level or resource material, and to eliminate redundancy of learning, which may involve being a risk-taker as well. Modeling a lifelong love of learning and having a sense of humor will be beneficial to all.

Professional Development

Parents also expect teachers to stay current in their profession, being up-to-date on scientific research and best practices in gifted education. They encourage teachers of gifted students to belong to professional organizations including the National Association for Gifted Children, state organizations that support gifted education, and local advocacy groups in order to enhance their ability to teach gifted learners. Parents would also like teachers to share their expertise and knowledge of gifted education with them and to help them understand the school system.

Classroom Structures

Probably the primary expectations of parents are that their children are appropriately educated, that they enjoy their teachers and schools, and that they are happy. On the surface, these expectations seem realistic. However, given that many classrooms include widely diverse abilities, interests, cultures, behaviors, and needs, coupled with the account-

Nevertheless, parents still expect that teachers will provide academic rigor, personal nurture, and social and emotional support to their children.

ability demands and prescriptions from the state and district, it seems less realistic that teachers can meet all the needs of every student in the class, regardless of class size.

Nevertheless, parents still expect that teachers will provide academic rigor, personal nurture, and social and emotional support to their children. Parents expect that acceleration will be used when appropriate to provide optimal education, including early admission to kindergarten, secondary school, or college when appropriate, and that their children will not be held back by age or grade limitations or by problematic logistics. They expect pupils to move through the curriculum at their own pace, and that the scope and sequence for gifted learners is articulated across all 13 grades. They want to see progressive growth commensurate with their children's abilities.

Parents recognize that their children need to be with those who are like themselves; they want and need to be with their mind mates to grow academically, intellectually, and emotionally. Most parents want their children grouped by ability, emotional, social, interest, and intellectual levels, not just by age. They are as frustrated with mixed-ability cooperative learning as are the gifted students who frequently complete entire group projects themselves out of frustration.

Some gifted students purposely underachieve in order to fit in socially. Others may be getting easy A's with minimal effort thereby preventing them from developing appropriate study skills. Parents want teachers to recognize these and other types of underachievement or at-risk behaviors, and work with parents to intervene early and provide more appropriate academic challenge.

Communication

Parents want open and frequent communication concerning their children and everything that impacts them. There are many ways this can occur including the ubiquitous email, which should be used cautiously to avoid misunderstandings. Teachers need to communicate and educate parents about gifted learners including the characteristics, social and emotional needs, and the myths and realities; district and school philosophy, goals, and objectives; board policies; identification procedures; teaching strategies used in the classroom and how they benefit children. Teachers should also encourage parents to gather information about their children including what books they read at what age, drawings, favorite activities, and difficult areas.

Sometimes parents and teachers see two different children, and it is helpful to share this information with each other.

Parent Participation

Many parents want to be helpful to teachers and schools in meaningful ways. Teachers should determine what assistance is needed. Possibly classroom volunteers would make it easier to meet the various needs of students. Or, maybe parents could assist in developing a newsletter, or typing Socratic dialogues into the computer. Possibly, parents could become mentors, or classroom presenters. Teachers need to match their needs with parents' strengths. Studies have shown that when parents are involved with the schools, student achievement increases.

If there is no group at the school that supports parents of gifted children, parents would appreciate help forming one. Such parent groups provide communication forums, avenues to identify strengths needed to build a cadre of volunteers, and a means to develop an advocacy base. Just as it is important for gifted children to have time together, so it is with parents, and with teachers. They too need their peer groups. In ordinary times, parent groups may seem nice but not necessary; but during times of budget crises, or when gifted programs are threatened, parent groups are essential.

Conclusion

Are these expectations realistic? The answer must be yes for the benefit of gifted learners. However, it is important for parents to understand that teachers are the most maligned of all professionals. Some, including a prominent talk show host, think public education is the root of all evil. Certainly there are problems within the educational system as there are in any system, but public education is a reflection of society. Parents need to understand and appreciate the demands imposed on teachers from state, district, and school decision makers regarding a multitude of different categories of students, with gifted learners being a small part of the whole.

Teachers and parents need to have an appreciation and understanding of each other and the experiences, qualities, and expectations that make them who they are. Each should assume the other has the best of intentions, and work to develop a mutually beneficial relationship. After all, parents and teachers have the same goal: student success.

References

Clark, B. (1997). *Growing up gifted* (5th ed.). Columbus, OH: Merrill/Prentice-Hall.

Dabrowski, K. (1967). *Personality-shaping through positive disintegration.* Boston: Little Brown.

Galbraith, J., & Delisle, J. (1996). *The gifted kids' survival guide: a teen handbook.* Minneapolis: Free Spirit Publishing.

Rogers, K. (1991). *The relationship of grouping practices to the education of gifted and talented learner,* University of Connecticut, National Research Center on the Gifted and Talented.

Szabos, J. (1989). Bright child, gifted learner. *Challenge* 34. Good Apple.

Walker, S. Y. (2002). *The survival guide for parents of gifted kids.* Minneapolis: Free Spirit Publishing.

Warren, S. (1999). *Parents of the gifted's guide to teachers—teacher's guide to parents of the gifted.* Unionville, NY: Royal Fireworks Press.

Winner, E. (1997). *Gifted children: Myths and realities.* New York: Basic Books.

Little Things Count:
What Teachers Wish Parents Knew

Elaine S. Wiener | SUMMER 2003

Elaine S. Wiener is associate editor for Book Reviews for the Gifted Education Communicator, in which she also writes a regular column, "Carpe Diem." She is retired from the Garden Grove Unified School District Gifted and Talented Education (GATE) program in Southern California.

Just as parents have expectations of their children's teachers, teachers have expectations of their students' parents. Elaine Wiener includes a list of fifteen requests to parents; these requests begin and end with an appeal to foster respect for education and educators. She points out that little things such as punctuality, backpack inspections, and tying shoelaces are small matters when involving only one child, but are magnified when teaching twenty to thirty-five children.

Teachers who are also parents know how difficult parenting is. Even teachers who are not parents are in awe of how difficult that job has become. It would be the most valuable piece of information for teachers and parents if they were to trade information and expectations in writing at the beginning of each school year.

Basic Premises

Please know that what is a small action for one or two children is a huge undertaking for twenty to thirty-six children. It will help teachers if parents can visualize dealing with a large group when a request is made of them for only one child.

Please also know that all requests can be more easily accomplished if you add twenty minutes to any of your plans. Everything takes longer than you anticipate.

There will never be anyone who has as much influence to develop a child's values and character as a parent.

Requests

Instill respect for education and educators. Children absorb all your attitudes. If you are angry at a teacher, please come to us and politely express your frustrations, but don't express them to your child because once your child has a negative attitude, respect is never again shown in class.

Develop a professional relationship. Talking takes a lot of time. Please make appointments with us just as you do with your doctor or lawyer.

Talk over the problem with your child at home first; then bring your child to school for at least part of the conference. We are then talking with the child, not about the child. All aspects of the problem can be seen together.

Talk, listen, and read to your child every day. Many parents say they are too busy but this is vital. Re-prioritize your life to accomplish this. The benefits will be seen five, ten, twenty years down the line. This combination—talking, reading, and listening—is the number one choice of all teachers for building skills and a child's feeling of being loved and valued.

Be the parent in your home. Bed times, habits, and discipline are determined by the adult, not by the child. It frightens children to be the boss. Getting enough sleep and eating breakfast affect how well your child concentrates on schoolwork.

Encourage punctuality. Being on time to school is a message that being organized is valued and that school is important. Plan ahead.

Foster organization. Create an organized time and place to look at school papers, and sign and return those that need attention. This is a message, again, that being organized is important. Consider this part of your job as though it were one of your responsibilities at work. Dig into your elementary child's backpack daily. It can be a ritual with humor and perhaps a snack, but do it daily.

Be aware that little things count. For younger children, the tiniest details are mountains at school even with as few as twenty students, but many districts have classrooms as large as thirty-six.

- Double tie shoe laces.

- Check the weather report, and dress your child appropriately.

- Pack or buy lunch, but be sure your child wants the food. She or he will throw away food not wanted regardless of what parents say at home. That is verified daily by thousands of teachers.

- Please keep your child home if he or she is sick. You must have an emergency plan already in place to deal with this. This is a home responsibility, not a school responsibility.

- Teach preschoolers their colors, how to count to ten at least, and nursery rhymes. You are their first teacher. Talk to them even when they are infants.

Promote self-reliance. For all children of all ages, please allow them to be independent. Do not make excuses for your children's errors. Allow them to pay the consequences and become strong from that.

Come to Back-to-School Night; or make an appointment to hear what was said. This is when teachers tell parents what is expected of the students and when you can ask questions. Arrive at conferences on time because there is another conference scheduled immediately after yours.

If you can, be an active supporter of the school. However, if you cannot, support the school with your words to your children. Join the PTA; it is a modest amount and is symbolic of your attitude.

Share important information. If there is a heartache or something you would like the teacher to know, write a note or call. Teachers love children. Knowing important information will help your teacher help your child.

Set priorities. Not having enough money is no excuse for ignorance. We are so privileged to live in a free country where libraries are available to all. You don't need a lot of money to be sure your child is clean and rested and loved. Wearing expensive clothes and buying expensive toys are not necessary items. Please remember who is in charge of character building. Say no easily and without guilt!

Be in charge of the TV, the computer, and electronic games. Remember, despite what children say, it scares them to be the boss. Start loving and consistent discipline early in life.

Foster respect for education. You do not need to have college degrees or have money or speak fluent English to impress upon your child that school is important. You simply need to tell your children that becoming educated is their number-two job. The number-one job is showing respect to their parents and teachers.

Consider additional requirements related specifically to the needs of gifted children. It is the obligation of a gifted program and its teachers to educate parents to the characteristics of gifted children and to the kind of curriculum and the methods used to educate gifted children. However, sometimes these explanations become educationese and sound like double talk. It would help teachers if parents would ask questions when they don't understand. This would force educators to be clear and succinct.

Recognize teachers' efforts. Simply be aware that teachers work long into the night and on weekends to keep a classroom going. They also spend thousands of dollars of their own money on those classrooms. This is the nature of the job and mentioning this is not done to complain or whine. However, the general public should know this fact to understand that teaching is a calling and a sacrifice.

The kind of person who would choose this profession is special and should be appreciated. The best appreciation of all is shown by sending a child to school who is loved, rested, read to, listened to, talked to, and disciplined wisely.

Parents as Learners and Teachers

Sylvia B. Rimm | SUMMER 2001

Sylvia B. Rimm, Ph.D., *is director of the Family Achievement Clinic in Cleveland, Ohio, and is coauthor with Gary Davis of the frequently used introductory textbook,* Education of the Gifted and Talented. *She has written numerous books on parenting, giftedness, and underachievement; served as a regular contribution correspondent to NBC's* Today *show; has appeared on ABC's* 20/20 *and* Oprah; *and is an internationally renowned speaker. She also writes a regularly syndicated column on parenting for Creators Syndicate.*

After many years of working with parents and gifted children as director of the Family Achievement Clinic in Cleveland, Sylvia Rimm reports that parents are generally eager to participate in training that will assist them in better understanding their gifted children's characteristics and needs. She outlines basic elements of a parenting class including topics and strategies for implementing parent training. She also lists numerous helpful parent guidebooks.

Parents and educators are partners in guiding gifted children toward self-fulfillment and in helping them contribute to society. If these partners communicate well, they are more likely to be supportive of each other. Parents should understand the educational goals of teachers, and teachers must acknowledge the perspective of parents.

Parents often feel intimidated about parenting gifted children. Faced with their children's high IQ scores, adult-like vocabulary, and exceptional wisdom or talent, some parents mistrust their ability to guide a child who is so different. Parents may worry that the children are smarter than they are and assume they must follow their children's direction instead of providing needed parental guidance. While it is true and often repeated that gifted children are children first and gifted second, it is also true that sometimes their unusual talents are so powerful and obvious that parents feel isolated and frightened about the whole parenting process.

It is wise for parents to join local, state, and national organizations for guidance and support. Schools, too, should provide training programs for parents that sensitize them to the ways gifted children are like and unlike other children. Such programs help parents gain confidence, prevent gifted children from internalizing pressure, and can enhance the communication between home and school.

Will Parents Participate in Parent Training?

Schools that hold parenting courses usually garner excellent participation and parent appreciation. Some parents may require prompting to take part; in general, however, parents of gifted children especially feel the need for support. Parenting courses improve communication between teachers and parents and also encourage achievement for gifted children.

Tried-and-True Formats

These classes can have a variety of formats. A basic or awareness-level format, held at least once during the school year, offers an evening meeting for parents to better understand the special needs of gifted children. A regionally known speaker attracts larger audiences. Advertising and communication, however, make the most difference in the size of the audience. If there is an accompanying program for the gifted children, more parents are likely to participate. Furthermore, if there is an art exhibit or brief performance by children prior to the program, more parents will be willing to leave the comfort of their homes.

In economically disadvantaged areas, it becomes even more important to attract and hold parents in order to provide their children with the support they need. Offering a light evening meal and child care for younger children can add to the likelihood of excellent attendance. A local business or industry might be willing to support such a parent-child evening.

A more in-depth format that includes six to eight weekly sessions provides a good follow-up to the introductory awareness evening. One-and-a-half- to two-hour sessions, combining presentation, discussion, and video material, permit parents to apply what they learn to their own families and give insight into the ideal home-school partnership. Such classes can be led by teachers, counselors, or school psychologists within the school district if they have appropriate training. Ideally, attendance could be between eight and twelve parents, and times for these meetings should vary to attract different parent audiences. Day, evening, or weekend classes may be effective for different audiences.

Attracting fathers may be more difficult; emphasize that they too are an essential part of parenting. Depending on resources, consider offering courses for fathers or single parents. The more parent involvement, the more likelihood of success for your gifted students.

The Content of Parent Training Courses

The content for a single presentation can vary, and can be based on any interesting topic about gifted children. There are also many books from which topics can be taken, including those listed in the resources at the end of this chapter.

Topics such as characteristics of giftedness, emotional and social adjustment, ADHD and gifted children, underachieving gifted children, creativity and giftedness, gender issues and achievement, your school's curriculum for gifted children, or assessment of giftedness, are all appropriate.

There are several books available especially for training parents of gifted children, including *Guiding the Gifted Child* (Webb, Meckstroth, & Tolan, 1982) and *Parenting for Achievement* (Rimm, 1994). The latter uses the accompanying books *How to Parent so Children Will Learn* (Rimm, 1996) and *Keys to Parenting the Gifted Child* (Rimm, 2001b).

In crafting a curriculum, I recommend including fundamental information found in any good parenting course along with some additional information specific to giftedness. Providing giftedness information without teaching basic parenting may lead parents to assume that certain behavioral problems—such as over-empowerment, emotional intensity, and perfectionism—must be acceptable behaviors of a gifted child. Too many children have been brought to Family Achievement Clinic for help after their parents have helped generate problems for them by misguided acceptance or fostering of inappropriate behavior because the children are gifted.

I recommend elements based on the Parenting for Achievement course, which I developed specifically for fostering the partnership between parents and teachers in guiding gifted children. It has been used with great success in many school districts.

Basic Elements in a Parenting Course

Following are a number of elements that make up the core of good courses for parents of gifted children.

Characteristics of gifted children. Sensitizing parents to the range of characteristics of gifted children will help them understand their own children's similarities and differences compared to other children. Characteristics of gifted children are shaped by both genetics and environment. The praise and attention given to gifted children helps establish their identity as being gifted in particular areas and encourages them to define themselves, their motivations, and their pressures. Parents and teachers dramatically affect the characteristics that emerge; therefore, educating adults to the power they have in shaping direction and self-concept is a priority. Too often gifted children are paralyzed by their self-definition as a "brain," and they can be crippled from developing as a total person. Adults set children's expectations early; parents who are aware of this power can save their children from some terrible pitfalls of giftedness.

Setting limits. There are philosophical differences as to how parents should set limits for their children, gifted or otherwise. Although there is considerable research that suggests that authoritative families—neither authoritarian nor too liberal—seem to raise the best-adjusted children, children's giftedness may mislead parents to over-empower them because they seem so adult-like at times. Parents who set limits positively, as coaches, not judges, were found to be important to the success of over a thousand women (Rimm, Rimm-Kaufmann, & Rimm, 1999). Avoiding over-empowerment is equally important for parents of all children, and over-empowerment is less likely to occur if parents feel more confident in their parenting. A course that grants parental leadership builds confidence in the parents and security in the children.

Parents and teachers working together. Because of the many variations in family structure today, the "united front" no longer means agreement between only two parents. The parenting team may include one, two, three, or four parents, grandparents, nannies, childcare providers, daycare providers, and teachers. With so many individual differences affecting gifted children, they can easily feel pressure, avoid effort, and manipulate adults in ways that will harm their accomplishment, learning, and self-confidence. When children can manipulate adults against each other, their power may make them oppositional and defiant. Although adults don't necessarily have to agree on everything, children grow in confidence when their guiding teams agree on the main principles for raising them.

Helping parents compromise with each other at home, and having parents and teachers support each other, are crucial components of raising all children. This becomes more complicated with gifted children because school curricula may not be sufficiently challenging, and parents, in their appropriate advocacy for their children, can become or seem oppositional to the school. Healthy advocacy requires some delicate balancing, and parenting classes give schools the opportunity to teach parents how to be positive advocates for their children without undermining the school's own authority.

Providing enrichment and acceleration. From the preschool years onward, parents must understand how to tie together what teachers and they themselves provide for their gifted children. Determining when to get professional intervention and how to find it also plays an important role in maintaining appropriate challenges in school and in life. A thorough understanding of available school programs will also help. Parents can also learn how they can volunteer to provide enrichment as adult mentors.

Social-emotional issues. Pressures, perfectionism, peer issues, emotional intensity, and underachievement are a few important awareness topics. How parents and teachers can support gifted children during periods when they feel alone is especially important in light of recent violence perpetrated by gifted individuals. Although there is no evidence that gifted children have more problems than others, they certainly have some different ones. Depending on the community, children known as "geeks" or "brains" may struggle with special peer issues. Parents need guidance to determine when these problems are within normal development and when there is pathology that requires special psychological or psychiatric help.

Role models and mentors. Parents, of course, shouldn't try to create children in their own images. But because we do know that children unconsciously copy other people in creating their own identities, it is important to realize that children are watching and copying parental behaviors and attitudes. Understanding what qualities are more likely to elicit unconscious copying is very useful.

Research from social learning theory suggests that there are three variables that make a difference in whether children identify with their parents. Once aware of these variables, parents can encourage children's identification with positive role models in their environment (Rimm, 1995). The three variables are:

- nurturance, or the warmth of the relationship between the child and a particular adult

- similarities that children see between themselves and the adult

- power of the adult as perceived by the child

When a parent cares a great deal about the child, the child feels a closeness that promotes the wish to be like that adult. This wish is enhanced when the child sees characteristics within him or herself that resemble those of the adult—for example, similar hair or eye color, personality, humor, or enjoyment of similar activities.

The issue of appropriate power is the most difficult to convey. Parents who deprecate themselves or who are demeaned by their partners are not great candidates for identification, because children are likely to see them as powerless. Parents who are seen as respected by their partners, by other people in the community, or even by their children's friends, are more likely to be figures chosen for identification.

In a divorce, if a parent compares the child to the other parent with whom the first parent doesn't get along, the child is more likely to see the other parent as a role model—not exactly what the first parent wishes. Also, parents who seem dependent and powerless, and who complain about the other parent not providing support, may find their children admiring the other more powerful parent.

Parents who feel good about themselves, who are interested in their careers, and who are respected by their partners, are most likely to garner the respect and identification of their children. Although life is not kind enough for parents to feel good about themselves all the time, the better they make their own lives, the better role models they will become for their children.

Although each of these main topics for the content of parenting classes could be the subject of a single class, leaders of classes will need to be sensitive to the special interests of the particular parents in their classes. When parents are both learners and teachers, there will be flexibility in parenting classes, and gifted children will benefit.

References and Resources

Benson, P. L, Galbraith, J., & Espeland, P. (1998). *What kids need to succeed: proven, practical ways to raise good kids.* Minneapolis: Free Spirit Publishing.

California Association for the Gifted. (1998). *The challenge of raising your gifted child.*

Davis, G. A., & Rimm, S. B. (1998). *Education of the gifted and talented (4th ed.).* Boston: Allyn & Bacon.

Galbraith, J. (1999). *The gifted kids' survival guide: For ages 10 & under.* Minneapolis: Free Spirit Publishing.

Galbraith, J., & Delisle, J. R. (1996). *The gifted kids' survival guide: A teen handbook.* Minneapolis: Free Spirit Publishing.

Rimm, S. B. (1994). *Parenting for achievement.* Apple Publishing Company.

———. (1995). *Why bright kids get poor grades—and what you can do about it.* New York: Crown Publishing.

———. (1996). *How to parent so children will learn.* New York: Crown Publishing.

———. (2001b). *Keys to parenting the gifted child* (2nd ed.). Hauppauge, NY: Barrons Educational Series, Inc.

Rimm, S. B., & Rimm-Kaufman, S. (2001a). *How Jane won.* New York: Crown Publishing.

Rimm, S. B., Rimm-Kaufman, S., & Rimm, I. (1999). *See Jane win: the Rimm report on how 1000 girls became successful women.* New York: Crown Publishing.

Smutny, J. F., Veenker, K., & Veenker, S. (1989). *Your gifted child.* New York: Ballantine Books.

Webb, J. T., Meckstroth, E. A., & Tolan, S. S. (1982). *Guiding the gifted child.* Dayton, OH: Ohio Psychology Publishing Co.

Counseling Issues for Gifted Students: More Issues? Special Issues?

Nancy M. Robinson | SPRING 2006

Nancy M. Robinson, Ph.D., is professor emerita of Psychiatry and Behavioral Sciences at the University of Washington in Seattle, Washington, and former director of what is now known as the Halbert and Nancy Robinson Center for Young Scholars. Her research interests have focused on effects of marked academic acceleration to college, adjustment issues of gifted children, intellectual assessment, and verbal and mathematical precocity in very young children.

While gifted children are no more susceptible to social-emotional ills than children at large, they do have some special or different challenges. Nancy Robinson delineates nine of those special challenges including the stress of being "different," the stress of high expectations, and the burden of perfectionism. She also provides detailed guidelines for selecting a skilled counselor with training and experience in working with gifted children if such counseling is needed.

Gifted students are no more intrinsically vulnerable in their social-emotional makeup than any other group of students—and in fact, as a group, they are probably a bit more robust and resilient. On the other hand, neither are gifted youngsters immune to any of the woes of childhood and adolescence except one: mental retardation. Parents of gifted children need to be as alert as other parents to the possibilities of depression, loneliness, anxiety, attention deficit, learning disabilities, delinquency, and the like. Seeking counseling for such issues is often wise and useful, as it would be for any student.

Special Challenges for the Gifted Student

On the other hand, there are some situations that gifted students face that other students don't, and coping with these situations can be stressful. Here are some:

A school setting poorly matched to the level and pace of their learning—typically, ordinary classes that cover old ground, move too slowly, and fail to provide the challenge and satisfaction of mastering something new. Among other things, such settings create relentless, low-level feelings of irritation even in the most kind-hearted students, draining energy that should be directed at growing and learning.

The stress of being "different"—not finding friends who "talk their language" or share their interests, pastimes, and aspirations. Bright students often feel that something is wrong with them if they are unlike their classmates. For example, they are typically less interested in spending time at the mall and more interested in talking about a great book they've discovered or playing a musical instrument. Far too often—beginning in grade school—they try desperately to be just like everyone else and wonder why they feel so disconnected from themselves. Those who are also "different" for reasons of appearance, learning disability, ethnicity, or sexual orientation have an extra burden to deal with.

Growing up a little faster than expected—because gifted children are often somewhat more mature than their age mates, they may be impatient for the next step—ready for deeper friendships, older friends, more independence, the next grade, even boy-girl relationships. They are "out of sync."

Lagging motivation and underachievement—especially because they meet too few genuine challenges that match their interests and vision, gifted children may be especially prone to underachievement. They may seem "lazy"; they may procrastinate (nothing like creating one's own challenge by starting a term paper the night before it's due); they may simply turn off.

The stress of "multipotentiality"—interests and abilities that pull the student in many directions at once. (Actually, although many gifted students feel as though they are equally good at a number of things, they are generally not really equally good at all of them, but have little opportunity to find this out.) Not only may students feel confused about their choices, but they may take on too many activities—too many AP classes, team sports, drama clubs, math competitions, yearbook, community projects—and rob themselves of sleep, leisure, family time, and the satisfaction of doing their best at something they love.

The stress of high expectations—because they are used to doing so well academically, the occasional B or—oh, no, a C!—can be very unsettling and cause them to conclude that they're not so smart, after all.

The burden of perfectionism—high aspirations that exceed everyone else's, working much harder on projects and papers than necessary, missing deadlines because something isn't "good enough" yet. Actually, the most pernicious part of perfectionism is not feeling that you don't measure up to your own standards, but fearing (usually unrealistically) that you don't measure up to those of others.

The "instant expert" expectation—avoiding activities that present the possibility of not being the best, or at least, not right away because too much of their self-concept rests on being so good at things without trying. Many bright students "hate" sports or physical education classes because of this—not because they are especially clumsy but because they are unlikely to be the star.

Some Issues for Younger Gifted Children

As bright as they may be, younger gifted children often do not understand that their classmates are doing the best they can; they are not being "stupid" or oppositional. Your child's impatience is understandable, and it's difficult to explain this situation in a way that is respectful to the other children. In most cases, your child is not as great at sports, or drawing, or singing—or something—as some of the other students are, and you can use this fact in your explanation. At the same time, you should be working to find a better educational match for your child.

And again, bright as they are, when they are moved into a class with other highly capable children, or into a more advanced grade, children may be disappointed that they are not automatically at the top of the class. Children need help understanding that they are using a different comparison standard than before—that they are now the same fish but in a bigger pond. It's best to prepare your child before the shift happens.

Furthermore, gifted students sometimes learn about events and develop fears that send them into a tailspin—for example, death, inconstancy of friends, terrorism, suffering by children who are the victims of natural or man-made disasters, the general unfairness of life. Gifted young children have the awareness but haven't yet developed the "calluses" that come from weathering such experiences. Often their classmates are blissfully ignorant of such matters. You may need to minimize graphic sights on TV, but to approach the issue head-on with your child.

Sometimes it helps to flood your child with more factual information than she is asking for! A little boredom with the issue may be good medicine.

Special Counseling Needs of Gifted Students

The import of the preceding list of special issues is that the counseling needs of gifted students are somewhat different than those most counselors are used to dealing with. It takes an understanding counselor who will say neither, "There, there, dear—it's all because you're gifted (and therefore there's something wrong with you)," or "Buck up, kid; with your assets you should be able to figure this out on your own (because there's nothing wrong with you)."

It may be that simply your understanding and warm support will help your student work through these issues, especially if you are able to advocate for school adjustments, facilitate your student in finding compatible friends, and help to clarify and moderate your student's unrealistic self-expectations. You may find matters improving on their own, but perhaps not. Professional help may be needed.

You may or may not be able to count on your student's school counselor for the services your student needs—not even the basic educational and career counseling that we think is integral to schools. School counselors are too often overwhelmed by sheer numbers of students and the severity of their problems. Good sources of referrals are the coordinator of gifted programs for your district or school, your physician, and parents of other gifted students who have worked successfully with a counselor.

Therefore, when looking for a counselor for your student—either an in-school person or someone in the community—ideally, you'll be looking for someone who:

- is well trained in a research-validated approach such as cognitive behavior therapy or interpersonal therapy. (Don't be afraid to ask.) The person you are looking for should have at least a master's degree in counseling, social work, or a similar profession. Persons who call themselves psychologists will have a doctoral degree.

- has experience with gifted students of this age.

- is reasonably bright and responsive to brightness in others, but not easily overwhelmed by intellect over emotions.

- recognizes your student's yearning for greater challenge and deeper friendships as normal.

- is aware that giftedness by itself does not produce problems and that high standards and aspirations do not necessarily represent maladaptive perfectionism.

- is willing to consider a broad range of questions, including some career and educational issues.

- is also willing to recommend seeing a physician about medication, if it seems called for.

Counseling/psychotherapy services, if obtained in the community, are unfortunately not inexpensive and may not be covered by insurance, especially because your student may not qualify for a mental health diagnosis that is covered by your carrier. (Talk with your physician about this.) Community mental health clinics are seldom equipped to deal with the kinds of special issues gifted children bring to the table, although they are worth investigating. If finances are an issue, it is worth being an active advocate with your child's school psychologist or school counselor, overworked as they may be. It's clearly worth the cost of being known as a "pushy parent."

So, don't be surprised if your gifted child experiences something of a rocky road. Childhood was never the blissful paradise it is painted to be, and you needn't panic if your ordinarily stable and upbeat child goes through rough spots from time to time. But if your child seems sad, anxious, or stressed for more than a few weeks, then do try to find professional help. And if the first person you find doesn't click with your child, keep looking. You may be able to avert a good deal of distress—and keep your child from making poor, even dangerous choices down the road.

No One Said It Was Easy: Challenges of Parenting Twice-Exceptional Children

Linda C. Neumann | FALL/WINTER 2005

Linda C. Neumann is the editor and copublisher of 2e: Twice-Exceptional Newsletter, *a bimonthly publication that focuses on twice-exceptional children, those who are gifted and have learning or attention difficulties. The audience includes parents of twice-exceptional children plus educators, advocates, and social service, medical, and mental health professionals who work with these children.*

Gifted children who also have one or more learning deficits are an enigma to all those around them. These twice-exceptional (2e) children display many of the characteristics of typical gifted children; but they are hampered by learning deficits that interfere with typical childhood development. Parents of 2e children must first seek professionals who can accurately assess and diagnose their children; come to terms with their child's twice exceptionality; and finally, find the right learning environment for their child.

Many years ago, as a college student, I took an introductory course in psychology. We were required to serve as guinea pigs in experiments that more advanced students conducted. In one, I had to give answers to some fairly simple questions and math problems. With each answer, I found myself completely out of sync with the four other people in the room. Before too long, I figured out what was probably going on. My reaction to the situation was the focus of the experiment: would I go with what I thought was right, or would I go along with the crowd?

I remember how uncertain and uncomfortable it felt to be in that situation, even when I knew what was going on. As the parent of twice-exceptional (2e) children, I often remember that experiment and the way it made me feel. In raising my children, those feelings have often returned as I ponder: should I do what feels right for my kids, or do I follow conventional thought?

Parents of 2e kids find themselves with a foot in each of two worlds: giftedness and special needs. Straddling these two worlds is what makes our experiences as 2e parents so unique and is often what leaves us so uncertain. Having this combined perspective affects many aspects of our parenting, in particular what we ask for and expect of our children's teachers, coaches, peers, relatives, and the professionals who work with our children. It often makes us feel that we need to explain their differences to others as well as protect them from the opinions and judgments of those who can't see what's hidden, be it their gifts or their disabilities.

In this article we'll consider some questions that all parents of twice-exceptional children face: What sets our 2e children apart from others and makes our job of parenting them such a challenge? What does it take to meet these challenges?

When Gifts and Deficits Meet: The Challenge of 2e Kids

Twice-exceptional children have two sets of conflicting traits, one related to their high capabilities, the other to their limitations. Like other intellectually gifted children, they are likely to think in different ways from average children and to experience the world differently. Often, they display many of the characteristics typical of gifted children, such as:

- intensity and sensitivity

- greater asynchrony than average children—that is, a bigger gap between their mental age and chronological age

- highly developed curiosity

- precocious development and use of language

- early interest in mathematics

- tendency toward divergent (creative and unusual) thinking

- ability, from an early age, to remember large amounts of information

- unusual sense of humor

- advanced moral reasoning about issues related to fairness and justice (Lovecky, 2005; Silverman, 2005; Webb, Amend, Webb, Goerss, Beljan, & Olenchak, 2005)

Unlike other gifted children, those who are twice exceptional find themselves hampered by deficits that interfere with their ability to perform the tasks that classroom learning requires. The deficits, often invisible to others, can do any of the following:

- interfere with their ability to make sense of visual or auditory information

- make it hard to correctly interpret social cues, like facial expressions and tone of voice

- limit the functioning of short-term memory

- take the form of language-based disorders that make reading, writing, mathematics, or verbal expression difficult

- appear as a mood disorder that leaves the child anxious or depressed or an attention deficit that makes it hard for the child to sit still and focus

- hamper fine or gross motor skills

- interfere with the way the child's brain organizes and interprets information taken in through the sensory experiences of touch, taste, smell, sight, and sound, as well as body placement and movement. (With deficits of this type, in sensory processing, a child experiences the world quite differently from others. For example, the lights, sounds, and smells of the classroom might be painfully intense for the child, making concentration on lessons difficult.)

As a result of deficits like these, twice-exceptional students may display behaviors and characteristics that can be baffling, annoying, or even infuriating to the adults around them. For instance, these students might:

- forget to do or follow through with tasks

- display an uneven academic pattern, with a typical profile being strengths in math and content areas and weaknesses in language arts, especially written language

- require more time to process language and respond than would be expected of someone with high intelligence

- have a poor sense of time and difficulty estimating the time needed to complete tasks

- have difficulty with personal organization and lose their possessions

- be unable to stay on task and stick to a schedule

- have difficulty with multistep instructions and tasks to be done sequentially

- find it hard to employ systematic strategies for solving problems

- have poor handwriting and spelling

  (Birely, 1995; Seay, 2005; Maker & Udall, 1985)

Such a combination of strengths and limitations leads to children with unique, and often quirky, profiles. They can have difficulty finding peers and, as a result, may have a small number of friends or no friends at all. Coping with their deficits can take a toll on their stamina, leaving these children exhausted from the strain after a day at school. Furthermore, having to confront these deficits day in and day out in the classroom can take a toll on the 2e child's self-esteem. As psychologist and author Linda Silverman (2003) states, "It's emotionally damaging to be unacceptable in the place you spend six hours of every day for thirteen critical years."

The Challenges That Parents of Twice-Exceptional Children Face

Perhaps the greatest challenge that parents of 2e children face is trying to make sense of what they're seeing—the uneven performance at school, the low self-esteem, the difficult behavior. These children are easy to label and pigeonhole. People do it all the time with statements such as: "They're just lazy; they're just troublemakers; they're disabled and we can't expect too much from them."

It can take a long time, plenty of money, and a great deal of frustration to get a more accurate picture of what's really going on with a 2e child. Parents often face a daunting task searching for professionals with the skills, experience, and insight needed to accurately assess and diagnose their children and then give parents the help they need. Oftentimes, the search doesn't end until children are in middle school, high school, or even college.

Another of the challenges that parents face is coming to terms with their child's twice-exceptionality. It's often a matter of letting go of the child you *thought* you had and learning to celebrate the child you *do* have. For instance, parents may see from early on that their child is very bright and creative. They might imagine what the school years will bring—the outstanding report cards, the honors and awards, the full scholarship. However, few 2e kids match that stereotypical image of a gifted child; and for parents, it may be hard to give up that traditional view of success. It may be even harder to continually answer the question that puzzled relatives and others in their lives often ask: "If that child is so smart, then why . . . ?" It is the same type of question that most parents of 2e kids probably ask themselves from time to time. There can be difficult emotions for parents to deal with as well—grief from knowing that their child has a disability and guilt that comes from not seeing it sooner or, on the other hand, from not recognizing the child's gifts sooner.

A third challenge for parents is finding the right learning environment for their children. According to the book *To Be Gifted and Learning Disabled* (Baum & Owen, 2004), this environment is one that provides "educational experiences that assure appropriate challenge, while offering instruction, accommodations, and compensation strategies that minimize the effects of the learning disability."

Some parents may be fortunate to live in districts with programs that meet this description, specifically designed for twice-exceptional students. Most parents are not. For those in the latter group, finding the right learning environment can be an elusive dream. Some years the mix of teachers, administrators, classmates, curriculum, and services work better for their child than others. For some children, it never works at all. When the blend is right, the child is happy, the parents are grateful, and the year goes well. When it isn't, grades can plummet along with the child's self-esteem, and stress can plague the family.

Ways to Meet the Challenges

Unfortunately, there is no handbook on the market titled *Successfully Raising Your Twice-Exceptional Child*. However, following some general guidelines can help parents meet the challenges they face.

1. Follow your instincts. You know your child better than anyone, as the old saying goes. Be skeptical of those who are quick to label him or her as lazy. Use your own knowledge of your child to question what might underlie problematic behavior. Keep in mind, however, that seeking the opinions and advice of professionals is often necessary; and listening to what they have to say with an open mind is essential.

2. Be willing to deviate from the accepted path. What's right for many gifted children may not work for your twice-exceptional child. Consider alternatives, despite the raised eyebrows or doubtful comments that others might offer. For example, you may find that you need to do some of the following:

- Consider leaving the public school system for a private school if your child's learning or emotional needs are not being met.

- Come up with different options for your nonathletic child to compete and excel, such as science and math competitions or chess tournaments.

- Abandon the pressures of structured schedules and homework for the more relaxed pace of homeschooling.

- Seek out alternative means of learning—virtual (online) schools, tutoring, mentorships, Talent Search classes, and specialty summer camps.

- Forget about traditional school timelines. Your child may need to take longer to finish high school or college; or, on the other hand, your child may benefit from acceleration, given the proper support and accommodations.

3. Educate yourself. One way to make difficult or unorthodox decisions concerning your child and feel comfortable about them is to learn as much as you can about who your child is, what he or she needs, who can help, and what options are available to you. Armed with a solid understanding of these factors, you'll be better equipped to take the steps that are right for your child.

4. Find support. Sharing with other parents of 2e children is perhaps the most important thing you can do for yourself and your child. Just as our 2e children need true peers, so do we as their parents. Joining groups that focus just on the gifted or just on learning disabilities probably won't provide the needed support. Parents of 2e children are likely to feel isolated in such groups because the gifted parents don't want to talk about accommodations, for instance, and the LD parents aren't concerned with issues like acceleration. Parent support groups and online discussion groups exist that focus directly on the needs of twice-exceptional children. Sharing with other 2e parents will open up possibilities for your child that you never considered before. When you learn about other parents who have veered off the traditional path of educating their children—and found success—you may feel less trepidation about doing the same.

As mentioned before, there is no handbook for raising a twice-exceptional child. You're writing your own as you go. You're bound to feel uneasy and doubtful at times, but having confidence in your instincts and judgment and the knowledge and support to back your decisions will bolster you for doing what you think is right for your twice-exceptional child rather than feeling pressured to go along with the crowd.

References

Baum, S. M. & Owen, S. V. (2004). *To be gifted & learning disabled: Strategies for helping bright students with LD, ADHD, and more* (rev. ed.). Mansfield, CT: Creative Learning Press.

Bireley, M. (1995). *Crossover children: A sourcebook for helping children who are gifted and learning disabled.* Reston, VA: Council for Exceptional Children.

Lovecky, D. V. (2004, April). Gifted children with AD/HD. *2e: Twice-Exceptional Newsletter.*

———. (2005, June). Gifted children with Asperger syndrome. *2e: Twice-Exceptional Newsletter.*

Maker, C. J. & Udall, A. J. (1985). *Giftedness and learning disabilities.* ERIC Clearinghouse on Disabilities and Gifted Education. (ERIC EC Digest #E427).

Seay, M. (2005, August). *Working with the gifted learning disabled child.* Session presented at the World Conference for Gifted and Talented Children, New Orleans.

Silverman, L. K. *Characteristics of giftedness scale: A review of the literature.* Retrieved August 21, 2005, from http://www.gift ed-development.com/ Articles/Characteristics_Scale.htm.

———. (2003, October). *The universal experience of being out-of-sync.* Keynote address delivered at the New England Conference for Gifted and Talented, Nashua, NH.

Webb, J. T., Amend, E. R., Webb, N. E., Goerss, J., Beljan, P., & Olenchak, F. R., (2005) *Misdiagnosis and dual diagnoses of gifted children and adults: ADHD, Bipolar, OCD, Asperger's, depression, and other disorders.* Scottsdale, AZ: Great Potential Press.

The Right Tool for the Job

Alexandra Shires Golon | SPRING 2003

Alexandra Shires Golon is director of Visual-Spatial Resource in Denver, Colorado. She is a former GT teacher, parent of two gifted visual-spatial learners, as well as an author and international speaker. Her books include Raising Topsy-Turvy Kids: Successfully Parenting Your Visual-Spatial Child, If You Could See the Way I Think: A Handbook for Visual-Spatial Kids, *and* Visual-Spatial Classroom: Differentiation Strategies That Engage Every Learner.

Another group of gifted children presenting special challenges to parents is visual-spatial learners. Since most schools are structured to teach children in verbal and sequential modes, a child who thinks and processes in images will no doubt be at a disadvantage. Alexandra Shires Golon includes many verbal pictures to illustrate common home and school situations that may call for alternative approaches for visual-spatial learners to be successful.

Imagine this: You've just tucked in your child for the night and—well, it seems as though you've just tucked him in, but, now that you think about it, the news is coming on and you've managed to fold the laundry, do the dishes, and tidy the family room in the meantime; so maybe it's actually been a couple of hours and, and—he's calling for you! Why isn't he asleep yet?!

You've been summoned for one last whisper, snuggle, and butterfly kiss. In your attempt to navigate the four feet between the bedroom door and the bedside, you manage to plant your unprotected left foot smack on top of a Mars colony created from Legos. As you attempt to regain your balance your right foot lands on and collapses the K'Nex version of the International Space Station. You are clearly losing the navigational battle of your child's bedroom floor and now, on your way to greeting that when-was-the-last-time-this-was-vacuumed-floor with your face, you notice that hurled under the bed frame like so much forgotten dirty laundry, is the homework assignment that was due three weeks ago!

Feel free to replace the Legos and K'Nex with puzzles, art or construction materials, books, blocks, marbles, beads, Play-Doh, ribbons, scissors, stuffed animals, chess pieces, or any number of other items. Then switch the misplaced homework with anything else that nobody but you seems to understand the value and importance of. If this scenario sounds even remotely like an evening from your life, you are probably the parent of a visual-spatial learner.

Visual-spatial learners are the delightful little darlings in our lives who crave for time with such joys as building, painting, drawing, daydreaming, dancing, music making, and letting their creative imaginations soar. They struggle to find the time or inclination to put their clothes away, maintain some degree of organization, and you can forget altogether about punctuality. They have the most incredible "a-ha!" moments of discovery, invention, and problem solving, but the skills of managing a time schedule or showing their work may absolutely elude them. They march to their own drummer and virtually nothing you do will convince them it may be offbeat.

Is Knowing Someone's Learning Style Important?

Does it matter whether you know your child is a visual-spatial learner? Well, one might just as easily ask, does it matter whether you know if they are right- or left-handed? When we know a child is left-handed, we don't insist on the use of right-handed scissors. We used to, but then we realized that lefties are born that way, that there's nothing wrong with being a leftie and we, the right-handers of the world, finally accepted lefties as they are. When given the proper tool, the task became easier, the job more interesting, and the end result more pleasing.

What if we're not giving the appropriate tools to specific learning styles? If you, your child's teacher, and others involved in this person's life, understand that people can have a preferred learning style, just like having a preferred writing hand, and that you can teach to that preferred learning style, wouldn't you be offering them the same advantage for learning that appropriate scissors are to preferred handedness?

I didn't know people actually thought differently until my son was old enough to describe for me how he thought. For instance, one night as I was tucking him in, I asked him which goodnight song he wanted. He sat straight up in bed and stared intently at the ceiling. "What are you looking at?" I asked. "My song list." "Oh, what does it look like?" He proceeded to draw with his finger in the air a sort of shelf holding every picture of every song he knew. He described the images of a number of songs for which he could also find a word, the song's name, to match his image. He could see the song he wanted but couldn't find its name. I asked him to describe the picture: a hand with two fingers up. While I was guessing songs with two items, songs with the number two, anything two, my hand—with two fingers raised—was bouncing and he got it: "Little Bunny FooFoo!" This was a song I had not sung to him in many years, maybe four or more, but the image, the picture he had created of the song, lived on in his mind's eye, on his shelf of songs.

What I discovered about my son's learning style was that he thinks in images. His brain is one gigantic filing system of pictures that symbolize words—like song names. Visual-spatials like my son can often solve complex math equations accurately, but they may not always be able to show their work. They excel in right-hemispheric talents, skills requiring aptitude from the right side of the brain: art, geometry, thinking in multiple dimensions, music, creativity, empathy, design and invention, and the sheer joy of creating something wonderful out of the trash you nearly threw away.

One evening, after enjoying a take-out meal from a local restaurant, my youngest couldn't wait to get his hands on some tape and the Styrofoam containers our food had been delivered in. He "saw" airplane propellers in the lids, an airplane body in the boxes and all the other pieces required to create his custom jet. They were all there, their potential being wasted just holding our food. When dinner was over, voilà, the airplane was created—food crumbs and all. I'm almost certain it still exists somewhere, probably under his bed!

Once, as we were headed out for some unmemorable chore, and still backing out of the driveway, Visual-Spatial Poster Child was obviously struggling in his seat. "What's up?" I called back. "I can't get the backward seven to work!" I'm thinking, "backward seven??"—what is it, how does it work, and why does he need it? "Uh, what's a backward seven, honey?" I cautiously asked. Meanwhile, I'm headed down the street and the panic level in his voice is rising. At the stop sign I looked back to discover that he had not been able to connect his seatbelt, which from his vantage point, coupled with his ability to see the image and not find the matching word, is clearly a backward seven!

I have learned that most people are a little sequential and a little spatial. My older son, for example, is very strong in both auditory-sequential abilities and visual-spatial abilities. For him, learning comes easily and rapidly. He can grasp complex concepts with little effort regardless of how they are presented. What a gift to be able to call upon the strengths of either or both hemispheres at any given time!

In an effort to meet the needs of children like mine, we parents and teachers must first recognize that there are distinct differences in how many people think and learn that are inherent in each individual, even in our learning styles. Many of us are strongly auditory-sequential or strongly visual-spatial. To require visual-spatial learners to conform to an auditory-sequential structure, in their home and school life, is equivalent to the archaic practice of forcing left-handed children to write with their right hand.

Visual-Spatial Abilities—Your Child's Gift

Think you've got a visual-spatial on your hands? What do you do now, right? As a homeschooling mom, I have the luxury of creating a classroom that is custom-designed to meet the unique needs of my children and their abilities. Whenever we approach any new learning material, we think about how to present it visually. Often my children come up with remarkably effective, visual ways they would like to learn new material. From maps of South America in multiple colors of clay (including transparency overlays of the ancient Aztec, Mayan, and Incan civilizations) to gigantic sheets of butcher paper (to trace the paths of the first Polynesian explorers and Lewis and Clark), we are always incorporating some interesting visual activity to accompany and expand upon our traditional curriculum. You haven't truly appreciated Shakespeare until you've seen it dissected, diagramed, and a cartoon version created of it!

Visual props such as math manipulatives, graphic organizers, the computer, good old paper and crayons, clay, transparencies, mnemonic devices, cartoons, and much more, serve to enhance the overall educational experience for every learner, visual-spatial and auditory-sequential. I've never met an auditory-sequential learner who didn't enjoy squishing and shaping clay to re-create ancient artifacts, but I've known several visual-spatial learners who couldn't recite the dates or the names if they had only learned the information by having it read or lectured to them. They remember what they see, not always what they hear. And for what they hear, they must be allowed time to create a visual image to accompany that new knowledge or it is lost.

VISUAL-SPATIAL LEARNERS LEARN BY OBSERVATION

When he was just 20 months, I discovered my older son playing on the computer. He had learned how to manipulate the mouse, get into a document, and ask the printer to do its thing just by watching me. I wasn't teaching him, but he had been on my lap and seen the process maybe two or three times, and he learned it. Today he approaches computers as many kids of his generation do, without any trepidation or concern, fully understanding how it performs pure acts of magic.

My son created a picture (see Figure 1) when I asked him to tell me how he was able to learn Spanish so well. (Foreign languages are not typically mastered by visual-spatial learners unless they are involved in a total immersion program.) Rather than try to explain, he proceeded to draw, in great detail, how his "satellites" (ears) received information which was then forwarded to the "picture-making-building" which transformed the signals into pictures. Those pictures then traveled to the "picture-stamping-area" which "put what the picture means" on the picture. Finally, the image traveled to the "filing building" where all images are stored for later recollection. What I particularly enjoyed hearing about was where all the employees who were responsible for receiving signals, stamping the pictures and filing, lived: "Employee Paradise," a fenced-in village complete with swimming pool and small store!

SUCCESSFULLY HARNESSING THE GIFT

If your child is a visual-spatial learner, one of your jobs as a parent is to work with classroom teachers to help them understand and teach to a known preferred learning style. Chances are your child isn't the only visual-spatial learner in the classroom; studies have shown that at least one-third of the population is

Figure 1: Visual-Spatial Learning Example

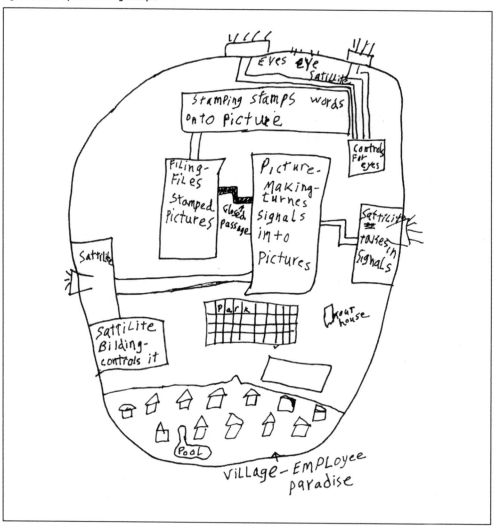

visual-spatial. By enriching the learning experience with a more visual, hands-on approach, and with activities that engage all students, the classroom teacher doesn't sacrifice, but only adds to everyone's learning. If the teacher can reach everyone, no one falls through the cracks.

At home, take a look at how you communicate with your child. Imagine it's time for the weekly "Clean-your-bedroom-or-else" ritual. Do you typically rattle off a list of "do-this, do-that" chores then leave the room believing that your picture of a clean living space will somehow manifest itself out of the reigning chaos? And that it will be done within a prescribed time frame?

Now think about your success rate with this approach. Next time try this: work with your child to create a poster of pictures—either drawings you create together or clippings from magazines—of what the end product should look like when the job is finished. The pictures might include one of a nicely made bed with all the stuffed animals aligned and waiting. Another could illustrate folded clothes neatly tucked into drawers that are still within the dresser, while another pictures matching shoes lined up nicely on the floor of the closet. Yet another shows similar toys gathered carefully into tubs. Okay, you get the picture; now help them get the picture!

Getting a visual-spatial child out the door can be an ongoing challenge. There are so many distracting and more entertaining options available. One technique that works, at least some of the time, is to create a picture of the consequences of not getting to your destination on time. For example, suppose you are running late to an afternoon Tae Kwon Do practice. You could create the following picture for your child: "If we are late for your class, that will upset the instructor and possibly interrupt the start of the lesson for all the other students who did arrive on time. How do think your instructor will feel? How will the other students feel?" If he can see the consequences of not arriving on time, you may actually stand a chance of getting out the door—and, with the shoes! Assure your child that whatever he was longing to do instead of getting in the car will still be there for him when you return. Visualizing what will happen, or not happen as a result of action, or inaction, is often an effective way to get results. Also effective, though militaristic sounding, are one-word commands: "shoes—car—please" conveys all the instructions needed.

Auditory-Sequential vs. Visual-Spatial

If you are not a visual-spatial learner and your child is, you must try to see from his or her perspective. Unless you have created a picture for the visual learner to remember, consider it lost. You could deliver an entire set of instructions regarding the laundry: gather it up, bring it down to the laundry room, sort by colors, fill the washer with detergent, turn on the water, add the bleach, put the clothes in, and so on; but if you have not planted the image of the chore's

Figure 2

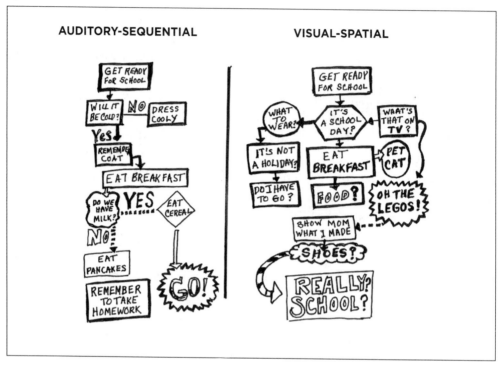

goal—clean laundry—your child will be stuck gathering the laundry in a room full of temptations that draw attention completely away from the chore at hand. Once you think you've created a picture, ask your child to describe the image for you. Make sure you both agree on the picture that will result when the chore is complete.

Imagine you are helping your visual-spatial child to master something new. Whether it's riding a bike or memorizing the multiplication tables, the greatest gift you can give your child is to present that new material visually. I once met an incredibly dynamic teacher who taught the thirteen colonies by having his audience memorize a ridiculous story—in pictures that each person drew—of a Jersey cow named Georgia, atop the Empire State Building. Are you seeing New Jersey, Georgia, and New York here? I taught my sons their times tables by reading them the silliest cartoons that exchanged the names of numbers for characters and other objects. What's 8 x 2? "Skate times shoe = Sick Queen, Sixteen!" from the cartoon story of a queen spinning dizzily while wearing a shoe on one foot, and a skate on the other. You can find the entire collection available at www.multiplication.com. There are a number of math programs that present material visually including Borenson's Hands-on Equations, Mortenson Math, Math-U-See, and more.

Maybe If We Ignore It, They'll Outgrow It!

Preferred learning styles don't affect just school-age children. My husband and mother-in-law recently learned there was a name to refer to how they think and learn. Neither knew that their way of thinking was different from others; they thought everyone learned and thought in images. And, while neither did well in elementary school, both are very bright. Understanding their uniqueness has helped to heal old wounds from their school days and to create confidence in their abilities and contributions.

The Future for Visual-Spatial Learners

Parents of visual-spatial learners everywhere, take heart! We are on the eve of an educational revolution and your child's time to shine has come. For the first time in perhaps centuries, their special gifts will be recognized and honored. How can I make such a prediction? Because in this new century, our reliance on the computer and the visually-oriented careers that will spring from it means the talents that come naturally to the visual-spatial learner will be of highest value. It can be exceedingly challenging for sequential, left-hemispheric thinkers to imagine objects in dimensional form, to create pictures in their mind's eye, to think in terms of space rather than time. But for the visual-spatial learner it is precisely how they think and learn.

Perhaps one day, there will be remedial courses in how to think sequentially because the talent for such will have been lost. Until then, we must honor the visual-spatial learners among us, learn from them, and offer them the tools they need for success in their academic work—the right tools for the job.

Can Parents of Gifted Kids Try Too Hard? And What Do Gifted Kids Want, Anyway? Some Possible Answers for Two Impossible Questions

Judy Galbraith | SPRING 2003

Judy Galbraith has a master's degree in guidance and counseling of the gifted. She has worked with and taught gifted children and teens, their parents, and their teachers for over twenty years. In 1983, she started Free Spirit Publishing and is the author or coauthor of numerous books, including The Gifted Kids' Survival Guide, When Gifted Kids Don't Have All the Answers, *and* What Kids Need to Succeed.

Without even realizing it, parents can sometimes overwhelm their gifted children and "create unintentional barriers." Judy Galbraith, with years of experience in surveying gifted youth and their parents, shares "Six Ways Gifted Parents Can Try Too Hard." She also includes survey results of "What Gifted Students Want (and Need) From Their Parents," and a "letter" from a gifted teenager to his parents, that could serve as an effective discussion starter.

My son would make a great lawyer someday. I think the rules I set are reasonable, but he comes back with arguments against them—and they make sense! Often I find I'm willing to compromise, but sometimes I feel as if he's the one making the rules, and I'm not comfortable with that.

They're always saying things like "You're gifted. Why can't you get straight A's in that class you're taking?"

Why can't my parents understand that I can be responsible and spend some time with my friends, too?

It's tough knowing just how far to "let go of the leash." We always worry about whether we're being too lenient—and maybe even giving the impression that we don't really care. I guess most parents question this type of thing.

I have a terrible time balancing what I want to do with what my parents want me to do.

Sometimes it can seem like gifted kids are from Mars while their parents are from Venus. Certainly they can seem to go out of their way to alienate each other. After years of hearing from both parents and kids, I can safely say that neither is as "off-planet" as the other might believe. Each thinks the other doesn't understand how hard it is to be a gifted kid or the parent of a gifted kid. The truth is, both are challenging positions, and both need and deserve the respect and support of the other.

Gifted kids and teens often complain that parents expect them to always study every night, always get A's (or higher!), always behave perfectly, and always, always put education above everything—even friends. Parents of gifted kids worry about everything from their children's ability to make and keep good friends to their need to be challenged (and the school's capability to keep them challenged) and focused on the future. Most of all, however, parents worry if they are doing all they can to help.

Certainly parents of gifted kids care about their children and want to help them succeed. But sometimes parents of gifted kids try too much. They have such hopes and dreams for their children, such a strong desire to help and guide, and a dedicated willingness to do "whatever it takes" to help their children succeed, that even the most beloved gifted child can feel a little overwhelmed by it all.

Six Ways Gifted Parents Try Too Hard

When do good intentions go bad? When parents are so intent on "paving the way" for their bright, wonderful, challenging gifted child that they, instead, create unintentional barriers.

1. If you raise it, they will jump. Set high expectations, and your child will naturally rise to meet them. Sounds logical, right? After all, it seems to work (especially with young children). You expect great things of your child; your child does great things, which proves you're doing a wonderful job as parents. *Unfortunately, kids, especially gifted kids, are unpredictable. Children can place so much importance on pleasing their parents that they obsess on the grade and not on the learning. (This can lead to anxiety or perfectionism.) They might think you value their achievements more than you do them as people. (This can lead to poor self-image and low self-esteem.) Teens, on the other hand, can leap overnight from appreciating their benevolent parents to resenting their Evil Dictator parents. (This can lead to underachievement or rebellion via unhealthy risk-taking.)*

2. My gifted child, myself. Gifted parents often see themselves reflected in their children. When someone says, "I can't help but notice that your son Agamemnon is so polite and well-mannered," a parent is more likely to say, "Thank you!" rather than, "I'll pass your comments on to Ag." And that's OK. It's quite possible that a measure of Ag's success can be linked to how his parents raised him and the values they share. *On the other hand, if your child doesn't get A's, awards, and commendations and is criticized by other adults for less-than-perfect behaviors, do you feel these "failures" brand you as a lousy parent?*

3. I didn't but my child can. Gifted parents might make demands of their children in an effort to fulfill their own hopes and dreams. If you wanted to go to a certain college—or any college—but never could, it's tempting to insist that your child attend, or that she become a doctor (just like Mom) or an artist (like Dad never had the chance to be)—whether she wants to or not. Even when you have their best interests at heart, parents need to remember that their children's lives belong to their children. *Before completely charting out your child's future, try* *to remember that your child might have an altogether different course in mind. You will always be there for support and advice, but, ultimately, it is her life, not yours.*

4. If I can do it so can my child. Parents of gifted kids who are gifted themselves tend to impose their own high standards on their children—regardless of their children's talents or level of maturity. *Remember: The gifted apple may fall far from the gifted apple tree. Better yet, think of your child as a gifted orange who shares a lot in common with his apple parents, but he has his own interests, talents, and ways of looking at things.*

5. Act your IQ not your age. It's easy to forget that gifted kids and teens are just that, kids and teens. After all, they might interact well with adults, have older friends, be well versed in weighty issues, and otherwise talk like an adult, think like an adult, and even act like an adult. But they're not and, smart as they are, they deserve the right to act like other kids and teens on occasion. In fact, you might want to encourage a little silliness. *Try to avoid saying "With your intelligence, I would have expected you to . . .*

. . . act more maturely" or

. . . be more responsible" or

. . . stop this silliness" or

. . . act your age"

6. Worried you're not worrying enough? All parents are worriers. Will Johnny go to college? Will Kim find a job and be able to support herself? Add in the ever-present factors of peer pressure, negative influences, advertising, pornography on the Internet, trashy TV, alcohol and other drugs, random violence, ad infinitum, and it's a wonder parents aren't paralyzed with worry about their children. Parents of gifted kids can turn worrying up a few more notches. (Will Johnny choose the right college? Will Kim ever set a career goal and stick with it? What's more important, a high GPA or a difficult class load? Just because Gabe is with older classmates in school, is he ready to hang out with them socially?) After all, you've already had to fight more than a few battles to get your child what she needs. *Slow down, and try to be realistic about what's got you* *worried and what you can actually do about it. Keeping gifted kids overscheduled so there's no time for trouble or trying to keep them isolated from the possibility of negative influences won't protect them or prepare them for life. ("An A- in science? Sure, an A- is better than a B, but if you hadn't gone on that overnight, you might have done better . . .") Neither will always expecting the worst. Help your gifted children to understand themselves and others, and to be confident, caring, and resilient so they can protect themselves by making healthy choices and taking healthy risks.*

What Gifted Students Want (and Need) from Their Parents

According to the survey conducted for *The Gifted Kids' Survival Guide: A Teen Handbook,* the top ten things gifted students wish their parents would do (or not do) are:

1. Be supportive and encouraging; be there for us; be on our side.

2. Don't expect too much of us; don't expect perfection.

3. Don't pressure us, be too demanding, or push too hard.

4. Help us with our schoolwork/homework.

5. Help us develop our talents.

6. Be understanding.

7. Don't expect straight A's.

8. Allow us some independence; give us space; trust us, because chances are we know what we're doing.

9. Talk to us; listen to us.

10. Let us try alternative education/special programs.

Why can't GT kids just tell parents what they want? Although they can often talk a blue streak about virtually any subject, it can be difficult for gifted kids to speak frankly about what they need from their parents with their parents. Some years ago, I taught a "Surviving and Thriving" class for GT teens. As part of that class, my students collaborated on an open letter (see page 292) that highlighted the things kids want parents to understand but that can be difficult for children to speak about. (I recently rediscovered this letter when it was reprinted in the *Minnesota Council for the Gifted & Talented* newsletter. And I agree with the newsletter's editor that the sentiments expressed still hold true for today's gifted kids—and are just as important for today's parents to hear.)

An Out-of-This-World Experience

While your gifted child may be the light of your life, chances are he hasn't been the world's easiest child. Perhaps even more than parenting a more typical child, parenting a gifted child can pose many, many challenges, not all of them pleasant.

No one really enjoys the get-tough aspects of parenting—especially with a child who could logically argue her way out of any situation. Nagging children about homework, reminding them to study, helping them cope with perfectionism and procrastination, grounding them for breaking curfew, asking them (for the thousandth time) to clean up their room, and coping with the emotional ups and downs of intellectually curious and emotionally sensitive children are not among the pleasures of parenting.

Your gifted child is just the kind of bright, interesting, capable, and intelligent person you'd like to spend time with. Unfortunately, just as that happens, that bright interesting child may seem more eager to spend the majority of his limited free time with friends than with you.

Don't worry. By listening to your gifted child, talking with (not to) her, supporting her interests, and making it clear that you love her—not just her ability and accomplishments—you will build a strong foundation that can weather the storms of roller-coaster emotions and conflict that typical adolescence provides. Best of all, you both will be surprised to learn that you speak the same language after all.

Dear Mom and Dad:

You are great parents and I'd like to take this opportunity to thank you for that. I'd also like to say a few things that are hard to tell you in person. (I'm afraid you'll get angry at me. I'm afraid that you wouldn't really hear what I'm saying.) But in hopes that you won't get mad, and that you might want to truly understand and know me better . . . here goes nothing.

If I could have a wish come true it would be that you would realize (and even be happy that) things are different for me than when you were a kid. I want to be my own person, not a clone of you when you were a kid.

That was then. This is now.

Even though I am young, and I don't know everything, and I do make mistakes . . . I do know some things, and sometimes I am right, and I am a good person no matter what. I would appreciate knowing that you care about me as a person (not just as a kid with a good brain), even though sometimes our beliefs, values, or ideas may differ. I especially like it when you focus on the positive things about me, instead of the things I don't do so well. (After all, I think I'd be a big bore if I were a perfect kid—whatever that is.)

I get maddest (ARGH!) about being asked (and asked, and asked) about what I do, where I go, with whom, and what I think . . . knowing that if you don't approve of what I say, I'll be criticized or punished. It makes it hard for me to be honest with you. If I detach from you, and turn to my friends, it's because I feel safe with them—I can be ME. Could you learn to be more accepting of ME, too?

Sometimes, I just need time alone

. . . to collect my thoughts,

. . . to reflect, or

. . . to relax.

Please don't take it personally.

I really get excited at times, thinking about the future and thinking about, or using, my creativity and talents. I feel good about my accomplishments so far. I like it when you're excited for me, too.

In closing, I have an idea. I will make a commitment to be more accepting of you, and your human (albeit imperfect) ways. Would you be willing to do the same for me? This won't be easy, I know. But it's a start.

P.S. I love you.

Thanks for your support.

Promoting Philosophical
Discussions with Kids:
Surefire Conversation Starters

Jennifer E. Beaver | FALL 2004

Jennifer E. Beaver is the associate editor for Parent Topics and prepares the "Student Voices" column for the Gifted Education Communicator. She lives in Long Beach, California, with her husband and gifted son, where she runs her own communication service business.

Children are often reluctant to offer information about their daily activities at school or in the neighborhood when asked. Jennifer Beaver suggests alternate approaches to promote discussion. Chief among them is selecting places and times in which kids feel comfortable and safe; these may include baking cookies in the kitchen or gathering at the dinner table; sharing common experiences such as working together as volunteers in a chosen activity can also lead to excellent discussions.

When you ask your child, "How was your day?" do you get a lively rendition about the morality of the founding fathers, a full report on the less savory behaviors of your child's friends, a contemplative look at the cycle of life . . . or the more succinct and common, "Uhhhh . . . okay, I guess."

If your children don't react with enthusiasm as you pepper them with questions, let me introduce you to "Jennifer's Communication Corollary," which states: The greater the amount of information you request from your child, the less you will receive.

It's not that they don't want to talk. They just don't like direct questions. They're also uncomfortable with the laser-focus of parental concern, much like a bug under a microscope.

So what can you do to find out how they feel about life's important issues? How would they react when presented with a moral dilemma? Getting them to talk about their views and perceptions is easier than you think.

Offer Food

There's something about being around meals and food preparation that makes kids feel safe and talkative. Try making cookies all by yourself in the kitchen and see what happens. I've had kids wander in and tell me how they feel about their parents' divorce, ask me what I think of the discipline system at school, and comment on the O.J. Simpson trial—all with no prompting from me.

Have dinner as a family. Invite your child's friends. Talk about the news of the day, but don't put them on the spot. We once discussed a newspaper article about a murderous young couple who left their newborn in a trash can. In the course of half an hour, we covered: Is nurture or nature responsible for the development of a moral compass? What part does fear play in committing an act you know is wrong? What role, if any, did karma play in the fate of the baby and its parents? Not bad for one news event.

Be the Designated Driver

A cone of silence surrounds a parent driving a car . . . at least as far as the kids in the back seat are concerned. Give them a chance, and they'll forget you're there. Volunteer to drive your child and his friends and you'll hear all kinds of interesting things that you can use as conversation-starters later. That's how I found out about marijuana use on the middle school campus, for example.

If you hear something like that, please refrain from yelling, "What? The eighth graders are smoking pot?" Bring it up again later in a different setting. Again, you can use a news item as a nonthreatening introduction . . . something like, "I read the other day that kids are drinking and using drugs earlier. Do you think that's true?"

Conversely, what you don't hear is equally telling. If one of the backseat crew introduces a fairly scintillating topic and your child doesn't respond to it, bring it up again later. You may have identified a troublesome or confusing issue.

Traveling together lets you see the world in a different way. Before our city cleared the homeless encampment, my husband and son often passed a woman who lived near the freeway overpass. They talked frequently about whether society was responsible for the homeless, what factors might cause someone to live on the streets, and where the woman might have gone during inclement weather and after her home had been dismantled.

Invite the Media

Since we're bombarded by media in all their various forms, we might as well harness it for good. On one of my favorite driving trips, we turned to books on tape. It was one of the Harry Potter stories, and we listened, rapt with attention as we wound around the curves of Big Sur. When the tapes were off, we talked about whether it was ever acceptable to do something that you knew was wrong, even though you thought it would be for the greater good; the meaning of friendship; the meaning of betrayal; and how true heroes are those that persevere despite their fear. The right book or movie can really lead to some amazing discussions.

You might also tap the power of your local advice columnist. I read recently about a mother who offered her several daughters the question portion of an Ann Landers column and asked them to come up with the answers. The mother learned some illuminating things about her daughters and how their minds worked.

In a recent article in *Better Homes & Gardens,* a perceptive author wrote of the joys of reading aloud, even when kids get older. Not only does it bring the family together, but it also promotes meaningful discussions.

Volunteer

Insightful philosophical discussions depend, in part, on the ability to look outside ourselves. One great way to expose kids to the world beyond their Playstations is to volunteer, particularly if you can do it as a family. Be alert for opportunities to discuss everything from pollution to poverty.

If you're wondering what types of volunteer activities are available, check out *Investing in the Future: A Resource Guide,* an age-specific program manual that suggests activities that are age-appropriate, safe, and legal for young people of varying ages from Habitat for Humanity. If your child is a high schooler, he or she probably needs to complete forty hours of community service prior to graduation. Why not volunteer with your student . . . and talk about it later?

Take the time and set the stage to talk to your kids. You'll be amazed at their perceptiveness and their creativity.

Resources

Berman, S., et al. (2003). *Talking with children about war and violence in the world.* Educators for Social Responsibility, www.esrnational.org/guide.htm.

Faber, A., & Mazlish, E. (1999). How to talk so kids will listen and listen so kids will talk. *Perennial Currents.*

Habitat for Humanity, *Investing in the future: A resource guide.* 800-422-4828, x2552, Item #3313.

Law, S. (2002). *Philosophy rocks!* New York: Volo Publishing.

Madison, R., & Schmidt, C. (2001). *Talking pictures: A parent's guide to using movies to discuss ethics, values, and everyday problems with children.* Philadelphia: Running Book Press Publishers.

Ryan, B. (1998). *Protecting the environment: Opportunities to volunteer* (Community Service for Teens). New York: Ferguson Publishing Company.

Shaefer, C., & DiGeronimo, T. F. (1994). *How to talk to your kids about really important things: Specific questions and answers and useful things to say.* San Francisco: Jossey-Boss.

White, D. A. (2000). *Philosophy for kids: 40 fun questions that help you wonder . . . about everything!* Austin, TX: Prufrock Press.

Weate, J. (1998). *A young person's guide to philosophy.* New York: DK Publishing.

Web sites

Educators for Social Responsibility
www.esrnational.org/guide.htm

Habitat for Humanity
www.habitat.org

Volunteer Match
www.volunteermatch.org

INDEX

Page numbers for figures and tables are in italics.

About the California Association for the Gifted (CAG)

CAG is an organization of educators and parents that has supported gifted learners in California since its inception in 1966. It provides leadership in a variety of ways including collaboration with the California Department of Education to devise standards for gifted education programs; publication and dissemination of information for parents and educators through its quarterly journal, position statements, glossary, and resource reading list; in-service training at its annual conference, as well as through teacher and parent institutes; and advocacy in sponsoring and supporting legislation benefiting gifted learners. CAG's quarterly journal, *Gifted Education Communicator,* is distributed nationally as well as in Canada and Australia.

About the Editor

Margaret Gosfield has been actively involved in gifted education for more than thirty years. Early in her teaching career she developed the GATE (Gifted and Talented Education) program at her school in Ventura, California; it became the junior high school model for the district. She served as the district's program coordinator from 1982 until her retirement in 1997. She holds a B.A. in History and an M.A. in Education from the University of California, Santa Barbara.

In 1985, Margaret was named the first recipient of the Teacher of the Year awarded by the California Association for the Gifted. She joined its Board of Directors as a regional educator representative in 1990. In 1994, she was elected vice president, becoming president in 1996, and has served as editor of the *Gifted Education Communicator* since 1998. She lives in Santa Barbara, California, with her husband, Amor.

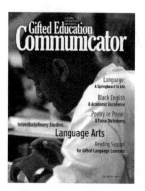

Other Great Books from Free Spirit

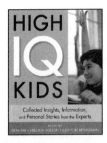

High IQ Kids
Collected Insights, Information, and Personal Stories
from the Experts
edited by Kiesa Kay, Deborah Robson, and Judy Fort Brenneman
Addresses the joys and challenges of raising and teaching, living with and
understanding exceptionally gifted kids of all ages. Recommended for any adult
who wants to know more about high-IQ kids and meet their needs.
*$19.95; 384 pp.; softcover; 7¼" x 9¼". Teachers, gifted coordinators, guidance
counselors, and other adults working with gifted kids (including parents).*

The Essential Guide to Talking with Gifted Teens Book with CD-ROM
Ready-to-Use Discussions About Identity, Stress, Relationships, and More
by Jean Sunde Peterson, Ph.D.
The 70 guided discussions are an affective curriculum for gifted teens. By "just
talking" with caring peers and an attentive adult, kids gain self-awareness
and self-esteem, learn to manage stress, and build social skills and life skills.
For teachers, counselors, and youth workers working with gifted kids in grades
6–12. The included CD-ROM (for Macintosh and Windows) features all of the
reproducible forms from the book.
$39.95; 288 pp.; softcover; 8½" x 11". Grades 6–12.

The Survival Guide for Parents of Gifted Kids
How to Understand, Live With, and Stick Up for Your Gifted Child
by Sally Yahnke Walker
Up-to-date information about giftedness, gifted education, problems, personality
traits, and more, written by an educator of gifted kids and their parents.
$12.95; 152 pp.; softcover; illust.; 6" x 9". Parents of children ages 5 & up.

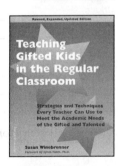

Teaching Gifted Kids in the Regular Classroom
Strategies and Techniques Every Teacher Can Use to Meet the Academic
Needs of the Gifted and Talented
Revised, Expanded, and Updated Edition
by Susan Winebrenner
Teachers call it "the orange bible"—the book they count on for insight, advice,
and strategies that work. Throughout, the compacting and differentiation
strategies that were the core of the first edition have been greatly expanded.
$34.95; 256 pp.; softcover; 8½" x 11". Teachers, all grades.

The Survival Guide for Teachers of Gifted Kids
How to Plan, Manage, and Evaluate Programs for Gifted Youth K–12
by Jim Delisle, Ph.D., and Barbara A. Lewis
Two veteran educators of the gifted share strategies, insights, practical tips,
and survival skills gleaned from years in the field. Includes advice on how to
set the foundation for a gifted program; how to evaluate, identify, and select
students; how to differentiate the regular curriculum for gifted kids; how to
extend or enrich the content areas; and much more.
$24.95; 176 pp.; softcover; 8½" x 11". Teachers, all grades.

When Gifted Kids Don't Have All the Answers
How to Meet Their Social and Emotional Needs
by Jim Delisle, Ph.D., and Judy Galbraith, M.A.
Gifted kids are much more than test scores and grades. Topics include self-image and self-esteem, perfectionism, multipotential, depression, feelings of "differentness," and stress. Includes first-person stories, easy-to-use strategies, survey results, activities, reproducibles, and up-to-date research and resources.
$17.95; 192 pp.; softcover; illust.; 7¼" x 9¼". Teachers, gifted coordinators, guidance counselors, and parents,

The Gifted Kids' Survival Guide
A Teen Handbook
Revised, Expanded, and Updated Edition
by Judy Galbraith, M.A., and Jim Delisle, Ph.D.
Vital information on giftedness, IQ, school success, college planning, stress, perfectionism, and much more.
$15.95; 304 pp.; softcover; illust.; 7¼" x 9¼". Ages 11–18.

Smart Talk
What Kids Say About Growing Up Gifted
by Robert A. Schultz, Ph.D., and James R. Delisle, Ph.D.
Quotes from real kids ages 12 and under and brief biographies provide insight into challenges gifted children face, like trying to fit in, dealing with adults' expectations, and being bored in school. Activities help readers relate the information and issues to their own lives. A must for any gifted child—and for any grown-up who wants to know about growing up gifted today.
$13.95; 128 pp.; 2-color; illust.; softcover; 6" x 9". Ages 12 & under.

More Than a Test Score
Teens Talk About Being Gifted, Talented, or Otherwise Extra-Ordinary
by Robert A. Schultz, Ph.D., and James R. Delisle, Ph.D.
A real-life look at what being gifted means to teens today. What is giftedness all about? What about expectations, mistakes, getting along, gifted programs, and dull days at school? Includes hundreds of quotes from teens ages 13–19, brief autobiographies, and activities. Essential reading for gifted teens and the adults who care about them.
$14.95; 176 pp.; 2-color; illust.; softcover; 6" x 9". Ages 13 & up.

To place an order or to request a free catalog of Self-Help for Kids® and Self-Help for Teens® materials, please write, call, email, or visit our Web site:

Free Spirit Publishing Inc.
217 Fifth Avenue North • Suite 200 • Minneapolis, MN 55401
toll-free 800.735.7323 • local 612.338.2068
fax 612.337.5050 • help4kids@freespirit.com • www.freespirit.com